economics of the new age

by

Dr. Berdj Kenadjian

With the best wishes
of the author

[signature]

DORRANCE & COMPANY

Philadelphia

To:
All those who strive
without reward or recognition
to help their fellow men.

Everyone who will make
a sincere effort to build
a better tomorrow.

And above all, I dedicate my book to

UNDERSTANDING

for, without it, there will be
more suffering in the world than
we dare contemplate.

CONTENTS

PREFACE

I have written this book for the layman, as well as the professional economist. Both may be surprised at what they find between these covers—perhaps they may even be shocked. But I have made no attempt to cater to any particular group. All I wanted to do was to stir the minds of my readers, the concerned citizen as well as the expert, and thus to strengthen their desires to build a better way of life.

I have chosen simple words to express the sublime ideas given to me to develop for this work. I say the ideas were given to me, because, as you will soon discover, this is not an ordinary book on political economy. The truth of the matter is that the most important ideas underlying this work were received as divine revelations and prophecies through extrasensory perception.

Until recently people would not believe that there can be divine revelations on the economics or politics of modern times. Fortunately, attitudes on this issue are gradually changing. Surely, in this age of turmoil, people who believe in God will not dispute the need for divine guidance on problems of government. In ancient times it was taken for granted that prophets could hear celestial voices directly which led men out of their social dilemmas. Why should this be impossible now when the need for divine instruction on world problems is so much greater?

Even though at times it may seem otherwise, God the Father has not lost His concern for the well-being of His children. Moreover, to have a peaceful and better way of life in the years ahead, it is evident that there must be fundamental improvements in the ideas, laws, and social institutions of the world. Without such reforms, civilized life may well plunge into chaos, causing humanity indescribable physical and mental pains. In the face of such prospects, is it logical to think that the divine forces would choose to remain silent?

This book declares without equivocation that there is a divine plan to rebuild the economic and political systems of the world on a righteous and honest basis. It outlines this plan, as well as the evils which must be eliminated before the sane and just economic systems of the next age can be implemented. What emerges from the pages to follow is a higher understanding of the form and meaning of human affairs. This new understanding alone can put the world on a road of healing its ills in a fortnight.

This preface would not be complete if I did not mention with gratitude the names of the recorder and the channel through whom the revelations and prophecies were received by means of ESP. The recorder was William D. Pelley, author and founder of the Soulcraft School of Divine Philosophy. The channel is Dr. Benn E. Lewis, author, artist, and leader of the Washington Cosmic Center. Without the dedicated service of these two great prophets, this volume could not have been offered to my readers for their consideration. I feel particularly blessed to have had the opportunity to spend many hundreds of delightful hours with Dr. Lewis who selflessly and patiently taught me more spiritual understanding and divine truth than any other teacher has taught me any subject any time.

Finally, I would like to thank Miss Ruth Marshall and my wife, Barbara Glenn Kenadjian, for their editorial and typing services. I am also grateful for the understanding and patience of my wife and son, Glenn, who missed my companionship during the many thousands of hours I had to devote to bringing this work to fruition.

Chapter I

THE CRISIS OF OUR AGE

However much people may disagree on the causes and effects of world events, one thing is certain. Our times are out of joint. We are witnessing a strange phenomenon. On one side of the ledger, we find world society in a stage of great and rapid development. Scientists are prying new secrets out of nature and opening up new possibilities for remaking human lives. This progression is bringing man to the verge of tapping the infinite.

On the other side of the ledger, we find the machinations of evil forces and catastrophic blunders shaking the very foundations of civilized society. The fears, anxieties, hatreds, and conflicts these forces generate are taking mankind to the brink of total slavery or destruction. Never before in history have the possibilities for good or evil been so great!

There have been many brilliant scientists, philosophers, and other world leaders who have written millions of words on the basic issues of the day. Yet, is it not true that the man in the street is more perplexed than ever? Should we not, therefore, go beyond the words of men to reach for the words of Spirit?

Some will say, with Shakespeare, that life is a tale told by an idiot, full of sound and fury, signifying nothing. The past two hundred tumultuous years that have toppled the old empires, produced an endless series of world wars, limited wars, civil wars, massacres, political revolutions, racial revolutions, financial crises, economic depressions, and a host of other calamities would seem to confirm such a point of view. All the same, can there not be a more optimistic explanation of these events?

Some optimists believe that ours is the best of all possible worlds. They would hear no evil, see no evil, speak no evil. Optimism of this type results from ignorance. There is, however,

1

another type of optimism, which is pessimism surmounted. Such an attitude results from knowledge. It reflects an awareness of both the immediate and ultimate effects of events. It takes into account both the visible and the invisible factors in life.

The anxieties people have stem from the fact that they do not have the proper awareness of things as they actually are. No one can be anxious about what he fully understands. Equipped with sufficient knowledge, a person can wait for the unfolding of events with poise and patience. Lacking insight, a person remains in a state of perpetual uncertainty about how to react to the situations confronting him. In our age, people who are despondent because of confusing circumstances are not rarities. They voice their lamentations in different forms. Yet their dilemmas are the same.

A middle-aged person in prosperous suburbia may say, "I have worked hard all of my life, observed the laws of the land, and have been a conscientious citizen in all other respects. I have helped the less privileged, and wished my neighbors well. Yet in return for such conduct, what do I get? I find myself accused and blamed for every fault under the sun. I am just about convinced that honest work does not pay and freedom is a needless burden, if not a curse. What good is it to toil and struggle, if in the end my life seems worthless, even to those who should care for me the most?"

The younger and the older people around this man have their own lamentations too. And, in a way, they all reason well. However, they do not reason well enough. This is not because there are flaws in their logic; rather it is because they are thinking narrowly and, by and large, strictly of themselves. Is it not true that a person is often served best by his greatest opponents who inadvertently develop in him the capacity to resist, endure and overcome? It is through a proper understanding of such hidden elements that the current crises can be seen as a positive force.

The greatest Teacher of all times taught His disciples to go among the multitudes two by two, taking with them neither

2

money nor expecting a return for their spiritual service. He advised them to let worldly affairs alone, to the point of refusing to assist in the burial of the dead. All of these admonitions were grossly misunderstood by those who heard Him then. They are misunderstood even today. When He gave these instructions, He did not want His disciples to be indifferent to the needs of their neighbors. Neither did he wish them to be accused by others for seeming hopelessly impractical. This would have been completely out of character. He had a higher purpose in mind, rooted in a deeper insight into human nature. Jesus knew that there are everywhere vast numbers of timid souls who live by sterile rules. They are the smug people of earth, satisfied with themselves and with their parochial interests. Being inhibited souls, they make it their business to interfere with other people's progress also. Such people resent change, not only for themselves but also for others. They prefer to depend on one another and to live in the narrow confines of obsolete tradition.

Thus, in advising His disciples to let the dead bury the dead, Jesus was protecting them from falling under the deadening influence of such small people. He wanted His active ministers to be free and independent. He knew that it is only through freely flowing, creative work that the weak are saved from themselves.

Today, as two thousand years ago, if mankind is to advance to greater heights of accomplishment, the small, parochial people must somehow be jolted out of their shells. They must be made to have new experiences whether they like it or not!

It is possible that some of the spiritually indolent multitudes can be inspired to raise their sights and look for new horizons. As a rule, however, man insists on learning the hard way. But learn he must, this being a law of life. We are told through ESP that it is for this reason, and this reason alone, that troubled times have been allowed to visit us. God does not punish. He educates.[1]

In periods of turmoil, it is easy to romanticize the past. Yet, much as we may decry the anxieties of our age, it cannot be denied that the world was far from perfect before the onset of the modern period. Testimony before a parliamentary committee in 1816 revealed that, in England, children as young as five years of age were employed in cotton manufacturing. The usual hours of work were fourteen, some mills requiring fifteen hours and others allowing no intermission for meals. A physician whose father-in-law owned a large mill testified "with the greatest reluctance" that there was no protection from the machinery, and that he "had too often" seen workers crushed to death, and that the mangling of the hands of the children was a "very common thing."[2] Before the Industrial Revolution, conditions under feudalism were often not much better. In Germany, Frederick William I declared that he himself had seen peasants beaten with cudgels and whips, driven to their work like cattle. An ordinance in 1738 forbade such mistreatment of the peasants under pain of imprisonment for the first offense and death for the second offense.[3]

There is no need to elaborate here on the well-known horrors of the African slave trade. Supplying black slaves—mostly prisoners of war—for white traders had become both a profession and recreation for many native kings. Slaves were wedged below deck like spoons in a sideboard drawer. Large numbers died of suffocation and disease. Often those diseased ones who did not die were thrown overboard so they would not infect the others. One could also prepare a long list of crimes and atrocities committed in the name of religion. But why go through this exercise?

My purpose here is not to take my readers through a chamber of horrors. Nor do I deny that wrongdoing has assumed increasingly more grotesque forms since the French Revolution. What I want to make clear is this: Without important lessons to be learned, there would be no reason for painfully disturbing world events. Consequently, the more chaotic the times, the greater must be the errors which men have been making in understanding how to solve their individual and social problems.

As time goes on, such cultural errors have a way of gathering momentum and multiplying. If this process goes far enough, it can cripple and ruin entire civilizations. Is this surprising? Not if we realize that what are often politely called errors are by no means innocent mistakes. At work also are willful and malicious influences. Moreover, most intellectuals will not lift a finger to correct mankind's errors of thought, if such corrections represent serious threats to their own earthly powers.

It is both naive and fallacious to trust exclusively what outstanding authorities claim to be true at any given time. The fallacy in this naive stance does not lie primarily in ignoring the fact that time has repeatedly proven the greatest authorities to be wrong. Rather it lies in failing to recognize that the great authorities may have become prominent precisely because they were willing to go along with the tide, supporting the ideas favoring the powers that be. Most intellectual leaders are very cautious in stating truths for which they may be criticized. In some instances they also fear economic reprisals. Therefore, it is understandable that, sooner or later, they give up challenging the politically explosive misconceptions of their times.[4] The few strong individuals who provide the exceptions to this rule are eventually recognized as benefactors of mankind. Unfortunately, as in the case of Socrates, they may be honored only after a shameful public trial and the executioner's hemlock.

It is because of such unpleasant facts that basic errors of thought continue. In the meantime, those with vested interests in falsehood keep on deluding themselves and others with more and more untenable, contradictory beliefs until the bubble bursts. Happy are those who know how to prevent the bubble from blowing up to unseemly proportions, or who know what to do after it bursts.

The immense crises facing mankind today do not originate from distortions in any single field of thought. All the same, wrong thinking in economics plays a particularly important role in the disorders of a civilization which makes men depend more and more on each other. It is, therefore, to economics that I turn first to discover some of the germs causing the convulsive diseases of modern times.

5

FOOTNOTES

1. The basic ideas expressed in the last six paragraphs come from a discourse recorded by William D. Pelley called, "The Cosmic Purpose Being Achieved by Periodic Ordeal and Mass Upset in Affairs," published around 1955 as part of *Soulcraft Scripts*. Vol. 9. Noblesville, Indiana: Soulcraft Chapels. This is one of 156 discourses received through ESP and published in twelve volumes by Soulcraft Chapels, now renamed Fellowship Press, Inc. I have drawn on these volumes extensively in writing my book. However, I refer to them in footnotes only when an important group of ideas can be directly traced to one discourse.

2. Witt Bowden, Michael Karpovich, and Abbott Payson Usher, *An Economic History of Europe since 1750*. New York: American Book Co., 1937, pp. 433-34.

3. Ibid. p. 162.

4. For a good illustration of both the techniques of intellectual fraud and a subtle persecution of individuals who offer to tell the truth despite opposition, see: Carlton Putnam, *Race and Reality—A Search for Solutions*. Washington, D.C.: Public Affairs Press, 1967, pp. 26-45.

For a second illustration of abuse by fellow scientists, see the article about Dr. Immanuel Velikovsky, who published a series of controversial books on geology: Eric Larrabee, "Scientists in Collision, *"Harper's* (August 1963). The methods of "smearbund" to suppress opposition thought to revisionism (to hide the real reasons for American involvement in World War I and II) are explained in detail by the eminent scholar, Harry Elmer Barnes, *The Struggle Against the Historical Blackout*. (By the author, 1951).

Chapter II

FALLACIES OF ECONOMIC REASONING

The study of the economic problems of man without reference to his spiritual needs is now taken for granted. In our age of specialization, such a state of affairs seems quite normal. Historically the study of how man creates the means with which he can enjoy a good life has seldom been separated from reflections on what constitutes the good life itself. In ancient times, economic ideas were woven into religious teachings, codes of law and principles of statecraft. The great classical philosophers considered economics as a branch of politics. And politics, which was defined as the study of what man must and must not do, included ethics as well as the practical sciences such as business administration.

Economics has now been largely divorced from ethics as well as from other related sciences and disciplines. A man may receive a Ph.D. in economics without taking a single course in philosophy or political science. As a result of intense concentration on a specialized set of problems, economists today understand better than at any previous time how economic systems operate. But are they putting their rapidly increasing knowledge to good use? When society is losing sight of the values which have given man meaning, beauty, hope, and the will to go on, the economist still equates the good life with an abundance of material things.

For how long can this type of thinking go on? After all, have not fabulous increases in income (considered by the economists as a prime measure of human welfare) often failed to lead to greater happiness? Is it not true that the richest nation in the world, America, has become the most bemused in its purposes and is most desperately homesick for the lost world of inner certainty? The average American would be appalled if he could look at this very moment into the private lives and thoughts of his most respected leaders.

Faced with the growing crisis of our age, even economists have started to question the validity of their premises. In a recent review of the history of economic thought, the reviewer pointed out that: "A science responsible for the study of human behavior as the relationship between ends and means which have alternative uses has the particular responsibility of continuously checking the validity of its assumptions."[1] All the same, few are the economists who are willing to squarely face the fact that, important as bread is, man does not live by bread alone. They love efficiency so much that they could be walking in chains to nowhere, while thinking of a more optimal way of accomplishing this feat.

There are, of course, exceptions. As one economist, famous for his wit, pointed out: "If we want the wrong things, then economic progress may enable us to damn ourselves all the more quickly and allow us to travel to hell at a hundred miles an hour instead of ten."[2]

The truth of the matter is that, in their basic reasoning, most economists today have not advanced beyond the concepts of an Englishman named Jeremy Bentham, who lived in the eighteenth century. This philosopher held that every social institution should be judged by its usefulness in increasing the pleasure or diminishing the pain of individuals. He conceived social good to be simply the algebraic sum of all individual goods.

The announced aim of Bentham was the greatest good to the greatest number. It may be possible to aim at the greatest good to a given number, or at a given good to the greatest number, but not at the greatest good to the greatest number. There was, however, a greater fallacy in his thought. Bentham's measure of the good things in life was essentially money. He reasoned that, since the lack of things measured by money was responsible for misery, enough of these things would bring happiness. It did not occur to him that unless human beings fulfill their divine destinies, they can under no circumstances be happy. Nor did it occur to him that life is a struggle between good and evil forces whose ideas about what gives satisfaction or what is reasonable are diametrically opposed.

Other defects of Jeremy Bentham's philosophy also gave rise to much critical comment. Benjamin Disraeli, for one, did not hide his disdain for this doctrine, which he considered completely barren. With Edmund Burke, Cardinal Newman, Thomas Carlyle, and William Blake, Disraeli conceived of society as a living, purposive thing. These thinkers intuitively recognized that men of common taste and hopes were so assimilated in their acts of thinking, feeling, and doing that, in effect, they formed a distinct unity. Moreover, they realized that this integrated social order had definite meaning not only for one fleeting generation but also for all generations who absorb, develop, and benefit from its traditions. They knew therefore that the meaning and purpose of society went much beyond achieving material prosperity or increased satisfaction à la Jeremy Bentham.[3]

Ironically, one of the most persuasive exponents of Bentham's materialistic philosophy, John Stuart Mill, also provided one of its most dramatic refutations. He did this when he said that it was "better to be Socrates dissatisfied than a pig satisfied." How could he have regarded dissatisfaction as valuable, unless he evaluated satisfaction by nonmaterial standards?

The socialistic thinkers of the nineteenth century also attacked Bentham's rational materialism (also known as utilitarianism) from a different standpoint. They pointed out that vested financial interests would not hesitate to block the adoption of proposals for general reform regardless of how beneficial they appeared to be in the light of pure reason. Therefore, they dismissed all measures designed to restrain, regulate, or improve the capitalism of their day as so much petty bourgeois nonsense.

The more Bentham's ideas were criticized, however, the more they seemed to flourish. Today, they are held in one form or another by most American economists in whose thinking Providence plays no part. In fact, many believe that utilitarian concepts are the only basis on which a science of economics can be built. All the same, I shall show in this volume that we need not be limited by the rational materialism of Bentham or by any other set of concepts accepted so far. We can go forward and build a system which will serve the spiritual as well as the material needs of man, while allowing people to remain thoroughly free and individual.

Modern economists, impressed with the achievements of physical science, emphasize the scientific aspects of their discipline at the expense of ethical principles, which are also involved whenever an economic choice is made. They see their basic problem to be to determine what the authorities or the people want and then show them how they can most efficiently go about getting it. Economists emphasize that their scientific opinions are, or at least should be, free from hidden value judgments. Subjective values, they say, should have no place in their scientific appraisals. Since they are human beings, however, their personal values and biases have a way of entering into their judgments anyway—often through the back door! That is why it is said that if three economists gather they are bound to have at least four different opinions about desirable policy.

Most economists trained in the West still believe that the ideal economic system is one which maximizes output with any given amount of inputs. This would happen if all productive forces in the economy are allowed to be in free competition with each other under conditions perfect enough to make all decisions rational. Under such a system, resources would be utilized so well that no one could be given an additional commodity without taking it, or its equivalent, away from someone else. This great emphasis on efficiency has been so much a part of their training that economists tend to lose sight of the fact that efficiency is a means to an end, and not an end in itself.

It is true that, in addition to the great efficiency free enterprise systems help to achieve, they also encourage individual inventive-

10

ness, initiative, and responsibility. Nevertheless, even free enterprise is not an end in itself but a means to the end of individual fulfillment. We know moreover that freedom can be abused particularly when people turn their backs on God, who is the author of their liberty. In fact, as we shall see later in this volume, the lack of vigilance and spirituality has allowed a most sinister satanic conspiracy to make great inroads in the freest of nations. We should also realize that when free enterprise is overly dominated by money values it can be quite cruel to those who have little or no money.

Some economists feel that they can correct this lack of compassion of the impersonal market with enlightened national goals in such fields as social justice, health, education, ecology, the sciences, and the arts. What they forget, however, is that the more a nation sets out to achieve collective goals, the less are the people allowed to pursue their individual goals. The reason for this is obvious. How can government hope to achieve significant national goals without regulating the people one way or another and taxing them more and more, thus leaving them with both less freedom and less income with which to achieve their own goals? If a government is to serve the people instead of dominating their lives, it must strictly limit its collective goals.

There is another fallacy in this approach to government by national goals and priorities. How can we decide what is good for a nation without reference to what people feel, or how they make up their minds? Men learn from their mistakes. This being the case, who would deny them the right to make mistakes from which they can profit? In a truly liberal system, is it not true that the evolution of the individual must go hand in hand with the evolution of a nation? Thus, while it is important to have concern for the ill, the illiterate, the hungry, and the underdog, would not attempting to do these things through pure handouts kill the dignity, the incentive, and progressive desire of those placed on the dole? At the same time, would not the people forced to support the needy grumble and get angry instead of learning the values and joys of giving voluntarily?

It sounds noble to say that we must satisfy the needs of people. But who can know what the real needs of any given person are? Which government or expert can be so presumptuous as to pronounce one set of human needs more important than another? The goals of a nation must forever relate to the just and proper means with which to ensure each person life, liberty, and the pursuit of happiness. Then each person can determine for himself what goals are worth attaining.

Economists are making another error which prevents them from restraining the evil influences which are causing the world crisis. An eminent economist expressed this error clearly when he claimed "the economist has little to say about the formation of wants: this is the province of the psychologist."[4] We might as well hold that educators should have little to say about what type of books their students should read. Especially in modern societies, what people want is shaped largely by the type of economic system they have. And the type of system they have is in turn largely shaped by those who control the breadbaskets, workrooms, and purse strings of that society.

The money powers who dominate the mass media would of course love to have the people think that they merely wish to satisfy popular wants. However, we shall show in subsequent chapters how they dominate the wants of the people to the point of tricking them into wanting war and serfdom in a regimented social system.

One American institutional economist, John R. Commons, did claim that, at the turn of the century, the largest owners of private property held the chief power in deciding the course of American society. His view was confirmed by men of wealth themselves who withdrew their support for the chair Professor Commons filled at Syracuse University.[5]

In the twentieth century, finding the best way to take advantage of the fears, anxieties, ignorance, sex desires, or vanity of the people for the pecuniary benefit of moneyed interests is developing into a science. We now have motivation researchers and analysts, Vance Packard's hidden persuaders, singing commercials, public relations experts, and a host of other forms of commercial propaganda whose purpose is to exploit cynically the irrational aspects of man. Advertising can be used to educate or to provide objective information to the public. Yet how often do we find it directed to enhancing the rational or critical faculties of the population who are considered the target?

What is worse, the same techniques of salesmanship have been applied to the political field. As the famous writer-philosopher, Aldous Huxley, has pointed out:

The political merchandisers appeal only to the weaknesses of voters, never to their potential strength. They make no attempt to educate the masses into becoming fit for self-government; they are content merely to manipulate and exploit them. For this purpose all the resources of psychology and the social sciences are mobilized and set to work. . . . Under the new dispensation, political principles and plans for specific action have come to lose most of their importance. The personality of the candidate and the way he is projected by the advertising experts are the things that really matter.[6]

Obviously the merchandising of candidates who are coached to look sincere requires a great deal of money. That is why it is said that those who command great wealth can collect congressmen and senators as a child collects butterflies. We are reminded here of a statement made by the founder of one of the most powerful banking dynasties, Meyer Amschel Rothschild. He said, "Give me the power to issue a nation's money; then I do not care who makes the laws."

13

The pursuit of wealth is a dangerous enterprise. Did not Jesus ask: "For what shall it profit a man, if he shall gain the whole world and lose his own soul? Or what shall a man give in exchange for his soul?" (St. Matthew 16:26) According to Plato, "In proportion as riches and rich men are honored in the State, virtue and the virtuous are dishonored."[7] To illustrate what too much concern for wealth can do to a man, I offer a quotation from Andrew Carnegie. At the time of his retirement, he said: "The amassing of wealth is one of the worst species of idolatry, no idol more debasing. To continue much longer overwhelmed by business cares with most of my thoughts wholly upon the way to make more money in the shortest time, must degrade me beyond the hope of permanent recovery."[8]

There is an old adage that every man has his price. If we offer a man in need $5,000, $50,000, up to a million, do we not eventually reach his breaking point? Furthermore, when a man conquers with the power of money, does he not become imbued with the spirit of domination, the spirit of control? For much too long have we blinded ourselves to the fact that the misuse of money is at the root of too much evil.

The time is approaching when people will recognize that economic values should not take precedence over spiritual and social values. The desire for money is not of itself evil, of course, but this desire often expresses itself in pure selfishness.

It goes without saying that most things that money can buy are reasonable and necessary for the well-being of people. But money tends to make its owner wish ever for more. All too often human beings do not want money to do constructive things for others or even for their own spiritual progress. They want it so they may not have to exert themselves as they go about their daily lives.

Affluence tends to make people think that no earthly effort is worthwhile. The rich devote themselves to dangerous pleasures and call these their privileges. They have an obsession that money will bring them happiness. Then they turn around and curse their wealth because it yields them no real contentment.

Utilitarian or money values, which are so central to economic

14

reasoning, are not without their benefits. They can provide the greatest incentive for getting things accomplished, as the history of the Western world has amply shown. However, we also know that money makes the rich despise the poor, whom they consider a nuisance. Money has often called forth Herculean effort. In the hands of truly spiritual men, it can also be the greatest force on earth for achievement of noble plans for the benefit of all mankind. In the right hands, money represents a power that is completely unnecessary to limit. In the wrong hands, virtually unlimited money can lead to the greatest calamities.

Few stop to think that in any enterprise of world significance, the profit motive is a secondary consideration, an enabling factor, rather than a prime mover. It is difficult to think of a single great advance in the history of civilization which was motivated solely by economic considerations. By the commercial standards of his time, when Columbus set out to discover a new continent, he was being foolishly visionary. What business did he have to attempt the impossible? Could he have explained to anyone exactly what profits he expected from his ventures? Yet history hails him as one of the greatest discoverers of all times.[9]

The world cannot evolve interminably along the lines that human life has appeared to go on in the twentieth century. The growing problems of wars or rumors of wars, ecology, crime, racial tension, drugs, anxiety, inflation, unemployment, never ending crises, abuse of money and power, corruption in high places, stifling controls and shortages are forcefully reminding us that unless we make economics serve the total man, the gains made on the economic front will have feet of clay. The times are drawing close when it will be brought home to men that the great ennoblers of the life experience are not money gains but spiritual gains. Men in large numbers will finally understand that economic progress cannot be an end in itself. If it does not become a means to a higher way of life, material progress will not even endure, let alone satisfy.

15

FOOTNOTES

1. J. M. Letiche, "The History of Economic Thought in the International Encyclopedia of the Social Sciences," *Journal of Economic Literature*, Vol. VII, No. 2. (June 1969): p. 424.

2. Kenneth D. Boulding, *Principles of Economic Policy*. Englewood Cliffs, N.J.: Prentice-Hall, Inc. 1958, p. 23.

3. W. J. Edwards ed., *The Radical Tory—Disraeli's Political Development Illustrated from His Original Writings and Speeches*. London: Jonathan Cope, 1937, pp. 23-25.

4. Milton Friedman, *Price Theory, a Provisional Text* Chicago: Aldine Publishing Co., 1970, p. 13.

5. George Soule, *Ideas of the Great Economists*. "A Mentor Book"; New York: The New American Library, 1963, p. 141.

6. Aldous Huxley, *Brave New World Revisited*. Perennial Library, New York and Evanston: Harper and Row, 1965, pp. 56-57.

7. Plato, *Five Great Dialogues*, trans. B. Jowett, and L. R. Loomis, ed. New York: Walter J. Black, 1942, p. 438.

8. Pitirim A. Sorokin and Walter A. Lunden, *Power and Morality—Who Shall Guard the Guardians?* Boston: Porter Sargent, 1959, p. 94.

9. The basic ideas expressed in the last six paragraphs come from Discourse 110 recorded by William D. Pelley called "Profits: The Cosmic Significance of Financial Gain and the Place of Loss in Matters of Spirit" in *Soulcraft Scripts*, Vol. 9.

Chapter III

NEW DIRECTIONS FOR ECONOMIC POLICY

The End To Be Served

If it is misleading to separate the study of economics from the total study of man, how then should this separation be ended? If the economic system of man are only means to an end and not ends in themselves, what then are the ends to be served by these systems?

No man or woman, however perceptive, can correctly evaluate the ends or purposes of the drama of life, while emotionally involved in it. In fact, it is questionable whether a person through his senses and reason alone can even begin to grasp the necessity for the drama at all. To feel the impact of a theatrical performance as a totality, one has to be out before the footlights, not behind them. To see the unity of the play as a composition, one has to sit in a place from which he can see the performance as a whole. One cannot do that while striding the stage. Thus a social philosopher who attempts to develop a valid theory about meaning and purpose of the drama of life while in the wigs and costumes of a social philosopher is trying something technically impossible. The same goes for others who refuse to go beyond the limitations of their reason or sense impressions.

That is why reliable knowledge about the direction or meaning of human life must ever descend for man's consideration from the loftier planes of heavenly thought. It must be based on knowledge of factors operating behind life as well as in life. In other words, a valid view about the ends of human life must always be the product of divine revelation. If it is not, we can accept it no more than the statement of a Sicilian who claimed that all Sicilians are liars!

It is often felt that revealed knowledge, being personal, is only of subjective value. On the contrary, sketching consistently the many exciting facets of truth with a detachment that is not possible in a world of desire thinking, divine revelation can attain greater objectivity than science itself. Moreover, the inspiration resulting from revealed information arouses an emotional response similar to the thrilled state of mind of a spectator which endures long after he leaves the theater.

Although many would prefer to ignore them, divine revelations have already been given with regard to the meaning of history and the destiny of mankind in modern times. Much of it has already been published, sometimes in the form of human stories which is in line with biblical tradition.[1] Others were given specially for this book. These new revelations should not come as a surprise to spiritual men who believe in a God of order and justice. However, they will provide little aid and comfort to those who think that man has been thrown into the world to do what he will with his life and then vanish into nothingness.

One thing is certain. World events, why they take place and where they are leading us, appear very different when viewed from a divine perspective. Unless we see them as they appear from the higher planes, any goals we may set for our economic system will certainly miss the mark. That is why before writing about economic policy, we must first understand the policies of the Almighty with respect to His children.

Much has been said about life being eternal, which it is. However, it would be most illogical to say that what one believes or does over one lifetime—a period infinitesimally short when compared with eternity—could determine a man's progress for the rest of eternity. The truth is that human beings exist on both sides of the veil of mortality, both before and after life on earth. Although belief in this principle of reincarnation, or repeat existence, has not enjoyed much popularity in the religious doctrines of the West, many famous Western thinkers have believed in it since ancient times. Among these believers one may cite Pythagoras, Plato, Virgil, Schopenhauer, Carlyle, Walt

Whitman, Ralph Waldo Emerson, Thomas Edison, and General Patton.

All of these famous men have known that we live not one, but literally thousands of lives, each related to the others in some logical way. We come as rich man, poor man, beggar man, chief, doctor, lawyer, merchant, thief, as the old nursery rhyme has it. Each life offers new lessons, and, therefore, new opportunities for growth. Consequently, the more and fuller lives a person has, the more he matures. In fact, life in all systems, no matter where it is found, has but a single meaning and purpose, a single power and wholeness. That meaning is the expansion of awareness. Only through a growing awareness of reality can a person know what he can do, who he can become, and, therefore, who he is. Thus, the aim and method of living is to know the full possibilities of attainment, so that over vast eons of time, each person can arrive at all the consciousness there is.

In other words, fantastic as it may sound, the end of man is to reach his own godhood! In the beginning, the Absolute, or First Cause, or Holy Spirit, existed unto Itself, with no thing external to Holy Spirit. In this self-contained state, the Absolute could not gain an understanding of Its possibilities. To achieve that, Holy Spirit had to divide and reduce certain parts of Itself to expression of form.

Thus Holy Spirit was divided into billions of units which were set in motion in areas where there would be limitations or obstructions. In this way contrasts and frictions would be generated between the particles of Spirit and their environment. And through the conflicts generated by these contrasts and frictions, these particles would realize their identity as well as their potential. Undoubtedly, some would advance faster than others, and thus set the standards by which others would measure their progress.

Thus, with further attainment, human beings were to see themselves in their manifold relationships to all other components of life. But the process leading to this end could not operate unless human consciousness stretches by pressing against the world of forms where everything is known because it has its opposite.

How can one know, for example, what light is, unless one can contrast it with its opposite, darkness? Without feeling the direct pressure of restrictions and prohibitions limiting one's conduct, how can one understand what it means to be free? If the sensation of heat cannot be contrasted with its opposite, coldness, by what standard can one evaluate temperature? We recognize a sensation, condition, or phenomenon to be what it is, as distinguished from something else, because we can place it on a scale, on one side of which is its most extreme manifestation and on the other side, its opposite. Various shades of gray are recognized because they fall on a scale one side of which is white and the other side black. Similarly, we evaluate a person's ethical development by placing the person on a scale with Jesus Christ, the most perfect person the world has known, on one side, and on the other, His most blasphemous and destructive enemies.

I know liberal intellectuals will object to having Jesus provide an absolute standard of conduct. However, we shall take their objections seriously only after they stop contradicting themselves. These intellectuals say that we have no proof or objective standards by which to determine whether one set of ethical values is better than another. They say that man has nothing but his own senses upon which to rely in judging questions of right or wrong. Therefore, they insist that we must be open to all ideas, viewpoints and ideals; then they turn around and systematically attack the viewpoints and ideals of all their opponents. To make some of their points, they say that one man's judgment of right or wrong is not any more trustworthy than another's. Then, to make another point, they scoff at the judgments of the common man because he is not sufficiently cosmopolitan or sophisticated.

There is, however, another and more fundamental contradiction in ethical relativism. If, on questions of ethics, all authorities are equally useful, do they not all become equally useless sooner or later? One philosopher stated that truth gets "shattered into a myriad of particles, each of which neutralizes and dulls the brilliance of the others. The result is not illumination but obscurity.[2]

In divine revelation there is no confusion or contradiction. In fact, according to this source, if man had not allowed his consciousness to sink into animalism, much of his confusion would not have come about in the first place. However, rebelling against divine order and his own nature, man did fall into animalism by cohabiting with bestial forms. It is through this original sin of Adam that the mark of the beast was introduced into the progeny of biological man. Since then man has been gradually extricating himself from his bestial appetites, in an ever upward climb. This climb, however, is at times difficult to perceive, since it is more like a spiral than a ladder.

The ever upward climb of man out of animalism into a path of glory to reach his own godhood is thus the key to a proper understanding of both the purpose of life and of man's social institutions. From this reality alone, we can derive all our general standards for judging which systems or policies help the advance of man and which hold him back. As for the specifics, they can be derived from the attestations of history.

A proper study of world civilizations will provide all the illustrations we need for understanding the consequences of both the right and wrong ways of solving the problems posed by man's lower nature. The wrong approach, which has always led to catastrophic results, would regiment man and control him so cleverly or treat him so brutally that he cannot seriously misbehave. This method the divine mentors call the satanic approach to government. The motto of this school is that the end justifies the means. More recently, satanic thought has expressed itself principally in cries for power and revolution.

The divine plan stands in eternal contrast to these grotesque conceptions. Those who implement the divine plan work through the goodwill of free men. They do not attempt to regiment the masses, so as not to hinder their ethical growth. They advocate change through love and evolution, always within reason and always according to man's ability to accept change and novelty.

This is because constructive growth comes about only through a roundabout process of trial and error.

Today the divine and satanic philosophies of life and government are in more universal conflict than ever before. It is not surprising, therefore, that there are those who fear that the final destination of human society may well be world government on the pattern of George Orwell's 1984. But, even if this happens, such an eventuality cannot prevail for long, because evil sooner or later brings about its own destruction and cure.

The Importance of Economic Policy

As man approaches a fatal crossroad, where momentous choices await him, it will become increasingly clear to him that the economic policies of his government can either reduce him to a robot or liberate him to follow the harder but more enriching path of individual growth. For too long economics has been taught without divine understanding. The power of money can be used for good or evil equally. It is futile to pretend that this is not so.

Economic organizations can induce people to become either grasping or generous. The example that leaders in business, labor, and government provide can either stimulate progressive desire or frustrate it. The economic policies of a nation can either encourage or discourage self-reliance, prudence, or rectitude. Even in normal circumstances, the social systems in which we live tend to blur our vision more often than we like to admit. The social conventions, with their subtle rewards or punishments, make such profound impressions on the mind, raise so many hopes, and induce so many fears, that it is very difficult even for a scientist to be completely objective about his social atmosphere. Moreover, when the mass communication media are given virtually a free hand to lead the public by the nose to any preconceived conclusion, it becomes even more critical to understand that our economic system can become either steppingstones or obstacles to a better way of life.

Economics is still first and foremost concerned with choice.

The most important choice, however, is almost never stated in public. It is the choice between God or mammon. There can be no escape from this choice. If life is a school for perfection, what can the service of God mean except to help His children gain the experiences which develop their talents, stretch their awareness, conquer their weaknesses, and induce them to amass the moral qualities which "neither moth nor rust corrupts, nor thieves break in to steal. (St. Matthew 6:19)

What, then, is the service of mammon? Surprising as it may seem, it is to a large extent what we see around us today. It is selling one's honor or future to the highest bidder. It is to glorify billionaires who hang to their fortunes—ill-gotten or otherwise—for generations, while the poor and hungry are despairing. It is the surreptitious use of public power for private gain. It is causing wars, financing revolutions, buying elections and legislators, controlling the money systems of nations—both large and small—for private gain. It is protecting the oil fields around the world with the blood and treasure of others.

The service of mammon is all these things and much more. It is demanding more and more compensation for contributing less and less effort to advance the welfare of man. It is justifying the ruses of the advertising business by saying *caveat emptor*—let the buyer beware. Is it any wonder that discontent and disorder are increasing instead of decreasing despite all the advances in the gross national product? We can and must change all this one day.

The classical economists had little faith in the power of benevolence where it clashed with economic interest. As Adam Smith pointed out: "It is not from the benevolence of the butcher, the brewer, or the baker that we expect our dinner, but from their regard to their own interest. . . . Nobody but a beggar chooses to depend chiefly upon the benevolence of his fellow citizens. Even a beggar does not depend upon it entirely."[3]

What Smith did not know at the time was that the butcher, brewer, and the baker would all serve their own interest best by being benevolent, and caring for the people they deal with.[4] Have there not been numerous examples of financial success which can be directly attributed to benevolence?

America's fabulous merchant prince, the late J. C. Penney, who went to work five days a week in 1970, at the age of ninety-five, said to a reporter that what brought him success was adhering to the Golden Rule. Actually, J. C. Penney Stores Co. was formed in 1913, when his Golden Rule stores were incorporated. Mr Penney opened the first of these stores with two partners in 1902 in a mining town of 1,000 people in Wyoming, where merchandise was sold at the lowest prices possible.

After buying up his two partners' interest in the store, Mr. Penney started an expanding chain store operation on his partnership idea. This idea was to allow a store manager to buy a one-third interest in a new store, provided he had trained a new man to manage it. The new man would invest one-third of his own capital in the store, or if he did not have the capital he would borrow it from Mr. Penney, who put up the remainder. After enjoying immense prosperity as well as grievous setbacks, a few months before he passed over, Mr. Penney observed: "We're going through a difficult period now, but if each man has the faith that I have, the opportunities are greater than ever."[5]

You may think, at this point, "Perhaps so, but not everyone has the faith of J. C. Penney." But why not? Is it not because false concepts, fallacies in reasoning, if you will, prevent people from seeking to help themselves by helping others? How many have actually tried benevolence as a principle of action in their daily work and found it wanting?

Night unto night, men have prayed wrongly to a God whom they did not understand for things which were by no means worth having. Century after century, people have cheated, robbed, or exploited one another with disastrous social consequences. Why? Was this not because of idolizing the wrong gods? Yes, it is the worship of the golden calf that has led men astray since the days of antiquity. When money becomes an object of worship, it is an insidious and diabolical state of mind which grips the people of the world. Ironically men little realize that the very things they wish to gain through selfish machinations can be created in an easier way through the pursuit of righteousness.

This principle was illustrated forcefully in the experience of an American businessman, who wrote a book about it and distributed 85,000 free copies.[6] Here is the story of a man, born in poverty, who fought for success and money for forty years, until he discovered that only when he abandoned his desire to accumulate money did things begin to gravitate his way.

In 1923, he organized a company with some friends, to distribute a mineral water with health-giving properties. Half of the $100,000 invested was paid for a fifty-year contract to the company owning the spring, which company proved to be in receivership.

Several other apparent misfortunes started to hit this businessman, one after the other. At one point, under pressure from the American Medical Association, the Food and Drug Administration seized the company's water under false charges, which did not hold up in court.

In the end, however, this honest man, who sincerely wanted to get the water to those who needed it, came to own a summer resort property near the spring water which eventually was valued at over a million dollars. Through his many trials and tribulations, this businessman learned a spiritual lesson which students of economics must also learn one day to make their science more useful. He learned that he had a Divine Partner Who can not only change financial failure to success but Who can also add to such success more happiness and love of people than he ever dreamed could be possible.

"When a nation forgets God, God sends an earthquake," said the French novelist, Victor Hugo. The new revelations tell us that there is no such God of jealousy and wrath at the head of the universe. There is only a Being who has a hundred times more tenderness, intellectual power, compassion, altruism and solicitude than Jesus Christ. And He has projected this material universe as a wise and kindly parent might found a school for his children.

This Holy Father, our Creator, has given man this earth on which to dwell and test the issues of life for himself. The Father says to men: "Be fruitful and multiply and enjoy your life as you will. There is, however, one condition you must observe. You shall suffer personally the consequences of any of your wrong thoughts or actions."

Thus a just God balances the give and take of life at all times. There can be no disruption of that balance. The slightest infringement demands compensation. Men have often been made aware that such a law of balance operates. But they continue to act as though somehow this law will not affect them as individuals. Through many centuries of living, man has learned to recognize that it would be good for each person to do unto his neighbor as he would have his neighbor do unto him. Yet for his narrowly conceived self-interest, man closes his mind to such considerations and proceeds to take advantage of his neighbor. But why? Is it not because he feels that he can get away with it, perhaps by dying out of life and allowing his children to suffer the retribution? If men really thought that they would individually have to pay for all damages done to others, how many would consciously want to harm their neighbors?

Consider a not-too imaginary situation in which a given class of people, say, in effect, to a group of politicians, "Give us all you can from the public's pocket, and in return, we shall do our best to keep you in office. Whatever trick plays or gimmicks you have to use is up to you, provided we end up getting what we want." Thus, for a while, monies which in no way belonged to those making this corrupt deal were placed in their hands.

In time, however, those favored with special privileges become softer or less vigilant, while those holding political office become craftier and more intoxicated with power. Consequently, there comes a point when they think it is safe enough to begin depriving their supporters of their traditional rights and prerogatives. When this goes far enough, protests are raised all over the country against the political leaders. Accusations are made that they are being preyed upon and having their liberties stolen.

By that time, of course, those whose actions eventually led to tyranny have passed over: the world calls them dead. However, as scientists are discovering, they do continue their existence on the invisible planes.[7] Therefore, they see that they have not been wise in their civic or social judgments. For a while, this may not affect them personally, except for the guilt they feel. But the time comes when they desire to enter life again. What happens now? Because they have to live under tyranny, which they do not like, they start to look for a convenient scapegoat on which to place the blame. So they blame their ancestors, society, or any god who may still be said to exist. What never occurs to them is to consider the possibility that they themselves may have been the sole authors of their fate!

Did the Father have any part in all this human tragedy? It was man alone who created the conditions which determined how life would be lived on earth. Some may concede that the Almighty is not implicated in such situations. Nevertheless, they may ask, if He is as merciful as He is said to be in sacred scripture, why then does He not send His messengers to rescue those who had their liberties stolen? From the celestial point of view the answer is that what was happened is not perceived as theft at all. It is seen as the natural result of a dishonest trade, which was motivated by nothing less than ordinary human folly and selfishness. The divine forces will not interfere with the consequences of such wrongdoing until the lessons they contain have been completely mastered.[8]

There is no mystery about divine justice and the balance behind historical events. There is only man's forgetting or ignoring or repudiating the fact of repeat existence. The day that men and women get this fully into their hearts, that day will true justice be administered unto this earth.

Once people realize that life is not accidental, that it fulfills a

27

divine plan worked out well in advance of birth with one's guides and loved ones to gain the experiences necessary for further growth, and that this growth is faster the more one gives and serves, they will try to stop thinking and acting negatively. This higher understanding is the key to progress and peace of mind. When men realize that they themselves have chosen their earthly careers, how can they continue to blame their troubles on either heredity or environment?

If we are not to be ruled by tyrants, we must learn to live by the Spirit of God, who says, "Ye must be born again." Man must learn the truth, and he must awake to his destiny, which is nothing less than reaching his own godhood over many lives. It is this truth which shall set him free. Then, and only then, will he be able to rebuild an economic house pleasing to the Heavenly Father, on the basis of justice and righteousness; for these are the foundations of God's throne.

However, before we delineate the principles that would make this dream a reality, let us glance back to see the stages man has passed through to arrive at today's system (which is bound to change one day as others have in times past).

FOOTNOTES

1. The one book which provides the best introduction to the new revelations is a novel by Benn E. Lewis, *I, John: The Reincarnated Apostle.* Jericho, New York: 1970. Exposition Press, Inc. For autographed copies of this volume readers should write to the author of this novel at 1327 Delafield Place, N. W., Washington, D. C. 20011. See also footnote 1 of Chapter I and footnote 8 of Chapter V.

2. E. W. F. Tomlin, *The Western Philosophers: An Introduction.* "The Perennial Library"; New York: Harper and Row, 1967, p. 25.

3. Adam Smith, *The Wealth of Nations.* "The Modern Library": New York: Random House, Inc., 1937, p. 14.

4. Research into the life of Adam Smith has shown that shortly before his death he had sixteen folio volumes of his manuscripts burnt. This was, of course, a pity, since the interests of this versatile genius ranged from rhetoric through the history of law and government to natural theology. (See, in particular, Letiche, pp. 417-18.? To the best of my knowledge, the reason Smith supervised the burning of his manuscript has not been explained in any of the published works on him. Through ESP we were offered the following explanation. Toward the end of his life, Adam Smith became convinced that reincarnation was an indisputable fact of life. Since this made him feel that many of his arguments were no longer valid, he decided to burn his works.

5. William E. Burrows, "J. C. Penney, at 95, Reflects on the Past and Looks to Future," *The Wall Street Journal,* (November 18, 1970).

6. Lou Austin, *You Are Greater than You Know.* Capon Springs, West Va.: The Partnership Foundation, 1955.

7. Ian Stevenson, "The Evidence for Survival from Claimed Memories of Former Incarnations," *Journal of the American Society for Psychical Research,* Vol. 54, (April and July, 1960) pp. 51-71 and 95-117; Francis Story and Ian Stevenson, "A Case of the Reincarnation Type in Ceylon," *Journal of the American Society for Psychical Research,* Vol. 61, No. 2, (April 1967); and Ian Stevenson, "Characteristics of Cases of the Reincarnation Type in Turkey and Their Comparison with Cases in Two Other Cultures," *International Journal of Comparative Sociology,* Vol. XI, No. 1, (March 1970).

8. This parable, together with its moral, was taken from Discourse 27 recorded by William D. Pelley called, "The Enigma of Events and Whether God or Man Is Their Maker" in *Soulcraft Scripts,* Vol. 3.

Chapter IV

THE EVOLUTION OF ECONOMIC SYSTEMS

Early Social Systems

The life of primitive tribes was governed by custom and impulse. Primitive man did not strike out on his own. He took to wandering with his kind. Living as part of close-knit groups was a necessity for him. In no other way could he have a chance to conquer his foes, procure his food and find relative security in his shelter of rocks and caves. However, this type of group existence in a primitive economy seriously limited the development of his intelligence and moral sense.

Primeval man was at times capable of the most arduous exertions, but he was incapable of engaging in a sustained effort. He was a good hunter and fisher. Yet, seldom, if ever, did he think of making provisions even for the near future. Without discipline and foresight, man in this savage state could not develop an economy of organized opportunities for individual development. And without individual growth he could not organize the institutions necessary to break away from his primitive life. Thus, caught in this vicious cycle, savage life remained bound by the double chains of rigid custom and a precarious existence at a subsistence level.

As we have seen earlier, the most primitive savage has within him the potential to reach the greatest heights of human achievement. Moreover, God never loses control completely of any situation. But, as long as primitive man remained isolated, what could he possibly create with his mind or hands? Where would he find a prototype, an example, to make him raise his sights, an ideal to stimulate his mind, an experience to fire his imagination?

In the absence of civilizing influences, savage life would have

31

remained the same for an indefinite period. However, the divine forces saw to it that a gradual transition took place from the isolation of primitive life to the stimulating interdependence of civilization. The settings chosen for this change were often the great river basins, with their potentials for transportation and agricultural production. In these favorable conditions, a certain surplus was created above the necessities of life, without which further progress would not have been possible.

True, in this stage, the masses were ruled by the few. Man was not yet ready for self-rule. Since the ruling elites had to give their energies primarily to law, making war, and religion, they set up dynastic kingships and hereditary priesthoods. Nevertheless, there were also other elites who attained positions of distinction by showing ingenuity in economic affairs.

Three thousand years before Christ, Mesopotamian merchants were seasoned in business practices, vigilant in drawing up contracts, and stout in litigation. By 2500 B.C., they were forming trading companies for penetration into distant realms to traffic in many kinds of commodities. It has been noted that they dealt in wool, spices, soda, silver, ointments, other wares, and even fair-skinned slaves.[1] However, these merchants, who opened many avenues for social progress, were nevertheless not allowed to trade entirely for private gain.

In fact, the economic practices and ideas of antiquity involved a great deal of governmental control of business. Sometimes the priest-king himself assumed the role of supreme enterpreneur. In Mesopotamia, the precious metals used in exchanging commodities were stamped with the guarantee of some temple or its deity.[2] Many transactions were covered by specific codes of law or religious teachings. The Holy Bible, reflecting the social teachings of the Israelites, provides, a good illustration of centrality of ethics in economic life.[3] The Mosaic laws and traditions are replete with injunctions against greed and extortion. They call repeatedly for justice and mercy in the economic relationships of the covenant people.

One Biblical law explicitly warns against seeing a brother's ox or sheep go astray and withholding help. Another prohibits lending with interest to a brother, although lending with interest to a foreigner is allowed. This edict has been called the famous Deuteronomic double standard on usury. Regulating labor relations was a law forbidding oppression of a hired servant who was poor and needy, and requiring payment to him before the sun went down. These laws definitely bear witness to the fact that among the children of Israel economic relations were governed by divine commandments.

In the ancient world, there were also glaring abuses when economic practices were dictated by religious and political objectives. In ancient Egypt, "every man was bound by a principle of religion to follow the occupation of his father, and was supposed to commit the most horrid sacrilege if he changed it for another," as Adam Smith noted.[4] Large proportions of the surplus production were used for noneconomic purposes not related to the people's welfare. For example, the wealth of the Incas of Central America was dissipated in elaborate sacrificial and ceremonial rites. In other civilizations, much of the surplus product created was wasted on needless wars. All the same, the ancient world did not have the modern problem of treacherous rule by mammon interests behind the scenes.

The Greeks and Romans tried to develop the principles of statecraft for the regulation of economic life in the structure of the state. In most of Athenian history, in Sparta, and later in Rome, the predominant interest was agrarian. The importance of trade and industry was not properly understood. Traders and workers in handicraft were often stamped with the disapproval of the community. They were excluded from the high councils of state. In other places, however, the trader rose to political power.

On the whole, the Greek city-states did enjoy economic prosperity. As Alfred Marshall pointed out, the Greeks were encouraged to work out new ideas without restraint, instead of being repressed by tradition, while their culture had absorbed the best thought of the Old World.[5] The Greeks never felt the extreme pressure of poverty, as a bountiful nature made it easy for them to obtain the requisites of a good life. Even their slaves did not have to work very hard.

However, this easy existence, instead of being a blessing, actually led to their decadence. Since they regarded slavery as an ordinance of nature and industry as somewhat degrading, they had their slaves do most of their work. Thus without the discipline of regular work, they lacked persistent resolution and self-mastery. Consequently the Greeks did not use their freedom to fullest advantage, and as "a genial climate slowly relaxed their physical energies...at last they sank into frivolity."[6]

The Romans were heirs of the Greeks in their practice of leaving work and commerce as much as possible to the slaves. They much preferred war and politics to economics. Even so, they showed much skill in developing trade guilds, joint-stock companies, and other forms of commercial association.

Largely because of the order and unity achieved by imperial Rome, there was much freedom of trade and movement throughout the entire civilized world. Huge fortunes were accumulated by individual Roman citizens. However, these were often won by the power of the sword, with much cruelty.

The Romans made their capital efficient and powerful, but they also made it hateful. Because they placed too much stress on money gain as their motivation for enterprise, the business life of the Romans progressively deteriorated. At one stage, public disdain for business showed itself in a law prohibiting Roman senators from engaging in all forms of business except those connected with holdings of land.[7]

The Roman endured the harshness of his life with a strong sense of duty. However, he was never reconciled to it; that is why he remained sad and stern. The intense religious feelings of the Jews opened new possibilities for reconciling the individual to society but the world was not yet ready to accept the higher Christ teachings which combine inner joy and spiritual growth with social and political improvement.

The Middle Ages

From the fall of Rome in the fifth century, Germanic and

Scandinavian tribes wreaked havoc in Western Europe. Thus passed the glory that was Greece and the grandeur that was Rome. During this dark chaotic epoch, Western civilization remained viable by the skin of its teeth. Then in the year 800, Charlemagne was crowned emperor of the Holy Roman Empire, the Frankish heir to Roman power, and blessed by the powerful Catholic Church. Charlemagne's influence served to unify the culture of Western Europe, which was to become the dominant force in human history. Thus civilization was enabled to endure the terrible disorders of the next two hundred years and to evolve into a social order known as feudalism.

With the loss of monarchical power in the former Holy Roman Empire, the prince of the domain became the key figure, because he was needed for military protection by the people. Since the towns, along with commerce, had largely disappeared, the great estates absorbed most of the lands and the people. With their castles and surrounding estates providing the main bulwark against complete chaos, the princes were thus able to usurp both the revenues and the land.

The authority on this period, Henri Pirenne, described the extremely active life of the prince as follows: "Not only did he lead his men to the wars and with them fling himself upon the enemy, he also presided in his court of justice, supervised the work of his tax-collectors, and gave his personal decision in all important questions; and above all, he watched over the 'public peace'."[8] In return, in addition to performing some minor duties to the lord of the manor, the serf gave a part of his produce and labor. This system of mutual obligation, made rigid by tradition, became the basis of the economic, political, and social structure of the times.

However, the manor house was not the only bastion of strength in the Middle Ages. The Christian church, after many power struggles with secular rulers, was establishing itself as a moral authority independent of the earthly princes of Europe. Beginning with Charlemagne's palace school in Aachen, most of the leading scholars were churchmen; their wide cultural activities greatly strengthened the church.

The church was the catholic one, the greatest single force that bound Europe together during the Middle Ages. The clerical scholars traveled without regard to political boundaries; their allegiance was to the mother church at Rome. Even powerful nobles yielded to its dictates, out of respect for religion or fear of God.

With strong emphasis on a promised life to come, the church thus was able to enforce her moral power over the life of the people. As it became a political force and an immensely rich landowner, the church was able to extend her power to the regulation of economic practices, not always for the better.

Recent historical research has also made it clear that the towns did not entirely disappear from the scene in the Middle Ages. All the same, in medieval times, the feudal domains were the main centers of economic, political, and social life. And this pattern of closed economy, basically devoid of outlets, reduced the bulk of the population to a condition of servitude.

According to Pirenne, the mode of life of the nobles was not especially refined. They were endlessly engaged in private wars and family vendettas, with no intellectual culture, except the embryonic code of chivalry with its emphasis upon devotion and honor. From an economic standpoint, the definitive characteristic of the nobility was their hereditary claim to land. To a certain extent, the ancient idea that labor is unworthy of the freeman was revived once more by feudal Europe.

When there was no strong monarchy and when the small villages of peasants were wide open to invasion, the basic benefit of the feudal system to the peasants was that it offered them security. The idea of security had other attractions also. The peasant class had centuries of experience living close to the soil as a part of nature's annual cycle of birth, death, and rebirth, which was consistent with the teachings of the universal church. The peasant's daily round, spent in turning the soil with a few simple tools and rotating crops within a prescribed strip, at least insured him a predictable life. He knew that his liege would take care of military affairs and that the village priest would care for his soul.

And yet his lot was grim. In such a closed agricultural system, there was hunger, sometimes starvation, and increasingly plague stalked the countryside. The typical peasant whose forebears toiled through the centuries of feudalism was described by Edwin Markham with great pathos:

> Bowed by the weight of centuries he leans
> Upon his hoe and gazes on the ground,
> The emptiness of ages in his face,
> And on his back the burden of the world.
> Who made him dead to rapture and despair,
> A thing that grieves not and never hopes
> Stolid and stunned, a brother to the ox?
> ....
> Whose breath blew out the light within this brain?
> ....
> Oh Masters, lords and rulers of all lands,
> Is this the handiwork you give to God,
> This monstrous thing distorted and soul-quenched?[9]

The destiny of western man could not be allowed to remain in such a cul-de-sac. As noted earlier, change and growth is ever the law of life. New social movements eventually disturb even the most stable social equilibrium and give men new chances for growth.

The growth of towns was one of the principal factors keeping alive the spirit of movement and freedom in the Middle Ages. When these towns were able to survive, they sponsored a growing culture of freedom and individuality, exemplified by the medieval university. The winds of change blew more from these centers than from any other. In the twelfth and thirteenth centuries, the principle town air makes free gave the right of asylum to men who were fed up with feudal restrictions.

North of the Alps, towns were built with a merchant quarter, where itinerant traders gradually settled, and where guild systems developed. South of the Alps, despite the Catholic church's stand against usury, thoroughly self-seeking financial empires were built in such cities as Florence and Venice. Good came out even from these bastions of mammon, however, as they became a force releasing man from the shackles of feudal restraint.

Another strong factor breaking up the mold of medieval life was the Hanseatic League in Northern Europe. The League with its 160 member cities turned the whole of Northern Europe into a unified trading area. Further impetus to economic expansion came from the geographic discoveries of the fifteenth and sixteenth centuries, which ushered in a period characterized by the term commercial revolution.

There was much good and much evil in both epochs of history. I do not condemn or condone either age. I only point out that the clashes of opposing forces were giving European society new chances for growth. How such transitions occur from one historical epoch to another is a question which has been forcefully and endlessly debated. Especially in modern discussions, the hand of God, which in the end predominates, is almost always completely ignored. At this juncture, however, we are more concerned with the interval between medieval times and the revolutionary era in America and France than in the theories of causation in history.

Feudalism Evolves Into Mercantilism

In the general view of European history, the Renaissance with the related Protestant Reformation tolled the death knell of feudalism. In truth, vestiges of feudalism survived for centuries afterward. In the agricultural system of Europe, feudal patterns persisted at least until 1700. Up to that time, European agricultural methods were on a level with those of ancient Persia, India, or China. The development of new agricultural methods and crops on a large scale did not start before the eighteenth century.

By the 1700's, the relations of the ruling and subject classes also had begun to undergo significant transformations. The process of social change had stretched the close bond between the nobility and the peasantry into a more tenuous one. By the eighteenth century, the noble "thought of himself primarily as a landowner collecting a money revenue from a portion of his estate and possibly holding a large farm directly administered for money gains."[10] Thus, even though the personal servitudes of feudalism had greatly diminished, land remained concentrated in the hands of the aristocracy through rigid entail or family settlement. Moreover landlords and peasant farmers alike found themselves entangled in a net of perpetual leases and other legal obstacles to changing methods of cultivation. It is conditions such as these which made eighteenth century reformers naturally wish for unfettered individualism, in order to grasp the opportunities opening up in scientific agriculture.

In the sphere of commerce, banking, and industry, remarkable developments occurred in the sixteenth and seventeenth centuries. In this period, the landed gentry continued as the dominant class. However, wealthy merchants and bankers also assumed positions of power in European society. It was during this period that goldsmith bankers learned to reap enormous interest payments on money which they literally created out of nothing. Before bankers discovered the immensely profitable practice of issuing paper money and other credit instruments backed only by a small amount of metallic money, the nations attached great importance to obtaining gold and silver to serve as liquid capital.

The Portuguese and Spanish solved this problem by plundering the natives of the New World and India and by developing mines in these areas. Other countries who could not gain control of the principal sources of the precious metals, however, had to depend largely on manufacturing and trade for securing gold and silver.

To succeed in their struggles, capitalists found it essential to be supported by the power of a strong and centralized state. At the same time, the kings and monarchs of Europe found it essential to rely on the precious metals and financial resources of the wealthy merchants and bankers. The gradual transition of government from feudal lords to nation-states required money in large amounts. The crown needed money not only to pay for armies and navies to engage in ambitious wars of expansion but also to hire civil servants in order to command the resources of its subjects.

The economic system which emerged along with these developments became known as mercantilism. It was at this time that the peculiar concept of regarding a nation as if it were an individual merchant was developed. This view is best expressed in the argument of the Englishman, Thomas Mun, who found the key to increased wealth in ever observing this rule: "to sell more to strangers yearly than we consume of theirs in value."

To secure this wealth, the power of the state was magnified. Eli Heckscher, the most acclaimed authority on mercantilism, wrote that the concept of Leviathan, or Mortal God, dominated the arguments of the mercantilists to such a degree that the interest in human beings was displaced by the interest in the State. He called mercantilist policies amoral in a twofold sense, because of their aims and the means chosen to attain their aims.[11] The fact is that mercantilists viewed people as economic resources to be managed. So they set out to arrange affairs so cunningly that people would have to act in directions to enhance the materialistic interest of the crown and its financial allies.

For example, a large population was encouraged and wages were kept low to effect a large export surplus of manufactures and a corresponding import surplus of gold and precious metals. Even unemployment was welcomed as it tended to lower wages. No limitations were placed on hours of work. Idleness was regarded as a crime, and relief under the poor laws was scanty.

Under this system, instead of the medieval nobility and the hierarchy of the church, the new master was the state. In terms of freedom, the individual fared no better than he had under feudalism. The supremacy of the State over the individual, the church, and any other groups was widely supported by mercantilist thinkers. Moreover, Machiavelli, in *The Prince*, argued with satanic cleverness that "a benevolent despot was above morality in his public acts provided he sought justifiable objectives." And what were the results of this type of crafty philosophy in action? Since there was no way to balance the disharmony between nations, mercantilism and rampant nationalism led to endless commercial and colonial wars.

On the plus side, even critics had to concede that the growth of power of the nation-states provided security against internal warring interests and extended free trade within the national boundaries. Heckscher was, therefore, right in claiming that it would be historically naive to think that modern civilization could have flourished if Europe had not gone through a stage of narrow nationalism in economic and political affairs. The predominant view among modern economists is that mercantilism was an age of error in economic reasoning. From a divine perspective, it appears as an age when evil in human affairs was allowed to run its course, to make people desire relief in an opposite direction.

The exponent and practitioner par excellence of mercantilism was Colbert, the statesman who served as minister of finance and virtual dictator under Louis XIV. Unlike the other states which were heirs to Charlemagne's empire, France had formed a unified kingdom as early as the first half of the sixteenth century. By 1560 Roman law had been accepted, as it had in most of continental Western Europe. With this background, France was the model state for the mercantilist work of unification during the disintegration of feudalism.

Colbert's attempt to abolish internal tolls and standardize weights and measures fitted into the mercantilist system of encouraging free trade within the country. To have his king wrest control from the towns and secular lords, the guilds, the most medieval of institutions, were utilized for the regulation of industry. The purpose of this state intervention was to create large sources of revenue for itself "under the more or less false pretense of guiding industry along the right lines."[12] Thus, in France, the privileged industry came to be the manufacturing of luxury goods, characterized by artistic workmanship, based not on people's needs but on the state's greed.

Within a decade, Colbert's policies doubled the King's revenues and made France the greatest nation in Europe. At the same time, the finest transport system on the continent was created and libraries and academies were built and subsidized to foster learning. Nevertheless, the increased public spending necessitated by these policies brought the kingdom close to financial ruin. In the end, Colbert passed away, an intensely unpopular man.

This French experience illustrates how fleeting the fruits of evil can be. The mercantilist state of Louis XIV and Colbert, with its clever deceptions and elaborate system of industrial regulation and subsidies, manifested what we called the satanic conception of government in Chapter III. In this conception, which is not without visionary idealism of its own, it is the ends and not the means which count. Ends pursued with the wrong means, however, never materialize. For example, to glorify the French state, new ideas in industrial techniques were eagerly sought after and stolen if necessary. Yet the revolution in techniques took place in Britain. Because of its carefully ordered system of law and government and its self-conscious intellectual and artistic supremacy, most Europeans felt the future must belong to France. Nevertheless, it was Britain, with her passionate adherence to liberty and practical approach to life which led the world in the successive age of industrialism and liberty.

FOOTNOTES

1. Miriam Beard, *A History of Business*, Vol. 1 *From Babylon to the Monopolists.* "Ann Arbor Paperbacks"; Ann Arbor: The University of Michigan Press, 1963, p. 11.
2. Ibid., p. 12
3. Bible, Deuteronomy Chap. 22-24
4. Adam Smith, p. 62
5. Alfred Marshall, *Principles of Economics.* New York: The MacMillan Co., 1952, p. 278.
6. Ibid., p. 730.
7. Ibid., p. 731.
8. Henri Pirenne, *A History of Europe,* Vol. 1, *From the End of the Roman World in the West to the Beginnings of the Western States.* "Doubleday Anchor Books"; Garden City, N.Y.: Doubleday and Co., Inc., 1958, p. 135.
9. Edwin Markham, "The Man with the Hoe", *American Poetry and Prose.* Cambridge, Mass.: The Riverside Press, 1934, pp. 1205-1206.
10. Bowden, Karpovich, and Usher, p. 64.
11. Eli F. Heckscher, *Mercantilism,* trans. Mendel Shapiro, Volume 1, New York: MacMillan, 1955, p. 285.
12. Ibid., p. 178.

Chapter V

AMERICA'S MANIFEST DESTINY

Divine Promise Fulfilled

Why it was Britain and not France which achieved the miraculous industrial revolution first has never been explained completely. True, such historical questions usually cannot be answered in terms of one simple set of forces in action. In this case, however, there is one overriding factor which clarifies many a mystery. This factor is divine intent as revealed in biblical prophecy.

I realize that in historical studies today the hand of God is seldom seen as a force shaping national destiny. This is because there are so few who understand how spiritual laws operate, and even fewer who have the keys to unlock the meaning of prophecy. Most people are not even aware of the fact that there has been a long record of fulfilled prophecy both in the Bible and in other sources.[1]

I do not deny that oracles have often spoken in riddles, but, with the proper keys, the most cryptic statements can become crystal clear. And the most important key, which explains many mysterious turns in world events since the eighteenth century, is the identity in modern times of the ancient tribes of Ephraim and Manasseh.

It will be recalled that the Father's promise of the birthright—the promise of vast material possessions and world dominance—passed from Abraham through Jacob (renamed Israel) to Ephraim and Manasseh. Referring to these two sons of Joseph, it was prophesied that, "A Nation and a company of nations shall come from you, and Kings shall spring from you." (Genesis 35: 11) and again: "I will multiply your descendants as the stars of

44

heaven . . . and your descendants shall possess the gate of their enemies, and by your descendants shall all the nations of the earth bless themselves, because you have obeyed my voice." (Genesis 22: 17-18) Also, "Your descendants . . . shall spread abroad to the west and to the east and to the north and to the south." (Genesis 28:14) Finally, speaking of Manasseh and his descendants, Jacob said prophetically, "He also shall become a people (nation), and he also shall be great; nevertheless his younger brother (Ephraim) shall be greater than he, and his descendants shall become a multitude of nations." (Genesis 48:19)

What nations have blessed most of the world since the nineteenth century, controlling the gates of their enemies—the Suez Canal, the Panama Canal, Gibraltar, Malta, Aden, Hong Kong, Singapore, the Khyber Pass? The world powers of Great Britain (Ephraim) and the United States of America (Manasseh). Toward the end of the eighteenth century, these two nations were small and insignificant, but at the zenith of their powers, the British Commonwealth of Nations and the United States possessed over two-thirds of the world's wealth and industrial might.

There are those who feel that the birthright promises were meant for the Jews. This view has been shown to be in error. After the division of the House of Israel (the full twelve tribes) about 3,000 years ago, the people of the ten-tribe northern kingdom, led by the tribes of Ephraim and Manasseh, were never called Jews. Rather the Jews are the posterity of the two-tribe southern kingdom of Judah. Besides, as Adam Rutherford has emphasized, "even the wildest flight of the imagination cannot magnify the Jews into 'a company of nations'.[2]

Then, with the aid of both biblical authority and an impressive body of historical evidence, Rutherford shows that the birthright promises were fulfilled and will continue to be fulfilled in the histories of Great Britain and the United States of America.[3]

The hand of God has guided the development of the British

people for centuries. It was not an accident which made Britain the only Western state to achieve national unification in the Middle Ages, beginning in the ninth century. Furthermore, Britain was blessed as a nation over the centuries with a legal system built upon the common law, which had its origins in the law of God, natural and revealed.[4] The common law established an elaborate system of rights outside statute law, based on the practice of the courts. Thus whereas Roman law, as used on the Continent, reinforced the monarch's power, the common law jurists were a most powerful force in resisting monarchy.

From the end of the sixteenth century onward, British common law protected the economic freedom of the citizen and refused to recognize restraints of trade associated with monopolies. Moreover, a very important principle of constitutional government, the rule of law, took root first in British soil. The basic concept of the rule of law is that the state is a subject of the law, on the same footing as all other subjects. Consequently, the state is obliged to prove the legality of its acts. This concept in practice greatly limited the British government's ability to regiment the people by means of industrial regulations.

Moreover, throughout the reign of the Tudors and the Stuarts, there was a consistent policy to aid the agrarian classes of society, who suffered from the new economic developments. In contrast, their counterparts on the Continent never paid much attention to the underdog. Because of such differences, the revolution in Britain came much earlier than in France and was much less disruptive. The doctrine of the divine right of kings was ended as early as the seventeenth century, with the final victory of parliament over the royal absolutism of the Stuarts. Thus, in 1689, when constitutional government was founded in Britain with the adoption of the Bill of Rights, absolutism was still being consolidated on the Continent.

The importance of these legal factors cannot be overemphasized. First, the limits which the British constitution placed on its government proved to be favorable for the rapid accumulation of wealth, which, in turn, encouraged invention and new technology. Secondly, after the triumph of parliament, the rising mercantile and industrial classes shifted the interest of the state from regulating domestic industry to regulating navigation, foreign trade and colonies. Eventually, the new emphasis made Britain the greatest naval and colonial power in the world.

According to the Father's timetable, the day of feudal restrictions of human activity was nearing its close. Thus, toward the end of the Piscean age, the island-dwelling Ephraim, with its free institutions and powerful navy, was guided to achieve the greatest world influence. Under the leadership of divinely inspired statesmen, Britannia ruled the waves, and planted its seeds of constitutional government around the world. There were, however, other prophecies to be fulfilled through another division of the House of Israel, the Tribe of Manasseh, branching over the wall of the empire of Ephraim.

The Uniqueness of America

The unique destiny of America has been played out in a historical drama quite different from that of the Old World. Likewise the American patriots were a different breed from their European forebears. While Thomas Jefferson admired and emulated his rugged frontier father of questionably Welsh background, he took scant note of his maternal aristocratic Randolph ancestors, saying, "They trace their pedigree far back in England and Scotland, to which let every one ascribe the faith and merit he chooses."

In developing a colonial society divergent from the mother country, America became a haven for refugees from the old feudal regimes of Europe. While the mainstay of early immigration was British, numerous Germans, Scotch-Irish, Frenchmen, Dutchmen, and other Europeans also sought a better way of life in the new world. From the beginning, therefore, the souls divinely guided to the shores of the North American continent came from a variety of backgrounds. It is

47

interesting, however, that half the Pilgrim fathers as well as thousands of colonists who followed them to New England came from the extreme eastern part of England known as East Anglia, in view of the fact that ethnological and historical research has shown East Anglians to be descendants of the Tribe of Manasseh.[5]

Even scholars who have shown no interest in spiritual history could not help observing something special in the spirit of those who came to the new world. According to the celebrated historians Charles and Mary Beard, "That something was a quality of energy, enterprise, daring, or aspiration that was to be a power in the course of American history, immediately and by transmission through coming generations."[6]

In Europe, no matter where a man had lived, the best lands had been tightly held by the nobility for generations. In America, the supply of farmland and virgin timber lying ready for development were so abundant that they were accessible to almost everyone. Thus abundance of land was a principal factor attracting the people who were destined to come to the new world. But something else was needed to bind these people into a cohesive nation.

Influenced by the mercantilist concepts discussed in the previous chapter, the British set out to use the American colonies primarily as plantations, providing the mother country with farm products and raw materials and serving as customers for manufactured articles. As the eighteenth century progressed, the economic conflict between Great Britain and the colonies became aggravated, because of more drastic policies affecting land holdings and trade, pressed by certain financial interests.[7]

However, the force of economic conflict alone, powerful as it was, could not have galvanized the thirteen colonies into united action. At a time when George III tried to assert his royal prerogative more vigorously than his predecessors, leading Americans such as Thomas Jefferson and John Adams were poring over the writings of Montesquieu, Voltaire, and Rousseau, to learn new concepts of liberty, social contract, and checks and balances in government. The spreading ideals of personal freedom and self-government enhanced the American desire to have a completely new start. At the same time, the opposition of George III to this spirit created a unity among the colonists which would have been unthinkable a generation before. Thus in this period also we find an illustration of how a clash between old and new systems of political structure can give birth to a creative new beginning.

To lead the American people during these critical times, historians say that great leaders emerged. These men amazed the civilized world with their genius for leadership, their strength in overcoming obstacles, and their innovative ideas in government. Yet, in all these developments, modern thinkers still refuse to see the hand of the Father. But how much luck or coincidence could there have been in the preparation of a man like George Washington for his position of national leadership?

Washington had a rugged boyhood, with much outdoor activities, and the fine traditions of a strong family. His formal education was limited, as was typical in his time and place. Early experience as a surveyor provided him with skills he would later need as a general. And his military experience in the British army made him aware of British weakness in land fighting. His years as a successful farmer and landowner gave him administrative experience. And what he learned as a Virginia legislator prepared him for the more important position he was to occupy later, as did his participation in the Continental Congress.

Washington had the stout soul to withstand the vicissitudes, the dangers and pervasive discouragement that were his lot as commander-in-chief of the long Revolution (1775-1783). Renouncing a practice often seen in Europe, he also had the strength of character to refuse a monarchy offered to him by the officers under his command. Washington returned his commission to the Continental Congress and became the first president of the free nation he helped to establish.

In truth, the character, background, and experience of this giant among men were specially tailored to set the American nation on its divinely intended course. The guidance Washington received was also evidenced in his religious life and his vision about the future of America, which formed another basis for the advice he offered his countrymen.

As though he could foresee all the major problems which would trouble his nation, Washington charted a safe course for the new republic. In his farewell address, he emphasized the "immense value of . . . national union." He warned against the dangers of excessive party politics. He advised restraining "the spirit of encroachment," which tends to consolidate the powers of government beyond constitutional limits and thus to create "whatever the form of government, a real despotism." Washington saw religion and morality as indispensable supports for political prosperity, adding that, "reason and experience both forbid us to expect that national morality can prevail in exclusion of religious principle."

"With respect to economic policy, his "great rule of conduct" was to extend commercial relations to foreign nations with "as little political connection as possible." Therefore, he advised the country forcefully "to steer clear of permanent alliance with any portion of the foreign world."

If one could free himself from the binding chains of preconception, how clear it would be that America has already paid a terrible price for having departed from the course charted by her truly inspired founding father.

America's current troubles are seldom seen as the inevitable consequences of departing from plans and principles set by divinely appointed men. Nevertheless, just because people refuse to see this relationship does not make it any the less true. The fact that social catastrophes are almost never traced to violations of spiritual laws should not be surprising in times when the most influential thinkers are either atheistic or agnostic. Sooner or later, however, it should become obvious that if there is a just God, He would never allow the innocent to suffer. In fact, there must be a just reason, or a good purpose for suffering of any kind.

Social scientists claim that it is environment which shapes the

50

lives of men. But does environment really account for one's triumphs or failures? Are men puppets of circumstance? Are nations simply aggregations of people jumbled together, in a hodgepodge, to work out any sort of destiny which happens to suit their caprice? If there is a God of order, would not each nation have a pattern of its own to follow? In the United States, it is revealed that the divinely ordained pattern was to set up a nation of many peoples to demonstrate the benefits of self-rule on what may be called the sporting basis.

Sportmanship goes much beyond what takes place in arenas of mass entertainment. It is a style of conduct with universal application. Essentially it involves honest rivalry and graceful acceptance of results—particularly when the results evidence superior effort. To acknowledge demonstrated superiority in an opponent without bitterness or ill feeling indicates a high degree of emotional discipline. If there is a just Father, such ethical poise or gracious command of self cannot be accidental. It can come only after a long series of lives in other ages and civilizations in which similar forms of emotional control have proven their beneficence. Thus, paradoxical as it may sound, the youngest civilization on earth was sponsored by the oldest souls in heaven!

Economic Growth of the "Young" Nation

I do not intend to imply that all Americans were equally advanced in their spiritual attainment. In fact, the founding fathers realized that they had a nation made up of many components, many of them almost primitive. Previously, some had not known anything but servitude or battle. Therefore, the early fathers knew that they could do no more than set down a nucleus that would have to be changed many times.

Much has been made of the fact that, at first, voting was mainly restricted to men who owned property or paid taxes. But even though the early American leaders serving in important offices were men of property, their thought and actions indicate that they had the nation's good at heart. Their basic aim, in contrast to the aims of some counterparts in recent years, was to serve the people, keeping always in mind the people's limited ability to accept changes which appear desirable to more enlightened minds.

The American economy through the first half of the nineteenth century was predominantly agrarian, with a population of about 2,500,000 people. Consequently, the distribution of the 3,000,000 square miles over which the central government held jurisdiction was basic to the development of the nation. Jefferson firmly believed that freehold farmers were the best and truest support for republican government. Following his lead, the popular democratic forces continually pressed for virtually free distribution of federal lands. Thus America was spared the problems associated with a servile peasant class. The notable exception was the large plantation system in the South, which perpetuated the curse of slavery. Elsewhere the emerging pattern was one of family-sized farms cultivated either by the owner or by a renter who aspired to ownership.

The wide distribution of lands inherent in this pattern was an important factor in creating the mass markets sustaining the mass production economy of the second half of the nineteenth century. During the early phases of national development, it was by no means certain that the country would experience the type of industrial growth taking place in Britain. There were shortages of capital as well as labor, i.e., both skilled and unskilled workers ready to accept a wage-earner's status. Moreover, Jefferson opposed an economic system which would tend to create a class of uneducated wage earners without property—a potential threat to free government.

It was Alexander Hamilton, first secretary of the treasury, who first set the nation on the path of industrial development. He planned the national currency, founded a mint, won approval for a central bank, established the nation's credit by having the federal government fund its obligations and assume state debts which might otherwise not have been paid. Hamilton also advocated measures to encourage immigration of skilled workers, to attract capital to manufacturing and to develop the nation's transportation.

On the whole, the aims Hamilton worked for did materialize. The nineteenth century did become a century of progress in transportation. Successive waves of immigration brought in the workers and the customers for the nation's industries. And the capital needed to build these industries was attracted first from successful merchants, land speculators, bankers and later from industrialists as well. In building the industrial might of the nation, the scope given to free enterprise in a huge unified national market was a great help. However, it would be impossible to explain what made America's economic development the success story of the world without reference to the inventiveness and resourcefulness of her people.

Here was an amalgam of optimistic, energetic, hard-working and generous people destined to prepare mankind for heaven. By means of their expanding range of free choice, swifter movements, and cumulative knowledge, they were to liberate man's earthbound mind so it could function with greater freedom on the spiritual planes. Such spiritual factors behind a country's economic development are seldom recognized, especially in recent years. Even inventions are explained as resulting from every conceivable factor except divine inspiration. People who understand spiritual law, however, know that without Him there would have been no new creations. "Great scientists, great artists in chemistry, great inventors of machines: who are these souls but my servants in flesh? They invent at My behest."[8]

The Industrial Revolution has been described essentially as the substitution of mechanical power for muscle. As energy released by machines freed Americans from limitations imposed by muscle power, Eli Whitney's invention of mass production techniques freed them from limitations imposed by scarce manual skills.

When Whitney had to manufacture several thousand stands of arms for the U.S. government, he faced a shortage of skilled craftsmen. At that time, the manufacture of a gun involved a whole series of delicate cutting and fitting operations to make and assemble a large number of intricate parts. There were not many craftsmen who could do this highly skilled work. Therefore, Whitney found a way to reduce drastically the range of skills required by one individual by dividing the manufacturing process into smaller, simpler, and standardized steps and assigning each step to one person.

Whitney's method of producing interchangeable parts by the repetitive use of simpler skills spread from one industry to another. Thus it became possible to raise the productivity of even relatively unskilled Americans by leaps and bounds in the course of the nation's industrial development. With the opening of such new productive possibilities in a nation blessed with the richest natural resources, if the American experiment in self-government had been allowed to proceed unhampered, it is virtually certain that a Utopia would have been reached long ago. But unfortunately this development was not allowed. It was difficult for some in the high financial circles in England and on the Continent to reconcile themselves to losing control of the rich resources of the new world. They had observed the critical flaw in the American character, the propensity of this optimistic and generous people to trust others too much. This was the handle they intended to use to accomplish their aims.

How these foreign financiers and their agents took advantage of the overly trusting Americans in order to step in and take over what they wanted will not be found in the history books our children study in schools. Many famous men such as Voltaire, Napoleon, Lamartine, and Ford have said that recorded history is often untrue.

Books on economic history refer to politicking and bribery of legislators to gain special charters for individual commercial banks which were given questionable privileges to establish local monopolies of credit in particular areas. They also refer to numerous frauds and much illegal profiteering which involved leading citizens and high government officials. The more daring books even mention the trade Americans carried on with the enemy during wartime.

The attempts to gain control over the entire banking system and the Treasury Department of the United States Government by international banking interests in order to be in a position to dominate the nation's economy have remained shrouded in mystery. I shall refer to these interests as international mammon in this book, on the theory that discretion is the better part of valor. These forces have known that they can press on sensitive nerves and assume controlling positions over a nation's finances much more readily during periods of severe stress and national emergency. Therefore, they have always had an abiding interest in wars or in rumors of wars.

The international mammon forces have not always caused the military conflicts from which they profit. Sometimes, seeing sentiment for a particular war growing in the land, they have encouraged it and channeled the destructive passions along the lines which serve their interest best.

Fanning the flames of a senseless war that they saw on the horizon was, in fact, the role international mammon played in the War of 1812. Thus, after the charter of the powerful first United States Bank was not renewed, the nation found itself declaring a needless war on Great Britain. This conflict accomplished none of its aims but left the United States government in a sea of financial troubles. Therefore, President Madison and his fellow Republicans had to establish a Second Bank of the United States on the same principle as the First Bank they had assailed. Moreover, they had to combine the scattered public debts into a consolidated debt larger than the one they had once condemned.[9]

However, even these concessions did not give the international bankers the control which they desired. Therefore, they set out to plunge the nation into a larger war, to exploit the type of power which makes governments bow to their wills. The role of financial intrigue in the Civil War, lasting four terrible years from 1861 to 1865, is becoming more widely known.[10] What is not yet known, however, is that this tragic fratricidal war was plotted for many years behind the scenes by the mammon interests, using the issue of slavery as a pretext. Their aim was to gain a surer stranglehold on the growing nation's monetary system. President Lincoln, however, took his stand and stopped the international moneychangers. This decision cost Lincoln his life. However, had he not taken that stand America would probably have been subjected to foreign rule long before the twentieth century.

In order to finance wartime expenditures, Lincoln decided to issue $450 million in U.S. notes, or greenbacks, instead of borrowing the money from the mammon interests. It has been estimated that had the United States borrowed the money, instead of printing it, a hundred years later the total interest cost to the taxpayer would have accumulated to an amount approximately five times the original amount borrowed.[11] Considering that the U.S. government alone borrowed about $200 billion to finance World War II, it is easy to imagine the financial burden the mammon interests impose on nations through the wars they precipitate in their relentless power drives.

On the whole, however, the nineteenth century was not a century of war. True, the seeds of trouble in future years were being planted. Even so, governmental power, especially in Britain, was increasingly moving to those serving the divine plan of individualism and evolutionary change by trial and error. And the negative forces in finance were being checked to a large degree, especially in America.

Toward the end of the nineteenth century, the center of financial power began to shift from Europe to America. Compared with European financiers, American capitalists were not as interested in imperialistic ventures and political dominion over foreign nations. Nevertheless, the enormous growth of American financial power was bound to pull the nation into the vortex of struggles for world power.

Much has been written regarding the history of the concentration of economic power in America. To some extent, this trend was associated with developments in banking. However, a more fundamental reason for the growth of financial empires of gigantic proportions was the indiscriminate legislative and judicial backing for business which led to the creation of a moneyed aristocracy stronger than the government in Washington.

In *The Truth about the Trusts*, John Moody described the dominant position of the American capitalist interests as follows:

> Around these two groups (The Morgan-Rockefeller interests), or what must ultimately become one greater group, all other smaller groups of capitalists congregate. They are all allied and intertwined by their various mutual interests. For instance, the Pennsylvania Railroad interests are on the one hand allied with the Vanderbilts and on the other hand with the Rockefellers. The Vanderbilts are closely allied with the Morgan group, and both the Pennsylvania and the Vanderbilt interests have recently become the dominating factors in the Reading system, a former Morgan road and the most important part of the anthracite coal combine which had always been dominated by the Morgan people... Viewed as a whole, we find the dominating influences in the trusts to be made up of an intricate network of large and small capitalists, many allied to another by ties of more or less importance, but all being appendages to or parts of the greatest groups which are themselves dependent on and allied with the two mammoth, or Rockefeller and Morgan groups. These two mammoth groups jointly...constitute the heart of the business and commercial life of the nation.[12]

Such powerful financiers had little difficulty influencing the very character of public life. They made their voices heard through newspapers, influenced public opinion in other ways and put pressure on governments at all levels. In such a distorted atmosphere, professional politicians continued to accuse each other of theft, corruption, and incapacity. The people, however, kept their faith in free government.

In fact, during the time of Theodore Roosevelt, governmental leadership moved once more in a righteous direction. Roosevelt challenged the abuse of power by his emphasis on honesty and dignity in public life. He denounced both what he called 'malefactors' of great wealth and 'anarchistic labor leaders.' He started effective enforcement of antitrust legislation and made many of his countrymen proud of their government, which they had previously regarded with suspicion.

Many of the reforms which Theodore Roosevelt backed, however, were blocked in Congress or in the courts. Moreover, as one textbook on economic history pointed out, the financial crisis of 1907 was used by the big money interests to check President Roosevelt's reform tendencies as indicated by the fact that he assured J.P. Morgan that he would not prosecute United States Steel if it took over the Tennessee Coal and Iron Company on the pretext of saving it financially.[13]

Nevertheless, social reformers succeeded in making some headway with limited measures of social improvement, even though they could not resolve the more fundamental problems of economic organization.

America's Destiny Tied to Its Currency

The lifeblood of a body politic is its currency. Disorders in the circulating medium of exchange flow from one part of the social organism to the other until the whole economic system is affected. Similarly, as the money flow is improved, the health of the entire economic system is restored. From the earliest colonial days, Americans have had problems with their currency. As a nation they had to go through several deflations and inflations, which influenced the lives and fortunes of practically everybody. In times of money panics and the ensuing depressions, hundreds of thousands of people were ruined, and millions suffered severe hardships. Yet Americans never bothered to understand adequately the ramifications of the currency systems of the past or the arrangements governing their lives today.

The colonists did not have banks because they obtained their credit from British merchants. But after the War of Independence and especially during the 1790's, several private commercial banks were chartered to replace the British sources of credit. These banks helped to provide capital for a growing economy. They also imposed severe burdens on many borrowers, who criticized the banks bitterly. From the beginning, because of the special privilege of creating money granted to private bankers, bank charters had to be obtained after much politicking or bribery of legislators. Later, actual fraud and severe personal and social losses resulting from bank failures also became common occurrences.

Hamilton had recommended that the First Bank of the United States act as fiscal agent of the national government and be subject to governmental supervision to protect the public interest, although he realized that it would have to be privately owned to a large extent. In practice, even this bank operated essentially as a profit-making commercial bank, thus dishonoring Hamilton's principle that the control of bank credit was an essential part of the federal government's constitutional function.

The establishment of the First Bank of the United States and its successor, as well as other parts of the nation's money and credit system, gave rise to an endless series of controversies. At times these resulted in the most bitter political battles. The basic problem was that the objectives of the monetary system of which the banks were a part failed to aim directly at supplying the nation with the required amount of money on an equitable basis, as Benjamin Franklin had advised with his usual common sense. Instead, reliance was placed on the operation of supply and demand in money markets, guided by rigid metallic standards or makeshift governmental regulations, all of which could have been and, in fact, were manipulated by unscrupulous financial interests.

The public was opposed to a powerful money monopoly like

the privately owned Bank of England. But many of the local banks which were allowed to spring up to prevent the rise of such a monolith were too weak to survive in years of strain. True, a large number of small banks continued to operate. But, in the end, enormous concentration of banking power developed in any case.

One way in which this happened was through what was called the pyramiding of deposits. To earn interest on their excess cash reserves, the smaller banks deposited them in larger banks, which, in turn, deposited them in the largest New York City banks, in which interest rates were the highest. The dangers of this situation were aggravated by the practice the largest banks had of making call loans to speculators on the New York stock markets.

Another element of instability was introduced by the humpty-dumpty way in which the banks reacted to fluctuations in business conditions. In a recession, to protect their reserves, banks tended to reduce their loans when more credit was needed to check the contraction of business. And when money and cash reserves were in excess supply, banks found it profitable to expand their loans, which, of course, tended to add fuel to the fire of incipient inflation. All the same, the need to stabilize the money markets did not receive much attention before the panic of 1907.

The facts unearthed by the Pujo Committee of the House of Representatives following this financial panic gave the public a picture of a "money trust," which gave "a small group of Wall Street tycoons control not only of all the big banks of New York City, but of most of the financial power in the whole country."[14] Despite this shocking revelation, there was no serious attempt to smash this extremely dangerous concentration of control. Instead, the congress chose to reform the monetary system of the nation by compromising with the very powers that had attempted to take over the nation's economy.

In 1913, by establishing the Federal Reserve System, Congress granted special privileges to the international mammon interests it could have and should have controlled with a firm hand. Had Congress not shown weakness in this year of destiny, just before Europe was pushed into World War I, international mammon would not have had its victories, and America would have escaped the tragedy of two world wars and a great depression, as well as the regimentation which inevitably followed these disastrous events.

Economists, who have seldom been good prophets, either as predictors of what the future holds or as spokesman for righteousness, tended to think that much good would come out of the Federal Reserve System. They have closed their eyes to the evils which have also infected this organization from the very beginning. The financial oligarchy which made sure that they would never lose control of the new central banking system, was able to transform a nation dedicated to freedom into one of the most thoroughly manipulated peoples in the civilized world.

Once again, it is becoming evident that if man shall not put his trust in God—as noted on the U.S. currency—he will have to depend on mammon to extricate himself from his dilemmas, until he learns his lesson the hard way!

FOOTNOTES

1. Those interested in this subject may wish to investigate some of the following books:
Adam Rutherford, *Anglo-Saxon Israel or Israel-Britain*. London: By the author, First Edition, 1934; Herbert W. Armstrong, *The United States and British Commonwealth in Prophecy*. Pasadena, Calif.: Ambassador College Press, 1967; Nostradamus, *Prophecies on World Events*, trans. Stewart Robb New York: Liveright Publishing Company, 1961; Raymond Neff Holliwell, *The World's Destiny according to Prophecy*. New Jersey: By the author, 1941; Hal Lindsey with C.C. Carlson, *The Late Great Planet Earth*. Grand Rapids, Michigan, Zondervan Publishing House, 1961; Mary Ellen Carter, *Edgar Cayce on Prophecy*. New York: Paperback Library, Inc., 1968.

2. Rutherford, p. 5.

3. Ibid., pp. 4-45.

4. Ibid., pp. 87-93. Regarding the Divine origin of the common law, Rutherford offers the following quotation from *The Common Law* by Dr. Wm. Pasdoe Goard: "Turning to British and American legal authorities, we may point out that Blackstone takes as the foundation of the common law, the Law of God, natural and revealed. We here quote from the Encyclopaedia Britannica (eleventh edition) under the heading 'English Law' as follows:

If we are content to look no further than the text-books ... we may read our way backwards to Blackstone (d. 1780), Hale (d. 1676) ... until we are in the reign of Henry of Anjou, and yet shall perceive that we are always reading of one and the same body of law, though the little body has become great, and the ideas that were few and indefinite have become many and explicit.

The other rivulet we may call Anglo-Saxon. Pursuing it through the code of Canute (d. 1035) and the ordinances of Alfred (c. 900) and his successors. This, it may be noted, gives to English legal history a singular continuity from Alfred's day to our own. . . . Alfred the great Saxon law-giver and administrator during the Saxon period, places the matter of the Divine origin of the law in the forefront. The following is taken from *Alfred the Great*, for it gives in a concise form just the thing we desire to show, viz., that the law of Moses was the basis of Anglo-Saxon administration:

Then the author proceeds to demonstrate in detail the close parallel between the Mosaic code in *Exodus* and *Alfred's Dooms* (or laws).

5. Ibid., pp. 81-82 and 4-21.

6. From *The Beards' New Basic History of the United States* by Charles A. and Mary R. Beard, revised by William Beard, copyright © 1944, 1960, 1968 by Doubleday and Co., Inc. Reprinted by permission of the publisher. p. 33.

7. How "protection for favored interests in England weakened the British economy by virtue of its injury to the Americans" is explained by: George Soule and Vincent P. Carosso, *American Economic History*. New York: The Dryden Press, 1957, pp. 47-55. These scholars, however, do not mention that among the "favored interests in England" were financiers who "had no direct interest in trade, and profited by the embarrassments of merchants as well as of princes and governments." See Bowden, Karpovich and Usher, p. 185.

8. *The Golden Scripts*. Noblesville, Indiana: Soulcraft Fellowship, Inc., (renamed Fellowship Press Inc.) 1961, p. 587. It is in this volume representing transcriptions of one called the recorder (actually William Dudley Pelley) that the profoundest and most beautiful of the new revelations may be found.

9. Charles A., Mary R., and William Beard, pp. 169-172.

10. Wylie C. Sampson, *The Patriot's Primer*. Delray Beach,

Fla.: Palm Beach County Conservative Club, 1970. See the sources cited on p. 10.

11. House of Representatives, 88th Congress, Committee on Banking and Currency, Subcommittee on Domestic Finance, *A Primer on Money*. Washington, D.C.: U.S. Government Printing Office (August 5, 1964), p. 48.

12. Charles A., Mary R., and William Beard, pp. 294-5.

13. Soule and Carosso, p. 271.

14. U.S. Congress, *A Primer on Money*, p. 57.

Chapter VI

AMERICA ENTERS
THE INTERNATIONAL CHECKERS GAME

The Tribulations of Manasseh

The disruptions of America's Divine destiny by financial influences are not often discussed in public. Without the aid of direct revelation, it would have been next to impossible to tell it as it was, since so much of what happened has never been told. When revelation is added to research, however, many seemingly unconnected events fall in place to form a consistent pattern.

A recurring theme in this drama is the conflict between national leaders who have sensed that the American people must be free to set an example to the rest of the world and powerful international forces who care little about such idealistic aspirations. As we shall see, it was not accidental that America moved away from her path of destiny.

Even before this nation was drawn into World War I, an era of independence was coming to a close. As Theodore Roosevelt pointed out with reference to the coal strike of 1902:

> A few generations ago, an American workman could have saved money, gone West, and taken up a homestead. Now the free lands were gone. In earlier days a man who began with pick and shovel might have come to own a mine. That outlet too was now closed, as regards the immense majority. . . . The majority of the men who earned wages in the coal industry, if they wished to progress at all, were compelled to progress not by ceasing to be wage earners, but by improving the conditions under which all the wage earners in all the industries of the country lived and worked, as well, of course, as improving their individual efficiency.[1]

Thus, in his inimitable way, Theodore Roosevelt was pointing to a new age of economic interdependence which called for collective measures. The changing economic system of the nation had also influenced the character of the immigration to America. At first, it was essentially independent and pioneering individuals, bent on developing the abundant natural resources of the new world, who were attracted to America. Later immigrants came in response to the heavy demand for labor to build canals or railroads. Starting with the 1880's, with the growth of capitalism, there was a marked change in the countries of origin of the later immigrants. In the 1870's more than eighty percent of the newcomers came from northern and western Europe. By 1910, about eighty percent of the migrants were being brought from the less advanced societies of southern and eastern Europe to work for low wages in the industrial urban centers of the nation. Many of these people were completely illiterate, and the great majority had no understanding of self-government.

In an early period, George Washington, Thomas Jefferson, and John Adams had warned against free migration of people from countries without experience in self-government. These warnings, however, were discredited by mammon interests who placed selfish gain above national ideals. Steamship companies anxious for passengers, employers looking for cheap labor, speculators hoping to gain from overcrowded housing, and machine politicians scheming to take bemused voters to the polls en masse all contributed to the confusion of American life through unrestrained immigration.

It was finally organized labor which put a stop to this unholy exploitation of immigrants. As Samuel Gompers pointed out, even though the generous American people wished to maintain their land as a free asylum to the oppressed everywhere, the United States could not solve all the problems of the world.

At the turn of the century, America had quite a few problems of its own to solve. All of these problems involved the rights of men or abuses of power. There were, for example, the difficulties of the former slaves who had been uprooted from their sheltered existence in the southern plantation system. Emancipation had set four million bondsmen free—the greatest act of liberation in the history of the world. However, the act also set them adrift in the country, illiterate, ill prepared for the competition of the outside world, and usually penniless.

After emancipation, which provided no compensation to the slave owners and no land to the former slaves, efforts were made to establish a wage system in southern agriculture. But these efforts did not succeed. The newly freed negroes did not want to work in gangs under the close supervision of the whites who had lately been their masters. The landowners, who were to be the employers, did not have the capital to continue making wage payments in periods of poor crops or poor markets. As a result, an inefficient system of share cropping tenancy developed on holdings which were often pitifully small. Thus, for many of the tenants—black and white alike—dependence on the landowner's animals and tools, lack of educational opportunities, and limited mobility resulted in a bondage not much more palatable than medieval serfdom.

Outside the South, the position of small-scale agriculture, as well as labor, left a great deal to be desired. Between 1864 and 1896, the wholesale price index of farm products had declined from 162 to an almost incredible low of 56. Again the price of what farmers bought did not fall nearly as much as the prices of what they sold. Moreover, because of the deflation, farmers had to pay back debts incurred to establish themselves in farming in dollars worth much more than the ones borrowed. This situation meant large windfall profits for Eastern bankers and other holders of farm debts. It was extortionate conditions such as these which led William Jennings Bryan to declare that the toiling masses were not to be crowned with thorns and crucified upon a cross of gold!

In 1892, the agrarians finally decided to make common cause with the disgruntled industrial workers. At the convention of their People's Party—called also the "Populists"—they declared with daring that: "Corruption dominates the ballot box, the legislature, the Congress, and touches even the ermine of the bench. . . . The newspapers are largely subsidized or muzzled; public opinion silenced. . . . The urban workmen are denied the right of organization for self-protection; imported pauperized labor beats down their wages. The fruits of the toil of millions are boldly stolen to build colossal fortunes for a few, unprecedented in the history of mankind."[2]

While Theodore Roosevelt disagreed with Brook Adam's prophecy of the death of civilization under the heel of capitalistic usury, he wrote that "There is in it a very ugly element of truth...there has been a large absolute, though not relative, increase in poverty...the very poor tend to huddle in immense masses in the cities...they constitute a standing menace, not merely to our prosperity, but to our existence."[3]

Were these conditions necessary in a land blessed with the richest natural resources and the most inventive, generous people in the world? Gladstone had declared the Constitution of the United States to be "the most perfect work ever struck off by the brain and purpose of man at any given time." Was the intent of the divine forces in offering America such a legal system to have her people huddle in immense masses in the degradation of poverty? What else other than mammon worship could have brought about such a deplorable situation?

Under the constitution, Congress had ample powers to legislate for the general welfare of the nation. In fact, John Quincy Adams had wanted a permanent body of trained and competent public servants to hold in trust for the nation the rich heritage of land, forests, and minerals so they could be used for the economic, intellectual, and moral improvement of the people. Certainly this was an inspired idea. The representatives of the American people, however, were not sufficiently perceptive to understand the profound beneficence of such an altruistic plan.

They chose instead to parcel out the national domain under legislation and procedures which became increasingly lax toward the end of the nineteenth century.

As a result, "millions of acres of valuable timber, mineral and grazing lands were literally stolen under the eyes of dishonest or negligent officials in the federal land office; and other millions were wrested from the government by chicanery of one kind or another. . . . Thousands of great fortunes in the East as well as in the West were built out of resources wrung from the government for a pittance or for a bribe to its officials, if not actually stolen."[4]

Toward the end of the nineteenth century, under pressure from powerful economic interests, American politicians also started reversing the traditional foreign policy of the United States. This policy of isolation from European imperialism was set by Washington's Farewell Address, Jefferson's messages, and by the Monroe Doctrine. Even so, toward the end of the nineteenth century, distinct attempts were made to steer the country onto a course of imperialism in Cuba, Puerto Rico, the Hawaiian Islands, the Philippines, and elsewhere. Americans were told that it was their responsibility to help the peoples brought under American jurisdiction by accidents of history. True, not everyone believed these arguments. Mark Twain, for one, ridiculed the idea of "giving civilization to the man who sits in darkness" and condemned the imperialist policies as "pious frauds devised to conceal commercial greed and lust for power."[5]

Nevertheless, despite all these economic and political problems, the nation prospered to an amazing degree. During the last three decades of the nineteenth century, real national income tripled. One invention after another opened greater and greater possibilities for economic and social development.

In Europe, the Middle East, and in the rest of the world, America was regarded as the land of opportunity, where the streets were said to be paved with gold. Yes, there was much provincialism and naivete in the thought of this people, set apart for a purpose. However, as long as America stood distant from

69

the checkers game of international intrigue, men everywhere felt instinctively that this nation was truly the "hope of the world." But it was not until the United States was drawn into World War I, fought to make the world "safe for democracy" that a period of disenchantment set in.

The False Prosperity of the Twenties

Since I explore the machinations of international mammon which plunged America into World War I in a subsequent chapter, that subject is deferred. By now it should be evident to the reader how needless such an entanglement was since it had nothing to do with Manasseh's destiny. The divine plan for America was to have her serve as a melting pot in order to demonstrate both the material and spiritual profits to be derived when people voluntarily choose to live under a system of self-government based on just law and fair play.

Losing sight of her divine destiny, Manasseh was deceived into moving away more and more from the intent as well as the substance of her sacred Constitution. Thus America would not curb the evil forces which threatened constitutional government both at home and abroad. Instead, she gave them free reign once more to continue their unholy work of world conquest and dominion. For this tragic error, the United States had to pay over and over again an enormous price, most of the time not even knowing why or how.

During World War I, the social order in the United States was disturbed by strikes, opposition to the war, and futile attempts to make the rich pay for the war. To deal with the economic crises and reverses expected to follow the cessation of wartime expenditures, President Wilson, reversing many American traditions, advocated a series of one-world policies. He strongly advocated that the United States join the League of Nations and promote world trade. Even in solving such domestic problems as labor-management conflicts, he wanted America to be guided by the new world order implicit in the covenant of the League of

70

Nations. He insisted that America follow this course as an alternative to ruin.[6]

The people, however, were not inclined to agree with Wilson on his one-world concepts. They chose instead a period of "normalcy" under Republican rule. The age of electricity and the automobile had arrived. With the aid of installment buying, these innovations helped to make the 1920's prosperous, despite the depression in agriculture. However, what appeared to be an era of permanent prosperity in the end proved to be a dazzling illusion.

The forces which were to bring about the economic collapse were so extraordinary and so unbelievable that few, if any, understood what was happening. This confusion was compounded because experts and layman alike, once more, decided to see no evil, hear no evil, and expose no evil in the highest councils of their lands.

During the First World War, the international mammon interests had seen to it that public and private debts reach astronomical levels. This gave them not only ample means with which to control financial and governmental policies in their respective countries, but also immense opportunities for unjust enrichment.

On the surface, it was apparent that in most countries the wartime expenditures were financed with progressive expansions of bank credit. This policy was called euphemistically 'following the line of least resistance.' What was not apparent, except to a few, was the fact that many private banks bought the securities to finance the war with money they created out of nothing.

As Reginald McKenna, who had been chancellor of the exchequer in England in 1915-1916, pointed out, "I am afraid the ordinary citizen will not like to be told that the banks can, and do, create money. . . . And they who control the credit of the nation direct the policy of governments and hold in the hollow of their hands the destiny of the people."[7]

In the United States alone, during the war, the national debt had increased from less than $2 billion to over $25 billion. Much of this debt was incurred to extend loans to the Allied Powers. These loans formed the largest part of a $20 billion system of inter-Allied indebtedness. This network was composed, first, of loans the United States had extended to the United Kingdom, France, Italy, Russia, Belgium, Yugoslavia, and other allies. Then there were the loans the United Kingdom had extended to France, Italy, Russia, Belgium, Yugoslavia, and other allies, amounting to about twice what she had borrowed from the United States. Finally France also was both a lender and borrower in this system, having extended credits to Italy, Russia, Belgium, Yugoslavia, and other allies.

Before World War I, the United States had been a debtor nation; after the war, she became a creditor nation. An export surplus helps a debtor nation repay her debts by bringing in more money than she sends out. On the other hand, a creditor nation needs an import surplus to make it easier for her debtors to pay back their obligations. In 1922, by raising her protective tariffs, the United States did not make it easier for the Allies to pay back their debts. There were, however, more fundamental reasons why the whole system of international indebtedness of the 1920's was on an extremely shaky basis.

Going against the wishes of President Wilson, Clemenceau, pressed by the forces of mammon, had inserted in the text of the Armistice agreements a severe reparation clause. Under this clause, the Allies demanded from Germany compensation for all losses suffered by their civilian populations. This demand was based on the false theory that the entire war guilt rested on Germany. Total reparations cost was set at $132 billion marks, or about half of Germany's total wealth in 1913. The transfer of payments, at least initially, would have absorbed eighty percent of Germany's annual exports.

When it became apparent that the Germans would not have the capacity to make such a transfer, the Allies claimed that, if they could not collect reparations from Germany, they would not be able to pay their debts to the United States. This position was too much even for President Wilson to accept. As he rightly

72

pointed out, he failed to see why the United States should pay part of Germany's reparation obligation or make a gift to the Allied governments to induce them to limit such obligations to a sum Germany can afford to pay.

Actually, in the early 1920's, some concessions were made to reduce the burden of the war debts as well as the reparation payments. Consequently, to help Germany transfer her reparations to the Allies and provide her with capital for other purposes, huge sums were raised in Wall Street and loaned to Germany on a continuing basis. Thus, for a while, the Germans paid their obligations to the Allies, who in turn made payments to the United States and to each other. But this system was bound to collapse as soon as money would cease to flow from the United States to Germany. Moreover, the nature of the obligations were arranged in such a way that no one was really approaching solvency as international credits were shifted from one account to another. Thus, after paying reparations for five years, Germany owed more in 1929 than she owed in 1924. But, because of these arrangements, "The international bankers sat in heaven, under a rain of fees and commissions."[8]

In the 1920's, other strange things were happening in the world of finance. During the war, the organization of both international and national money markets were gravely disrupted throughout the world. The piling up of debts, monetary inflation, emergency wartime pegging of exchange rates, and the speculative buying and selling of foreign currencies which followed the unpegging of these rates had made it difficult to restore the prewar gold standard. Sooner or later, it became apparent, however, that what the central banks in the United States, United Kingdom, and France were attempting to restore was not the prewar standard. Rather it was a pseudo gold standard, which was being manipulated recklessly without regard to either national interest or accepted banking practices.

There had been a long tradition of secrecy and independence of monetary authority from governmental control. For over three hundred years, to pry publicly into the business of the Bank of

England—which established and ran the traditional gold standard—would be "unseemly, shocking behavior not worthy of loyal Englishmen."[9] During the nineteenth century, however, the gold standard was managed with considerable caution and restraint—so much so that many economists thought it operated on an automatic basis. Moreover, it contributed to, or at least did not hinder, economic gains in the Western world hitherto undreamed of in any other civilization known to man, along with unprecedented moral-humanitarian progress and freedom.

According to the unwritten rules of the gold standard system, it was expected that inflows of gold into a country would be allowed to bring about expansions in the money supply. This, in turn, would tend to lower the value of the country's currency by raising the general price level (and therefore reducing the currency's purchasing power). Similarly, outflows of gold would be allowed to cause contractions of the money in circulation, which would tend to increase the value of the country's currency relative to others. Consequently, under normal circumstances, movements of gold from country to country would serve to regulate the trade and investments of business organizations in different lands by shifting demand from one area to another and bringing the cost-price structures of all participants into a mutually beneficial equilibrium.

After the world's gold supplies were concentrated more and more in the vaults of the Federal Reserve System during World War I, the financial authorities in the United States were no longer satisfied with playing by the relatively passive rules of the traditional gold standard. Instead, they started neutralizing the impact of gold flows on the money supply to gain greater control over the finances of the nation, and of the world for that matter.

As an outstanding authority on money pointed out, "When the Federal Reserve was established in 1913, it never entered into the minds of the people establishing it that the System would really have much effective control internally in ordinary times."[10] It was taken for granted that the policy of the System would be governed by the gold standard principle of maintaining a passive equilibrium between the dollar and the value of other currencies. The main function of the Federal Reserve System, as its name implies, was to serve as a source of reserves for the commercial banks to draw on when faced with unusual demands for funds. Then, the "Fed" was established to give the nation an elastic currency, responsive to the ups and downs in the demand for money and credit. What the international power structure wanted to do with the Federal Reserve is another story.

During President Wilson's time, most bankers and statesmen were convinced that an organization like the Federal Reserve could be made to operate only with the cooperation of private bankers. They had not realized what shenanigans were possible in a system which opened the door for private financial interests to dominate its policies. There has been a very naive attitude toward these questions. Even now, students of money and banking are almost never taught how much central banking powers can be abused.

In 1920, for example, the nation experienced the sharpest decline in wholesale prices up to that time or since. This sudden deflation, which threw millions of people out of work, caused a particularly severe depression in agriculture. In textbooks on money and banking, the catastrophic monetary contraction which caused this depression is simply called a mistake. William Jennings Bryan was more nearly right, however, when he said that it was a crime against the farmer "deliberately committed." In congressional testimony, it was pointed out that the deflation was intended to "smash labor's standard" by forcing farmers off their farms. It was also pointed out that the agricultural depression ruined many state and joint land-stock banks which had been opposed to the Reserve System, while it lowered the values of farmlands and ranches by $20 billion, creating immense opportunities for unjust enrichment by the moneyed interests.[11]

In the 1920's, the Bank of England also started to depart from practices accepted earlier as essential parts of the gold standard adjustment mechanism. It broke the traditional connections

75

between gold, money, and prices by offsetting the impact of gold flows on the nation's monetary reserves by varying its securities inversely with gold movements.

True, by 1925, the appearance of the gold standard was maintained. But its most useful function—bringing the value of the pound into balance with other currencies—was lost in the shuffle. In an economy as much dependent on foreign trade and investments as that of Great Britain, allowing its currency to be overvalued on international markets could easily have led to a depression. This, in fact, is exactly what happened. Was the overvaluation of the pound a mistake or a tryout for subsequent moves to precipitate worldwide depression, as well as a means of executing the plot against the British Empire spotted by the Duke of Northumberland?[12]

Actually, the return to the gold standard after the war was not necessary. By that time, banking structures and practices had evolved sufficiently to permit any advanced country to operate without a metallic standard. Equilibration of exchange rates to promote investment and profitable trade among nations did not require that the separate currencies be bound up with gold. It was the international financiers who had by that time acquired fairly effective control over both the gold supply and the central banking systems of the world who needed a standard based on gold.

In the 1920's, to exercise more effective control over the stocks of monetary gold, the international mammon interests had also created an artificial scarcity of gold by keeping its price at a ridiculously low level. The price of gold in terms of dollars or pounds was kept at its prewar level, even though the general price level had doubled in the United States and gone up even more in Britain. This protected the gold value of billions of dollars worth of bonds held directly or indirectly by the super rich. However, it did not help the liquidity of monetary systems, the breakdown of which caused severe hardships for millions.

Despite all these monetary ills and a series of economic dislocations in Europe, engineered by the tricky Versailles

Treaty, the surge of technology and production continued in the United States. Between 1919 and 1929, output per man-hour in America increased at a normal rate, as mass markets kept expanding. A big factor in this progress was the public's fascination with automobiles and electrical products. During the 1920's, the radio industry also grew like Jack's beanstalk, while motion pictures became standard entertainment.

The House of Cards Tumbles

Thus, what otherwise might have been a happy, vigorous period of economic growth was marred by financial machinations which were sure to spell disaster. The damage done was not always obvious. Actually millions closed their eyes to surrounding dangers, and concentrated on the seeming advantages of the moment.

And one of the most deceptive of these attractions was the stock market. Share prices in New York rose continuously for six years from 1923 to 1929. At first, the trend of rising prices seemed innocuous enough. Toward the end, however, the market was the scene of a frenzied boom. In 1923, there were 236 million shares traded; in 1925, 460 million; in 1929, 1,125 million. This feverish demand for appreciating securities was not spontaneous. It was stimulated and exploited in the most reckless way by those in control of the nation's finances.

After a bull market was created with money borrowed from banks, reckless financiers obtained control of companies, reorganized them, piled them one on top of the other in holding companies, to increase with each step their possibilities for profit and power. Leading banks formed investment affiliates to sell with one hand what they bought with the other, using of course the money of their depositors. Many new shares were created, not to meet the legitimate needs for capital, but to feed the greed of the bankers and brokers selling them.

Some investment counselors continually sounded notes of caution, especially in the last phases of the bull market. But the public was mesmerized by the quick gains to be made. Those on the inside of world money plans, knowing that a big break was to come, got out of stocks. Others who were warned about the crash planned by the mammon interests through ESP also disposed of their equities. The ones remaining in the market, however, had the shock of their lives on October 24, 1929, when the break, or crash, finally materialized. On that one day, 12,894,650 shares were traded; five days later, 16,410,030 shares. Much of the trading on both days represented short sales on which tremendous profits were made.[13] During these darkest of days, the cynical few were lining their pockets, as those ruined by the crash jumped from the nearest windows. The crucial first step to bring down the tottering economic order of the Western World had been accomplished.

With the sudden collapse of confidence, prices, industrial production, employment, and incomes started to tumble. The deepening deflation and depression also caused a series of runs on banks and bank failures, the most dramatic of which was the failure of the Bank of the United States in the fall of 1930. The Federal Reserve System had been set up primarily to deal with such liquidity crises. But, when the time came, for reasons economists cannot or do not want to understand, the Federal Reserve System would not act.

Worse was to come. By the spring of 1931, there were hopeful signs of a recovery on the horizon. The gold standard, such as it was, had remained intact in the United States and Western Europe. Industrial production had recovered slightly in the United States and Germany. Credit was easy in all principal financial centers. Just when conditions appeared as though they might start to improve, the forces of international mammon dealt their second major blow to the world economy—by creating the international financial crisis of 1931.

With a revaluation of the assets of Credit-Anstalt, the largest commercial bank in Vienna, a faction of the mammon interests created the impression that they were insolvent. This led to an avalanche of immediate withdrawals of gold and foreign credit from Austria, and then also from Germany. To protect her reserves, Germany introduced exchange controls which froze large amounts of British funds in Germany. Capital withdrawals then shifted to Britain. Attempts were made to save the pound in London, New York, and Paris. They were of no use. On September 21, 1931, the gold standard was suspended in Britain disrupting the oldest bastion of the world's currency system. The shock was profound. But the forces of chaos and disintegration had not yet finished their work.

For their next move, they used as their principal instrument an organization they had worked on for years—the Federal Reserve System—which at the time was said to suffer from a lack of leadership. As usual, the plotters behind the scenes made their carefully prearranged diabolic moves appear as perfectly understandable human errors. Consequently, the most unjustifiable deflationary action—a sharp increase in the discount rate charged to banks in need of money—was interpreted as no more than an overreaction to a loss of gold when Britain went off the gold standard. Some said the Federal Reserve panicked, without stating the reason.[14] America had more than ample reserves of gold to meet any crisis. There was no reason to panic. And yet, the "Fed" did cause another wave of commercial bank failures to hit the nation. As the most acclaimed authority on the subject pointed out, "Never was there a more unnecessary collapse or one which did more to undermine public acceptance of liberal principles."[15]

By the winter of 1932-33, when cooperation was blocked between the Republicans who were defeated at the elections and the Democrats who were to assume the reins of government, the bank failures reached catastrophic proportions. After his inauguration, one of the first things President Roosevelt had to do was to close all U.S. banks by executive order. At the same time, he placed embargoes on gold and silver, which took the United States off the gold standard.

The deepening world depression and the impact of the collapse of the monetary systems of the principal trading countries was nothing less than disastrous. Down came not only an economic order based largely on principles of freedom, but also the binding structure of reparation payments, borrowed capital, and foreign credits. In the process, down came also the Weimar Republic in Germany, as Hitler rose to power, dashing any hopes which might have remained for restoring free governments in Central and Eastern Europe.

FOOTNOTES

1. Charles A., Mary R., and William Beard, p. 384.
2. Ibid., pp. 314-15.
3. Ibid., pp. 354-55.
4. Ibid., p. 281.
5. Ibid., p. 329.
6. Ibid., p. 409.
7. Carroll Quigley, *Tragedy and Hope: A History of the World in Our Times.* New York: The MacMillan Co., 1966, p. 325.
8. Ibid., p. 309.
9. Robert Oetking, "Peek behind Closed Doors of the Bank of England," *Bankers Monthly Magazine,* July 15, 1970, p. 30.
10. Milton Friedman, "Should There Be an Independent Monetary Authority," *In Search of a Monetary Constitution,* Leland B. Yeager (ed.), Cambridge, Mass.: Harvard University Press, 1962, p. 231.
11. Eustace Mullins, *The Federal Reserve Conspiracy.* Union, N. J.: Christian Educational Assn., 1954, pp. 65-68. See also: A. N. Field: *The Truth about the Slump.* Hawthorne, Calif.: Omni Publications, 1962, pp. 103-105.
12. Nesta H. Webster, *Secret Societies and Subversive Movements.* Hawthorne, Calif.: Christian Book Club of America, 1969, p. xi.
13. Curtis B. Dall, *F.D.R.: My Exploited Father-in-Law.* Tulsa, Okla.: Christian Crusade Publications, 1968, p. 113 and 119.
14. Ross Mr. Robertson, *History of the American Economy.* New York: Harcourt, Brace and Co., 1955, p. 559.
15. Milton Friedman, "Real and Pseudo Gold Standards," *The Journal of Law and Economics,* Vol IV, October 1961, University of Chicago Press, p. 72.

Chapter VII

THE ERRORS OF PRESIDENT FRANKLIN D. ROOSEVELT

Background of the New Deal

What had the money manipulators dared to do and why? As Gottfried Haberler, famous economist, said, "At the time when it happened, most economists did not know what had hit them."[1] Three decades after the event, it had become apparent, at least to him, that it was "the wholesale destruction of money" which had caused the exceptional malignancy of the Great Depression. And this destruction Haberler attributed to "institutional weakness and incredibly poor policies on the national and international level."[2] Why should the policies pursued seem incredible to him? No doubt because he was assuming that the steps taken at the time were aimed at stabilizing the monetary situation instead of plunging it into chaos. And who can blame him for assuming that?

As a rule Western economists will not even consider the possibility that the Great Depression could have been engineered by a few devilish men in order to advance their long-range plans for world dominion. They do not reject such a theory merely as a matter of caution, taste, or self-interest. They reject it because they are not accustomed to thinking in terms of spiritual concepts. They do not ask themselves why, if there is a compassionate God, mankind had to endure such a catastrophe as this depression. Is He, perhaps, incapable of preventing honest mistakes of policy from causing boundless misery for millions? If those in authority had high motives, as school children are led to believe, why would they not reverse policies which prove to be appallingly destructive? The fact is that most of the so-called mistakes which have ruined entire societies have not even been properly investigated.

Why do we have to assume that whenever things go wrong it is because well-intentioned people are making mistakes? Perhaps such mistakes are the only means by which some can hope to line their pockets or magnify their power.

Honest scholars cannot help sensing that somehow wickedness always plays a part in social catastrophes. After stating that each of the currency devaluations of the 1930's could be defended as "unavoidable," Haberler nevertheless concluded that "their time pattern stamped the whole approach as a sadistic policy, calculated to maximize pain and destruction."[3]

Then why the sadistic policy, the wanton destruction, the planned chaos? Even most of the leading statesmen of the time could not answer this question. Nor can it be answered unless one becomes aware of some forces which are not generally known to the public.

In the heyday of financial capitalism, international bankers, who had organized their banking systems independently of government checks and balances, used their vast holdings of gold as weapons of political control. As a rule, academic economists do not think in these terms. Nevertheless, many volumes have been written regarding how international bankers made use of their immense financial resources to control governments, the press, and the people, in order to carry out their plans of world conquest hatched behind the scenes.[4]

As we shall see later, such evil conspiracies did not originate in financial circles. All the same, having accumulated great wealth, some financiers, who will remain nameless in this volume, turned their thoughts to power and control over the vast multitudes of the world.

At first, their manipulation formulas and machinery had centered around control of banking systems, channels of information, and diplomatic or political intrigue, including the financing of revolutions. When Zionism became a force, the leaders of this movement approached a faction of the interna-

83

tional mammon interests for financial backing. To interest the bankers, the Zionists told them of the tremendous hidden wealth of the Dead Sea area, referred to in the Talmud and in the instructions of the Kabbala. The bankers were skeptical and would not respond. However, when the oil discovered in Mesopotamia seemed to validate this ancient knowledge, their attitudes changed. Thus a faction of international mammon started backing the Zionists to gain a firm foothold in that area. Other factions sponsored further explorations and political negotiations of their own.

By the 1920's, the despotism of gold was being challenged. It was becoming increasingly evident that the value of gold as money or as a base for money rested merely on a gentlemen's agreement. The better informed recognized that money need not necessarily be tied to gold. At the same time, it was also becoming evident that, in the future, it would be the coveted black gold, or oil, that would be king in the economic sphere.

In 1917, Clemenceau had argued that oil would be "as necessary as blood in battles of tomorrow." According to Lord Curzon, "The Allies floated to victory on a wave of oil." The French industrialist and senator, M. Henri Berenger, went further and simply declared that in the future the owners of oil would own the world. For not only could the oil barons control transportation by sea, air and land, but also they could rule over their fellow men by reason of their fantastic wealth from oil. [5]

In the 1920's, therefore, those with aspirations to rule the world decided to bury the gold standard and rise to power by means of promulgating a planned economy geared to war. The necessity of economic mobilization to fight World War I had demonstrated the feasibility of directing industrial operations by central government decrees. The authoritarian fixing of prices, wages, and rationing schemes had worked without too much protest even in America. In Soviet Russia, socialism as an economic system had already been established. In short, the tools for regimentation in the framework of a planned economy had finally been forged. They were available to anyone who dared to use them. True, the tools for collectivism were still primitive, but the improvements could always come later.

Under these circumstances, a sudden forced change in the social balance caused by a grave banking crisis could transform the whole system of liberal laissez faire economics, unified by free trade and freely convertible currencies, into warring camps of collectivist states, each led by a strong man. In the United States, a prolonged depression was bound to change the temper of the people and reduce their resistance to economic and political regimentation. To encourage this trend, the planners made sure that the citizens turned to their government not only for their livelihood but also for other needs. Eventually these developments were to make it easier to lead an essentially isolationist people into World War II.

Meanwhile what was needed was a national hero who could be repeatedly elected in order to give the nameless forces behind the scenes enough time to carry out their long-range plans. The popular hero then was chosen—Franklin Delano Roosevelt.

This choice was remarkably clever. First, he had all the charm and social prestige needed to sell people on a radically new program. Secondly, he was a Democrat who believed in the Wilsonian ideal of the League of Nations. True, he was to some extent aware of the evil plans behind such international organizations, but he was not allowed to know the more sordid aspects of the plans. To him a one-world order portrayed a great ideal. He asked himself, "Did not Jesus also preach the brotherhood of man?", forgetting that the brotherhood of man is meaningless without the fatherhood of God. The latter concept is rejected by those who use evil means to promote international government.

What makes the choice of Roosevelt sad is that when he came to power he had hoped that his charm, cleverness, and power of persuasion would overcome stumbling blocks. Little did he know what he had to face. From the beginning, his chances of solving the nation's problems were severely limited. His advisers would not have him cooperate with the outgoing President Hoover to restore confidence in the nation's financial system. Consequently

85

wave after wave of bank failures continued to paralyze the country's economy. Moreover, after he assumed office, Roosevelt was misled by his advisers to emphasize social reforms instead of economic recovery, which was by far the more urgent need.

Even so, he was a great humanitarian, full of self-confidence and a persuasive salesman. Thus he succeeded in having the nation adopt an extensive package of reform and recovery measures which were collectively known as the New Deal.

Looking Through the False Bottom

The literature on the New Deal is full of references to the many contradictory policies which were pursued simultaneously during the 1930's. As early as 1934, one author prepared a list of no less than ten policies—such as pledging higher prices and then asking businessmen to keep them low—which were apparently inconsistent.[6] Political foes of President Roosevelt or lesser academic lights who delight in intellectual games make much of these paradoxes of public policy. But approaches of this type are essentially superficial. If we dig below the surface, we find that the contradictory policies of the New Deal were not primarily the products of ignorance or expediency.

There were, of course, those who wanted to weaken criticism by giving every vocal group something they would like, and this was bound to lead to some degree of inconsistency. However, the most fundamental contradictions of policy in the 1930's stemmed from pursuing hidden aims which could not be discussed in public. Once again, it was what was happening under the false bottom of the glass which helps to explain what transpired in the 1930's as well as in the decades to follow.

With one quarter of the labor forced unemployed, with the national income of the country cut in half, and with stocks in New York selling at one-fifth their price before the crash, when the Democrats came to office, the immediate need was for a rapid economic recovery. At least in retrospect, this seems very clear. Furthermore, the first essential of any substantial recovery from such depressed conditions was obviously a restoration of confidence in the future. At the time, it was particularly important for businessmen to feel optimistic, in order to assume the risks of enterprise.

As one authority on the period pointed out, an administration that would have frankly taken a pro-business stance might have sparked off a strong recovery, with relatively modest subsidies to producers.[7] If this had occurred, there would have been no need for much of the vast relief programs to follow.

Despite much elaborate theorizing to the contrary, in the 1930's there was nothing *fundamentally* wrong either with the U.S. economy or with the other major capitalistic economies of the world. As I pointed out earlier, the trouble stemmed mainly from perverse financial manipulation. The best evidence in support of this view is the fact that in whatever country the deflation of money was stopped without sharply raising costs in the process, the economic dislocations which were said to be structural swiftly disappeared.[8]

A return to normalcy, however, was not in the interest of those directing the international conspiracy. They were counting on a prolonged period of distress to make people want, even demand, a bigger government. This bigger government would promise them many things, help them somewhat, and at the right time, plunge them into another war, regardless of the isolationist sentiment in the country. As President Roosevelt had once remarked about affairs of state, they do not happen—they are planned. But even he was not allowed to know that the proposed world union planned to follow the war was to consolidate despotic rule over all nations by the insidious use of mammon power.

From the soup kitchens to the PWA, the intent of the world conquerors was to build Franklin D. Roosevelt as the national hero, who could be trusted to usher in the new social order. The President was cleverly promoted as an enlightened reformer, opposed to economic royalists, to unearned privilege, to bigness in industry and finance, and in favor of the little man, the hard-working farmer and worker and the exploited everywhere.

FDR was to chase the money lenders out of the temple, end the "Hoover Depression" and offer a New Deal to the Nation as a means to a more abundant life.

In the meantime, those in control behind the scenes promoted an absurd theory according to which prosperity was not possible without a prior increase in commodity prices, to be induced by an increase in the dollar price of gold. On the basis of this theory, devaluing the dollar—by about forty percent in terms of gold—did not, of course, bring about prosperity. But it did bring about what the government behind government wanted—an avalanche of gold flowing into the United States. As a result, the value of the gold stock held by the monetary authorities increased from $4 billion in 1933 to $22 billion in 1940, the largest amassing of gold the world had ever seen.

Under the monetary system of the nation, an inflow of gold meant increased loanable reserves for the commercial banks. Therefore, with each new shipment of precious metal, the self-confidence and power of the international bankers increased more and more. This was how President Roosevelt was chasing the money changers out of the temple! In the government of the future, which we can have if we become worthy of it, there will be no need for such hypocrisy.

However, back in the thirties, the world still had much painful experience to endure. The President who had said to the nation, "You have nothing to fear but fear itself," soon afterward started sowing the seeds of the most profound fears, directed toward a mortal enemy which he knew his financial supporters were rapidly creating through hidden international cartels. Germany did not have the oil, iron ore, or other economic necessities for a major war machine. Without pulling in critical war material and capital resources from outside her borders, Hitler would have gotten nowhere. That is why the support of the mammon interests in the United States, no less than their associates in Germany, was essential for the rearmament program of the Nazi dictator. There was, of course, much reluctance and hesitation. However, the gold which kept pouring into the

United States produced such a warm feeling of security and strength to key financiers here that they finally gave the nod to their counterparts across the ocean to proceed with their plans, not caring what thunder might break out in Europe.[9]

President Roosevelt had realized, at least to some extent, what consequences might flow from such international intrigue. Therefore, toward the end of his first administration, he thought of cracking down on the mammon interests implicated in the hidden cartels paving the way for war. In the end, however, he decided against it. Had Roosevelt taken his stand against the international mammon interests, as Lincoln had done before him, he would certainly have prevailed.

At the time, Roosevelt had the nation with him. For many he had become almost a god. True, his policies had failed to spark a rapid economic recovery, but he had won the loyalty and affection of a large majority of the people. Some said that his success was due to the greatest of his many talents, namely, to say all things to all men and actually believe them as he said them. All the same, much good came out of his many programs: his accomplishments in such fields as deposit insurance, unemployment compensation, collective bargaining, rural electrification, and social security contributed to his standing as a great public figure. But Roosevelt did not use his immense popularity to advance the divine plan for an America isolated from Europe's wars, as outlined by the founding fathers.

As early as 1935 the potentials of atomic energy were becoming appreciated. Here, the internationalists thought, was a source of energy which could unify the world; one more war and the world union concept could become a reality! This in turn would make the cherished dream of Zionism come true, and would also bring wily old Stalin back into the concert of nations again. Roosevelt was to preside over the new world order, once it was established; at least that is what he was told.

Partly brainwashed by the shallow, Godless humanism of his advisers and therefore partly innocent, and partly through boundless ambition, President Roosevelt flirted with the international mammon interests. The temptation to become a benevolent world Caesar, which was constantly made to dance before his often blurred vision, was an influence too strong for him to ignore. As he was torn between opposing forces, the pain of his physical disability would increase, to cloud his judgment even more. Thus, failing to make a clean break with the negative influences surrounding him, before he realized it, he was hooked.

Ambition Beyond Reason Never Pays Off

During his second administration, Roosevelt became more and more enmeshed in international intrigue. Convinced that the nation had been needlessly drawn into World War I and wishing to prevent a repeat performance of a similar involvement, as early as 1934 Congress had started passing protective legislation. These laws imposed restrictions on practices similar to the ones which resulted in U.S. entry into World War I. Among these restrictions were the export of arms and munitions or the granting of loans and credits to belligerent states. Throughout the 1930's, the popular sentiment was overwhelmingly in favor of isolating the nation from involvement with warring states in Europe. All the same, the government behind government would not allow Roosevelt to lose sight of the long-range objective he was to pursue, namely, uniting all nations in one organization. If this was to be, the ideas of neutrality and isolation were untenable, and sooner or later they would have to be abandoned.

Nor could the nation be allowed to prosper without placing it on a war production basis first. Here we have the explanation for the economic reversals of 1937-38 which gave rise to so much controversy among economists. The gradual economic recovery which had started in 1933 had developed into a mild prosperity during 1936 and through the summer of 1937. This made the Roosevelt administration feel cheered and encouraged. The money power, however, did not wish the Democrats to feel too independent. Consequently between August 15, 1936, and May 1, 1937, in three steps the authorities of the Federal Reserve

System were pressured to double the reserve requirements of member commercial banks, raising them to the maximum levels permitted by the Banking Act of 1935. A few months after these restrictive monetary brakes were applied, the boom was lowered on the stock market. The declines in stock prices in September, October, and November were so drastic that financial analysts could find "few instances on record where a larger percentage decline has occurred in so short a period of time."[10]

Economists have never really understood the reason for such a collapse of confidence, which led to a new depression from already subnormal levels of activity. Some explained the Federal Reserve system policies by saying that at the time the monetary authorities feared inflation, even though over 6,000,000 people were still out of jobs! Others called the monetary policy ill advised. The official explanations seemed to indicate that the Board was concerned about an injurious inflation arising, not immediately, but at some future time.[11] No one seemed to consider the possibility that the restrictive money policies could have been calculated to prevent Roosevelt from succeeding prematurely on the domestic front before making America an arsenal for the next major war, which Hitler was being encouraged to fight.

Yet undaunted by the ill-advised policies of the monetary authorities, the nation was still behind Roosevelt. Moreover the people never lost their humor or faculty to sing and dance, as was brought out so well by the then current Broadway and Hollywood musicals. The people sang first "Happy Days Are Here Again" and then:

> Though we ain't got a barrel of money
> Maybe we're ragged and funny
> So we'll travel along
> Singing our song
> Side by side . . .

So few seemed to suspect that these songs were sponsored by

the powers behind the scene to keep the public from thinking about the storm which was breaking out in Europe. How thorough are the ways of those who have set out to conquer the world while posing as benefactors of mankind!

At any rate, as the day follows the night, came the evil consequences of what had been planned for years. The greatest shock to Americans was the act of infamy—Pearl Harbor—in which the Japanese had been maneuvered into firing the first shot. Here was the first of a series of events which raised the practice of subjugating the military to the control of international intrigue to the level of a fine art. Then came the opening of the gates to the Soviet Union and the release of the nation's most precious military secrets. In the Far East, the same obvious potential enemy was given enormous fruits of victory in exchange for almost nothing. Finally the wolves in sheep's clothing succeeded in introducing the United Nations—the handiwork of and shelter for many subversive agents—into the city of mammon. Need I elaborate? Many volumes have already been written to explain how all these things were allowed to happen.[12]

Yes, President Franklin D. Roosevelt did make a few errors, which we must correct before it is too late. And what were the fruits of these errors? Let us review the record.

Despite all the excesses and inequities of the 1920's, the economic situation of the average American was far better than in the 1930's. Moreover, all the welfare measures notwithstanding, the failure to have a quick recovery from the Great Depression hurt the poorer classes much more than the richer classes in America. Thus the New Deal ended up imposing the greatest hardships on the very people it was supposed to help the most. True, the recognition of labor's right to bargain collectively gave the working man an added security. However, when Hitler's armies marched into Poland in 1939, unemployment in the United States was still above 17 percent of the labor force. This was a dismal record indeed, a record "worse than that of almost any other country except France, which had a similar 'New Deal' of its own."[13]

Much, if not all, of this failure must be attributed directly to

New Deal policies. During the Roosevelt era, the people who were needed the most for a quick recovery—the average businessmen and corporation executives—were the ones villified with the greatest enthusiasm. Moreover, the managers of American enterprise were continually confronted with the specter of government controls or monetary and fiscal experiments which they could not understand or support. Production was restricted and private initiative crushed in every direction. The cartellization of industry carried out by private code authorities under the National Industrial Recovery Act of 1933 was declared unconstitutional in 1935. Even so, in other areas the restraints on economic initiative were continued, while the surreptitious mammon interests, which had caused the depression of the economy in the first place, were allowed to continue their disruptive work with virtually complete immunity.

In the 1930's while the psychology of mass unemployment favored acceptance of state controls, both depressed prices and bankruptcies made it easier to accept takeovers by private interests in industry and finance. As a congressional report on concentration of economic power pointed out in 1941, "The dreaded trusts of the past century are but pygmies in comparison with our present day industrial giants."[14] Nor was this development inevitable. Noting that "laws to a large extent are only as effective as the men who enforce them," the authors of the report found that success in fighting monopolies was limited by lack of appropriated money and manpower to enforce the antitrust laws of the Nation.[15]

To counter the power of giant business empires, labor unions were encouraged to grow in power also. And as governmental bureaucracies increased in size, and executive orders increased in frequency to counter the power of both business and labor, American society became a society of pressure groups.

And what were the fruits of the foreign policies pursued during the Roosevelt administrations? First, as Secretary of State George C. Marshall pointed out in 1947, the nation after World War II had a cessation of hostilities but no genuine peace. The cold war and the series of hot wars on three continents which followed bear ample witness to the lack of genuine peace. Second, the treatment of the peoples in Eastern Europe, China, Indo-China, Germany, and elsewhere showed beyond any doubt that the noble principles of the Four Freedoms and the Atlantic Charter, which Roosevelt said would form the basis for a better world after the war, could be discarded with complete immunity as expediency required. Third, "out of the War came the triumph of another totalitarian regime no less despotic and ruthless than Hitler's system, namely, Russia, possessing more than twice the population of prewar Germany... and insistently effectuating a political and economic ideology equally inimical to the democracy, liberties, and institutions of the United States."[16]

In the meantime, President Roosevelt had managed to have Congress adopt conscription as a permanent policy, increased the national debt by an additional $220 billion and raised tax rates to heights never seen before. More ominous than any of these developments, however, was the obscuring of truth in government and tampering with the sacred processes of representative government under the Constitution of the United States. The extent to which realities can deviate from appearances and how clever tactics of deception can lead to "personal and arbitrary government, the first principle of the totalitarian system against which, it has been alleged, World War II was waged—while giving lip services to the Principle of Constitutional government" has been shown with masterly scholarship by one of the most eminent American historians.[17]

Finally, how does the personal record read? Toward the end of the war, President Roosevelt's health deteriorated more and more. Pictures in the newspapers and the newsreels showing his emaciated appearance gave the public a glimpse of his intense personal suffering. Why say more? It was a sad ending to what could have been a glorious life.

Franklin D. Roosevelt was a product of his times and a servant of national and international destiny in that he was allowed to do what he did to demonstrate to the world how not to rule. He should be an example to all future statesmen who may be tempted, as he was, to take shortcuts to political success. Those who can tune in to his mind today in the spiritual dimensions of life will find that he will be the first one to admit that boundless ambition, beyond reason, never pays. It has never worked in the past. It will never work in the future. Statesmen of the future, beware!

FOOTNOTES

1. Gottfried Haberler, "Integration and Growth of the World Economy in Historical Perspective" (Presidential address delivered at the Seventy-sixth Annual Meeting of the American Economic Association, Boston, Dec. 27, 1963), *The American Economic Review*, Vol. LIV, No. 2, Part 1, (March 1964), pp. 7-8.

2. Ibid., p. 8.

3. Ibid., p. 9.

4. See, for example: Arthur Kitson, *The Bankers' Conspiracy! Which Started the World Crisis*, Hawthorne, Calif.: Omni Publications, 1967; A. N. Field, *All These Things*. Hawthorne, Calif.: Omni Publications, 1963; George Knupffer, *The Struggle for World Power*. London: The Plain-Speaker Publishing Co., 1963; Boris Brasol, *The World at the Cross Roads*. Hawthorne, Calif. Christian Book Club of America, 1970; C. H. Douglas, *Warning Democracy*. London: Stanley Nott, 1935.

5. Ludwell Denny, *We Fight for Oil*. London: Alfred A. Knopf, 1928, p. 16.

6. Ralph Robey, *Roosevelt versus Recovery*. New York and London: Harper and Brothers, 1934, pp. 1-2.

7. Paul K. Conkin, *FDR and the Origins of the Welfare State*. New York: Thomas Y. Crowell Co., 1967, p. 33.

8. Haberler, p. 33.

9. The mysteries which surround the ownership and control of war-related cartels may be illustrated by the case of General Aniline and Film Corporation. This case had become a legal headache for every administration from Franklin D. Roosevelt to John F. Kennedy. The company was seized by the federal government in 1942 on the ground that it was German property. A Swiss holding company, Interhandel, challenged the seizure, claiming ownership of ninety-three percent of General Aniline's

stock. The experts in the Justice Department had traced through a legal labyrinth the ownership and control of Interhandel, formerly known as I. G. Chemie, to I. G. Farbenindustrie, the mammoth German chemical trust. The Kennedy brothers, however, agreed to a compromise settlement of the case out of court. The stock of Aniline was to be sold to Americans on the open market, and, after payment of taxes and fees, divided equally between the Interhandel stockholders and the federal government. The settlement, which cost the U.S. Government an estimated $60 million, was criticized in Congress. One critical Congressman, who asked why complete restitution had not been made if Interhandel were really Swiss, revealed that Swiss banks had refused to provide his subcommittee records to support Interhandel's claim that it was a Swiss company. (Reports on this story were published in 1963 in the *New York Times* Mar. 5, 9:1; Mar. 6, 8:2 and 11:2; Mar. 7, 4:5 and 9:8; Mar. 8, 13:1 and 11:5; Mar. 15, 13:7; Mar. 30, 9:l.) For all we know the real owners of General Aniline might have been neither Swiss nor German, but Rockefellers. For an amazing story about how millions of tons of French iron ore were being exported to be transformed into German cannons, tanks, shells, and other weapons of war in the 1930's despite an embargo which was placed after demands to stop this traffic became irresistible, see: Frank C. Hanighen, "Selling to the Enemy," *Harper's Magazine* (March 1940). There is another interesting story relating to the rearming of Germany. When American troops reached Frankfort, they found that all the buildings of the German I. G. Farben Chemical Trust had remained intact despite the heavy bombing of this industrial city by American planes. It was observed, therefore, that the Secretary of War in Washington at the time of the pinpoint bombing had recently left a position with an international banking firm in New York which had financed German I. G. Farben before the war and which had a hand in forming the coverup General Aniline and Film Corporation mentioned above. See: Morris A. Bealle, *Super Drug Story*. Arlington, Va.: Columbia Publishing Co., 1971, p. 9.

10. C. A. Beard, M. R. Beard, and Wm. Beard, p. 427.

11. Lawrence Smith, *Money, Credit,* and *Public Policy.* Boston: Houghton Mifflin Co., 1959, p. 546.

12. See, for example, John Howland Snow, *The Case of Tyler Kent.* New Canaan, Conn.: The Long House, Inc., 1965; George Racey Jordan with Richard L. Stokes, *From Major Jordan's Diaries.* Boston and Los Angeles: "The Americanist Library"; Western Islands, 1965; Frank A. Capell, *Treason Is the Reason.* Zarephath, N.J.: Herald of Freedom, 1965; Pierre J. Huss and George Carpozi, Jr., *Red Spies in the U.N.* New York: Pocket Books, 1965; John A. Stormer, *None Dare Call It Treason.* Florissant, Mo.: Liberty Bell Press, 1964; G. Edward Griffin, *The Fearful Master: A Second Look at the United Nations.* Boston and Los Angeles: Western Islands, 1968; James Burnham, *The Web of Subversion.* Boston and Los Angeles: "The Americanist Library" Western Isands, 1965; Arthur Bliss Lane, *I Saw Poland Betrayed.* Boston and Los Angeles: "The Americanist Library"; Western Islands, 1965; Ralph de Toledano, *Seeds of Treason.* Boston and Los Angeles: "The Americanist Library," Western Islands, 1965; John T. Flynn, *While You Slept.* Boston and Los Angeles: "The Americanist Library"; Western Islands, 1965.

13. Gottfried Haberler, *Inflation: Its Causes and Curses.* Washington, D.C.: American Enterprise Institute for Public Policy Research, 1966, p. 2.

14. 76th Congress, Senate Temporary National Economic Committee, "Investigation of Concentration of Economic Power," Monograph No. 38, *A Study of the Construction and Enforcement of the Federal Anti-trust Laws.* Washington, D.C.: U.S. Government Printing Office, 1941, p. 1.

15. Ibid., p. 1 and 90.

16. Charles A. Beard, *President Roosevelt and the Coming of the War, 1941; A Study in Appearances and Realities.* New Haven, Conn.: Yale University Press, 1964, p. 577.

17. Ibid. p. 584.

Chapter VIII

THE EVIL FORCES SPREAD

What Is Evil?

According to the folklore of modern social science, there is no such thing as evil. Scientists speak about ignorance, prejudice, irrationality, mistakes, or miscalculations, but not about evil. Anthropologists especially pride themselves on studying and analyzing objectively the most wicked forms of human behavior and insist that we cannot judge the behavior of others by our own moral standards. The economists take human wants as givens; while tracing the consequences of these wants, they refrain from calling them good or bad. Nor does the economists' training help them to understand what human beings really want. Thinking of people largely as rational calculating machines who seek to maximize their material benefits, they fail to see the highly emotional nature of most human aspirations. Their standards of welfare are derived from abstract theories developed by economists for economists.

While such economic conceptions and the culture free judgments of the anthropologists have had their benefits, they do not improve upon what spiritual men have held to be good for centuries. According to sacred Scriptures, the world was made in six days. Whether this work was done in six days or in six mammoth epochs, man was the crowning glory of that achievement. Man was the highest work of God because he was of God Himself, a part of God's thought projected into the universe and therefore ruling it according to His desires.

At first, man was not limited in function as were the beasts of the field. Nor was he of the dust of the ground, except in his body, which he lays down periodically, life after life. Moreover in

99

his spirit he was free, transcending all things earthly, unprofaned by any matter, moving about exactly as it pleased him. But there arrived a time when he expressed himself in matter in this fashion, when he wallowed in such deceits and malpractices, mixing his celestial power with the vilest of beastly orders, that he took upon himself a great onus. It is this onus which man must cast off to regain his original felicity, and it is to help him cast off this onus that man has always needed and still needs a Redeemer.

One might think of life as a never-ending score played by a master musician on the keyboards of the worlds. The tones and harmonies resulting from his playing often take the form of orthodoxy, causing man to see his future darkly. But man receives a new vision from times of trouble and change, and the continuum of time acquires a new meaning for him.

As an earthly father permits a child to go through a series of trial and error experiences to develop his character, so does the Heavenly Father allow His children to err so they may learn from their errors. Thus He allows them to come back into the world's schools for growth time after time, until they reach such levels of perfection that they would never again want to use their powers wrongly.

This process may at times seem to be interminably long. Fortunately the time for graduation is far nearer than men suppose. We are creatures of habit. Having once fallen into the habit of ignoring the God power within, we have been blocking our own progress. But further advances in science will sooner or later make people realize that they not only have the power to control their environment with physical instruments, but also with their own minds directly. A number of creative psychologists as well as laymen have already become aware of this.[1] However, the divine forces will not allow this power to flourish before men develop their ethical faculties to such an extent that they will not be tempted to use it to cause evil injury.

And what do I mean by such injury? I am not referring merely to physical lesions or economic reverses. These are usually temporary and sooner or later completely remedied. Even if they prove to be more serious, however, in the perspective of eternity, such injuries can only be considered unpleasant episodes while they last and perhaps educational in the long run. When Jesus said, "And fear not them which kill the body, but are not able to kill the soul," was He not expressing the same thought?

Damage to a person which results from evil thought falls in a different category. It causes one to live his life in such a manner that, instead of progressing, he retrogresses, becoming increasingly more animalistic, confused, or dependent on others and less of an individual.

We live in an expanding universe. The Spirit of God is the Spirit of Expanding Consciousness, which enables a person to function in the ever-widening fields of thought and action with ever greater competence. Whatever circumscribes or introverts such growth is evil, and we might as well call it so. The forces of evil are, therefore, those persons who deceive, pervert, or destroy, and tend toward a return to slavery enforced by totalitarian control.

These evil souls are of many types. Some are excessively brutal, not having overcome their animalistic traits dating back to the Sodomic era. In the higher ranks of society, such persons appear as willful, domineering men to whom the things of the world have an irresistible, hypnotic appeal. What they want first of all is power over others, giving little thought to the interests of those they want to dominate. A good example of this type is Mao Tse-Tung. Then there are the so-called black art specialists, like Al Capone. These function as arch criminals, perverters of the social conscience, anarchists, and various other malefactors of the human race. They are intent only in serving their own ends, ignoring all social obligations or decent human relations.

But neither of these two types have done nearly as much harm as a third type of mischiefmaker, who are often regarded as benefactors because of their cultivated ability to deceive their contemporaries. These personalities, who became important about the time of the French Revolution, have been fomenting

101

revolutionary departures from established norms in every field of knowledge and action. I call them evildoers not because they are psychopathic destroyers, but because they are meddlers and perverters of social issues. A good example of this type is Vladimir Ilyich Lenin. Often the meddlers are promoting harmful schemes with great zeal, forcing on society ideas which people are not ready to accept, not because they ignore others but because they are too blind to see that each individual must develop according to his own inner law.

The Role of Secret Societies

Since ancient times, men have known that when they unite in secret societies, they generate a power which greatly magnifies their influence. Over the centuries, the power of occult associations has been used for both good and evil purposes. During most of man's history, the power of secret societies has been a matter of common knowledge. Over the past two hundred years, however, the influence of secret associations devoted to subversive, revolutionary ends has been so potent that their members have almost succeeded in convincing the general public that such organizations have had nothing to do with the turmoil which has gripped the world. The truth happens to be the opposite.

To the English-speaking world particularly, even if there were no organized effort to discredit the conspiratorial view of history, there would still be reluctance to believe in the existence of sinister movements directed against the existing social order and against all accepted religions. This is not because of lack of evidence. Plenty of such evidence has been presented both to public officials and to the general public.[2] Rather it is because most people find it hard to conceive that a few devilish people do indeed exist and do implement their plans through secret associations.

In any case, my objective here is not to prove the existence of Satan or his many plots, secret or otherwise, directed against humanity. This would be much like offering proofs for the existence of God—an effort wasted on those not sensitive to spiritual matters and not necessary for those who are. What I feel I must do is to share with my readers revelations given to us for the benefit of all men, and for no other reason. I know that these revelations are consistent with historical facts because I checked them out. I do not feel compelled to prove them, however, beyond pointing out that they fit the facts better than any other explanation which has ever been advanced for the many unusual events which transpired over the past two hundred years.

As mentioned in Chapter IV, in the early stages of recorded economic history, man was not ready for self-rule. In those times, it was given to some men to rule and guide other men, since these men had made faster progress than others, as is still the case. These rulers were to lead their subjects into righteous paths. Moreover, those among them who remained true to their calling never led inconsiderately or brutally, although sometimes a bit harshly when events and the reactions of men called for it. It is this type of authority which established the concept of the divine right of kings.

But man, being a mixed breed and having animalism in his consciousness, the appointed guardians soon saw possibilities of personal aggrandizement in the exercise of political power. And so what was meant to be an enlightened and progressive leadership often turned into a burdensome, if not loathsome, rulership.

We saw in Chapter IV that political authority in Medieval Europe was exerted both by the princes of the universal Church (the priests) and by the princes of the particular realm (the nobles, lords, and kings). The feudal system offered the peasants a basic security and a predictable life. However, it also reduced their existence to a pathetic, grim routine, making them in Markham's words, "dead to rapture and despair . . . a brother to the ox."

Even in this ossified setting, the winds of change continued to blow through God's grace. The stultifying security of a static agrarian community and the ascetic, dogmatic teachings of the

Catholic Church were replaced by the excitement of exploration and the pursuit of material gain or imperial power. Through all these changes, however, the spirit of rigid and repressive rulership remained much the same.

The bankers and merchants amassed their fortunes and lent them at interest to the crowns, to obligate them financially and to establish a claim to the privilege of ruling. These alliances between gold and sword brought about far-reaching changes in the character of the state. But they did very little to change the servile status of the subject populations. Under the new system which followed the Renaissance and Reformation, instead of the medieval nobility or the Catholic Church, the new master was the state. In France, Louis XIV said, "I am the State," and his rule with Colbert's participation shows that this new master can be more crushing than the old.

In the meantime, as Western man was achieving a higher spiritual and cultural development, he no longer needed the restrictive tutelage of guardians appointed over his political destiny. He had advanced to a stage in which he could shake off that mild form of slavery and rule his spirit according to his own understanding.

As mentioned in Chapter V, the Father's blessing and birthright promises (of material prosperity and political dominance) had passed from Abraham through Isaac and Jacob to Ephraim and Manasseh—the leaders of the ten lost tribes of the House of Israel. In one of the most fascinating historical discourses ever written, Adam Rutherford has shown that, after wandering among many nations, after "bearing many different names, and yet in the end, as if impelled by instinct,"[3] the tribes of Ephraim and Manasseh finally settled in the British Isles and North America respectively. In these events we have amazing proof of the marvelous fulfillment of the prophecies of Amos, Hosea, Samuel, Ezekiel, Jeremiah, and Isaiah![4]

Thus in the divine plan of the ages, it was Anglo-Saxon Israel which was to spread abroad to the west and to the east and to the north and to the south to be a blessing to all the nations of the earth by giving them the torch and the institutions of liberty. To do this, Ephraim had to plant the banner of freedom first into her own soil. And this she did perfectly. As I mentioned earlier, despite the cultural splendor of continental Europe, constitutional government was first established in England as early as 1689.

Soon after this event, another long-range plan—part of the Master's malicious opposition—was also to be implemented under the protective cover of secret societies on the continent of Europe. As historical research into subversive movements has established, this longstanding plan to conquer instead of to bless all nations also dates back to earliest times.[5] In fact, this plan of conquest through political intrigue is part and parcel of what I called the satanic approach to government in Chapter III. In the eighteenth century, this approach, with its central concept of world domination, found its primary focus in the Bavarian Order of Illuminati, established by Adam Weishaupt on May 1, 1776.

Weishaupt was a professor of canon law at Ingolstadt University in Germany. His concepts and methods provide the beginnings of not only what became known as communism, but also of other international programs of social revolution. Also while he drew on Jesuit plans and methods and invoked the name of Christ at every chance to impress the gullible, his doctrines represented a complete negation of Christianity. As the French historian, Henri Martin, summed it up, Weishaupt, who had no other god than Nature herself, "had . . . proposed as the end of Illuminism the abolition of property, social authority, of nationality, and the return of the human race to the happy state in which it formed only a single family without artificial needs, without useless sciences, every father being priest and magistrate. . . . "[6]

Actually the motive power behind the Order was neither religion nor humanism. It was the spirit of revolt against all existing social and moral order to pave the way for despotic and atheistic world government. But the diabolic aim of the Illumiati—to rule the world—was revealed only to those in the highest degrees. Those in the lower degrees were told that the purpose of the Order was to advance the cause of humanity against the repressions of kings, princes, priests, and their accomplices, who were supposed to have exploited their subjects ever since men lost their so-called original liberty and equality in their savage state.

The Illuminati used the forms of Freemasonry to attract prominent intellectuals, writers, publishers, financiers, noblemen, clergymen, and visionaries of all kinds. But the constant aim of the Order was to infiltrate and control all Masonic lodges through a multiplicity of ruses. "More than this, Illuminism was not only the assemblage of all errors, of all ruses, of all subtleties of a theoretic kind, it was also an assemblage of all practical methods for rousing men to action."[7]

The points made above about this secret order and its founder, Weishaupt, have by now been carefully documented.[8] The existence of such a conspiracy came to light when a messenger galloping from Frankfort to Paris was struck dead by lightning. The documents found on him were turned over to public authorities, and, after proving their authenticity, a Bavarian court of enquiry banned the Illuminati in 1786. As Weishaupt had predicted, however, the Order went underground and continued its evil work.

Their first major "accomplishment" was the French Revolution of 1789. Not only did they provide the sparks to kindle the flames of this conflagration, but they also gave it its international character, its militant atheism, and an atmosphere of terror and hatred which horrified civilized people everywhere.

The role of the Illuminati in promoting the French Revolution, for the first time in history openly declared to take in the whole world, has been demonstrated in more than one way. First, associations have been shown to exist between the Order and the leaders of the Revolution, and also between the Order and authors, publishers, and distributors of atheistic and seditious literature. Moreover, from dozens of sources, a strikingly close

106

correspondence has been established between the doctrines and methods of Illuminism and what was so often proclaimed or done throughout this tragic era.[9]

On the eve of the Revolution, right-minded men were properly critical of the follies and repression of the old regime. The succession of wars associated with the eighteenth century struggle for empire, the extravagances of court life, the growing ranks of nonproductive holders of sinecures and royal pensions, the privileges of nobles, clergymen and of monopolistic guilds, the oppressive system of taxation, and the increasing dependence on foreign loans were without doubt ruining the country. Something had to be done to correct these anomalies. But many of the actions during the French Revolution did not have much to do with reforming the French system. They had everything to do with advancing the aims of the Illuminati.

A well-known economic history textbook notes, for example, that in the period preceding the Revolution, "a multitude of . . . writers, not only in France but in other countries as well, advocated ideas which were essentially destructive."[10] Augmenting this approach, a plan called "L'Infamie" was also implemented for the systematic character assassination of every person who stood for the more attractive features of church or state. The fabrications about a fabulously expensive diamond necklace allegedly sent to Marie Antoinette, the queen, by a secret lover in exchange for her favors, was part of this plan. Worse than L'Infamie was the Reign of Terror, symbolized by the guillotine. What were the resounding cries for blood and more blood, the arrests, detentions, murders, massacres, except to terrorize the populace into submission? What could such disruption and despotism have to do with Liberté, Egalité, and Fraternité, as proclaimed by the leaders of the Revolution?

And what happened to the prominent Frenchmen who let themselves be used as pawns in the game played by the international forces who gained enormously from the upheavals they created? It is said that Mirabeau, who had been trapped into becoming one of the principal agents of the Illuminati, was poisoned when he tried to save his king from the execution his masters had decreed. The Duc d'Orleans, falsely led to believe that he would be made the new constitutional monarch, shortly after he voted for the death of his cousin, the king, was himself beheaded. In the end, after sending the aristocrats, and then the moderates, to the guillotine, the radicals also started turning on each other. As a result, Robespierre, Danton, and Marat were all murdered in their turn.

I am mentioning these events because such tactics have been repeatedly used by those promoting world revolution for the past two hundred years. After the visible leaders were made to play the roles assigned to them, they were all considered expendable. Whenever they presented difficulties, perhaps because they would not cooperate, or maybe because they knew too much, they were eliminated at the first opportunity. Moreover, their deaths were made to look accidental, natural, or the work of a fanatic.

Can you blame people for not knowing what has been going on all these years? It certainly did not cross my mind to study these situations until we were informed about them through ESP. Since then I have learned that students of secret societies have known all along that "the real authors never show themselves" and that "one thing never admitted is the identity of the individuals from whom one is receiving direction."[11]

And yet there have been some who have dared to speak and write and thus give the world glimpses of what might have caused the effects which have left the wise and prudent wondering.[12] In fact, during my personal researches on these questions, I was impressed more with how much has already been said on the secret forces than with the gaps in knowledge which continue to exist.

Reasons and Methods of Takeover

Despite the horrors of the French Revolution, the forces of disruption and revolution kept alive the delusive hope that mankind can have universal freedom and brotherhood through class war and violent upheavals. They managed to do this because they learned how to work with a new monarch who rose to prominence about this time. This monarch, mightier than the king of France and seated on a more permanent throne, was to govern mankind from then on. His name was Public Opinion. The old sovereigns of Europe, failing to learn from experience, continued to wage a feeble war against this new, powerful ruler. Consequently they gave their enemies chance after chance to topple them in needlessly tragic ways.

The social changes following the French Revolution and the imperialistic ventures of Napoleon Bonaparte speeded up the process of clearing away feudal restrictions. The main permanent economic change was the emancipation of the peasants in Western Europe. Freedom of enterprise and new techniques of production also spread with the rise of the middle classes. These developments in turn made it possible for bankers and financiers to extend their influence not only over European trade and industry, but also over the fiscal policies of their governments.

It will be remembered that the immediate cause for the downfall of the old regime in France was the collapse of its finances. On May 5, 1789, the service of the French public debt and allied charges amounted to fifty-three percent of the public revenue.[13] When governments get into debt to that extent, the possibilities of banker control of public policy are obvious.

In the nineteenth century, with the fantastic growth of commercial and investment banking to finance the immense increases in foreign trade and investment, a small number of overly ambitious financiers also became intoxicated with the dream of world domination. As mentioned earlier, this dream did not originate with them. Their association with the Illuminati, however, showed them how they could form an international fraternity, rising above national rivalries, to stand on commanding heights, to trick the most powerful governments into doing their bidding.

This was not a vain hope or plan. In fact it was soon realized. By opposing the archaic feudal privileges and the often selfish rulership of the priesthoods of the time, these clever servants of mammon also seemingly became the new champions of the underdog. Thus, once more, the evil conditions which governed men became the open door for other evil forces to enter and take over.

The international financiers were quite pragmatic in all their dealings. They allowed the kings in Austria and elsewhere to have their palaces as long as they would offer no meaningful opposition. They dealt more harshly with the stronger rulers, such as Czar Nicholas or the Kaiser. Not being religious themselves, they nevertheless supported Zionism, which relies on religious principles for its success.

True, they were hoping that if they were eventually placed openly in the driver's seat, the world would be a more decent place in which to live. We recognize and admit this. At the same time we still say that no one can make the world more decent by regimenting and manipulating men. Decency and progress spring only from responsible decisions of free individuals. What is decent about doing something which one is compelled to do?

Let us also not forget that, on the whole, during the nineteenth century, the world was becoming a more decent place in which to live, although not in the way the mammon forces had hoped. The one-hundred-year period between the Napoleonic Wars and World War I (1814-1914) was truly a period of progress. Rapid gains were made not only on the scientific and economic fronts, but also on the political and cultural. Theories about the inalienable rights of man and natural liberty did gain acceptance. The emphasis placed on free competition made even the people living under the more sordid forms of capitalism have some recourse to individuality. And, as Arnold Toynbee pointed out, individualism is a "pearl of great moral price." Therefore the world prospered.

International division of labor and specialization, nurtured by foreign trade and investment, plus able British diplomacy, led to unprecedented economic gains. The destinies of Ephraim and Manasseh were indeed being fulfilled, and the world was being blessed as prophesied. In fact, things were going so well for the average man, that the mammon forces thought they might never have a chance to attain their objective of world control. Consequently, with greater determination than ever, they decided to be all things to all men and thus to realize their boundless ambitions for power.

By using the age-old diabolical theory—any means to an end—they released the scourges of communism and socialism, knowing that behind the scenes they had the power to make both serve their own ends.[14] They succeeded in having people call all who opposed them "reactionaries," "bigots," or "hate mongers." This shows how well those persons with moneyed interests could manipulate the new monarch, Public Opinion, as they had the monarchs who had preceded him.

Thus, having both the intention and the means, they set nation against nation, Gentile against Jew, race against race, church against state, while caring for none of them. Difficult as it is to believe, these souls, only about 300 in number, managed to dull their consciences completely. So they falsely promised man Utopia, where all share alike and all are provided for, where there are no wars, not even policemen. They pretended to be for the businessman and for free enterprise, turned radical when that tactic paid off, resorted to brainwashing where the going was more difficult, threatened and actually caused personal ruin and murders where the resistance was too strong. That is how they set out on their "merry way" toward their envisaged "victory" of an enslaved world. The strange thing is that mankind, so far at least, appears to like it.

In this bird's-eye picture, questions about when, where, and how become picayune. To those interested in this matter, I say, seek and ye shall find your answers.[15]

In 1848, when the *Communist Manifesto* was published, it declared that Germany was "on the eve of a bourgeois revolution which would involve the fall of the 'reactionary' classes." It was after this that the Communist Party was to lead the movement for a proletarian revolution. And this revolution of the workers in turn was to lead to the fading away of the state as an agency of oppression and the establishment of the classless society. Needless to add, the real directors of this world revolutionary movement had no intention whatever of relinquishing their power.

The uprisings of 1848 on the Continent, inspired by the secret powers, prepared the way for further extensions of economic and political freedom, which obviously helped them advance their cause, even though others benefited also. However, outside of France, which was largely dominated by wealthy bankers and industrialists, the principal immediate effects of these revolutions were agrarian. Consequently while the teachings of Marx and Engels at the time were not without some influence, historical conditions had not yet changed sufficiently to make them a significant basis on which to formulate a program for world revolution.

So the mammon forces continued to work essentially through capitalistic institutions, such as the Bank of England, and other private banks in France, and then Germany, Austria, and Switzerland, before coming finally to our shores in these United States. Being perceptive, although cynical, students of human behavior, they noticed that the British had great talent for colonization and for bringing modern civilization to primitive or slumbering ancient peoples. Therefore, they decided to work with British colonialism, on the theory that after the backward lands are softened up with commercial culture, they would be easier to take over.

Along the way, however, they encountered brilliant opposition in the person of Benjamin Disraeli, who became the Earl of Beaconsfield. Known as a radical Tory, he was appointed prime minister twice, the second time from 1874 to 1880. I know that today he is not universally admired, and he has been called a clever rogue and worse. But Disraeli in all his dealings, financial or otherwise, was forever loyal to England. Perhaps he did not understand banking or economics as well as his opponents, but he excelled in understanding something much more important— human nature. Therefore, better than anyone else in his time, he was able to grasp the skulduggery and intrigues of the mammon forces in all their amazing complexity. Moreover he was sufficiently intelligent to enmesh his enemies in the very same traps they had set up to catch him. This is illustrated by the way he gained control over the Suez Canal for his government. Many attempts were made against his life, but since he was under divine guidance and protection at all times, none of them succeeded.

Although he has rarely been acclaimed for it, Benjamin Disraeli forestalled the mammon takeovers in Great Britain. That is why the international financiers decided to gain stronger footholds elsewhere. They were determined to succeed in their endeavors one way or another. At stake was much more than their own enrichment. They were fighting the battle of the ages between the forces of Darkness against the forces of Light. Therefore literally compelled by devils on the spirit side, they schemed and worked for war, war, war, and revolution to bring the last of their enemies down to their knees. Thus would they prove that the struggle of the human spirit for freedom was a colossal failure.

Their method was first to observe the strengths and weaknesses of every nation or group which could serve their purpose. Next through a quick judo-like action, they would turn the strength of the strong against itself. As for the nations going down on the seesaw, their method was to pull them further down until they would find it a relief to submit to the dictates of their front men like Lenin or Trotsky. And if they could not bring their own men to power, they would, nevertheless, attempt to control the Napoleons and Stalins who made it largely on their own with their holds on finance or diplomacy. That is why, over the past two centuries, the visible leaders of the world have never really been the true powers.

It is again through cunning and intrigue that the evil ones enlisted international Jewry to serve their own ends. As the Jewish writer, Bernard Lazare has shown, anti-Semites are not right when they see the Jew as "the preparer, the machinator, the chief engineer of revolutions." But, as he also points out, "The

Jew has the revolutionary spirit; consciously or not he is an agent of revolution."[16]

In Talmudic as well as Biblical literature there are references to the eventual world rule of Israel which have seldom been properly understood. As mentioned in Chapter V, the Jewish people compose only a part of the House of Israel. Zionists, however, made the error of identifying the part (Judah) with the whole (Israel), which, as shown earlier, includes Anglo-Saxon people also. Consequently Zionist thought became tainted with exclusive messianic dreams of world rulership. This fitted into the overall plans and international takeovers of the mammon forces who will use any means, any avenue, to attain their ends.

The international mammon forces used the Germanic mind in a different way. The German people had been disciplined to obey their superiors too sternly for too long to make good revolutionaries. However, the stubborn, militaristic streak in their personality makes them willing to conquer for gain. Moreover, since they excelled in methodical thinking, and in mechanical, chemical, and related scientific fields, they were specially well qualified to build the industrial base for an efficient military machine. Therefore, the Germans were the ones chosen to plunge the world into the chaos of World War I, out of which would come what had been years in the planning, that is to say, the Communist Revolution and the League of Nations—two closely related tools needed to establish international government. The former was to be used as a hammer to crush the opposition while the latter provided the framework in which to pick up the pieces.

The revolution would be started in Russia, which happened to be going in the downward direction on the seesaw at the turn of the century. Unlike the disciplined Germans, the emotional Russian peasant could be easily stirred into a mass revolt which would make him feel important. Besides, as the evil powers assessed the situation, it would not take too much to buy off a poor nation with a basically autocratic tradition. They thought, "Promise them three full meals a day and a watch, and you've got them." Russia also represented a vast land of rich resources, not the least of which was the large army of hardy, healthy peasants who made good laborers.

In short, the evil schemers went from people to people, adding and subtracting the pluses and minuses in their conditions, to come up with a blueprint of action that would shake the world to its foundations, until they were placed in the driver's seat. Can this be true? Read on and decide for yourself.

After Bismarck's rule ended in 1890, the international mammon interest found it easier to help Germany challenge the ruling superpower of the time, Great Britain, with aggressive commercial and colonial policies, and especially with a most ominous naval policy. The mammon forces knew that such German adventures would alarm and alienate the British Lion, and that war would be the inevitable outcome. However, the powers behind the scene did not intend for Germany to win. The basic reason is that they were afraid that, if victorious, the German leaders would not hesitate to betray them. Therefore, it made better business sense for the evil ones to play their cards with France and England, whose governments were more vulnerable to manipulation. After they decided this, the most reasonable alternative was to advance the Zionist interest through the democratic countries and, of course, through the League of Nations, yet to be established.

These blueprints for conquest were not free from problems and complications. It will be remembered that on the eve of World War I, the nations of Europe were divided into two antagonistic camps—the Triple Alliance, composed of Germany, Austria, and Italy versus the Triple Entente, composed of Great Britain, France, and Russia. This meant that, as England and France would be helped, Czarist Russia would have to be wounded to weaken it for the planned revolution. It also meant that the United States of America, this great isolationist giant, would also have to be drawn into the war. Otherwise, after the arranged holocaust ruined all the major European nations, America would come forth with so much financial and moral strength that she might never consent to being tangled in the webs of a united world.

Recognizing that the United States and Great Britain were blood brothers, the mammon interests calculated that it would be easier to bring America to fight with the Entente allies. Consequently they stepped up their efforts to establish the Federal Reserve System, so it could be used to mobilize the funds the Allies would need to fight World War I. It was not accidental, however, that the United States did not enter the War in April 1917 before President Wilson had committed himself to advancing the League of Nations concept, before British Prime Minister Asquith, opposed to political Zionism, was forced to resign in favor of Lloyd George, a longtime friend of Zionism, and before Czar Alexander of Russia abdicated following the uprisings in St. Petersburg and elsewhere, financed with foreign money.

Arranging for these outcomes necessitated a number of mysterious and, on the surface, contradictory events. Note, for example, the use of British influence to release Leon Trotsky, captured off Halifax, although his revolution would lead to the collapse of the Eastern front and enable the Germans to concentrate on fighting British troops on the Western front.

All the same, whether what happened made sense or not, the war proceeded more or less as planned. Huge fortunes were allowed to be made from armaments and otherwise upon the ruins of nations, while higher taxes and inflation ate into the hard-earned incomes and savings of the general population. Public debts piled up higher and higher to give the financiers more control over their governments, and nations with splendid traditions of individualism became thoroughly regimented, setting precedents for planned developments to come. Above all, however, the spirit of destruction, despair, and confusion—which is the spirit of the Anti-Christ—spread and spread. Yes, things were going according to plan. From then on, the forces of evil could operate with much greater ease.

FOOTNOTES

1. See, for example, W. Clement Stone and Norma Lee Browning, *The Other Side of the Mind*. Englewood Cliffs, N.J.; Prentice-Hall, Inc., 1964; Charles T. Tart, ed., *Altered States of Consciousness*. New York: John Wiley & Sons, Inc., 1969; Elmer E. Green, Alyce M. Green and E. Dale Walters, *Progress of Cybernetics: Proceedings of the International Congress of Cybernetics,* ed. J. Rose. London: Gordon and Breach, 1970.
2. Nesta H. Webster, *World Revolution: The Plot Against Civilization*. London: Constable and Co., Ltd., 1921; Robert Wilton, *The Last Days of the Romanovs: From 15th March, 1917*. Hawthorne, Calif.: Christian Book Club of America, 1969; Francois Coty, *Tearing Away the Veils: The Financiers Who Control the World*, trans. E.N. Sanctuary. Hawthorne, Calif.: Omni Publications, 1967; Denis Fahey, *The Rulers of Russia*. Hawthorne, Calif.: Christian Book Club of America, 1967; William Guy Carr, *Pawns in the Game*. Glendale, Calif.: St. George Press, 1967; *Collective Speeches of Congressman Louis T. McFadden, as Compiled from the Congressional Record*. Hawthorne, Calif.: Omni Publications, 1970; A. H. M. Ramsay, *The Nameless War*. London: Britons Publishing Co., 1962; Mary M. Davison, *The Secret Government of the United States*. Omaha, Nebr.: The Greater Nebraskan, 1968; A. K. Chesterton, *The New Unhappy Lords: An Exposure of Power Politics*. Hawthorne, Calif.: Christian Book Club of America, 1967; Garry Allen with Larry Abraham, *None Dare Call It Conspiracy*. Rossmoor, Calif.: Concord Press, 1972; W. Cleon Skousen, *The Naked Capitalist* (A review and commentary on Dr. Carroll Quigley's book, *Tragedy and Hope*). Salt Lake City, Utah: by the Reviewer, 1971.
See also the works mentioned in footnote 11, Chapter V;

footnotes 11, 12, and 13 in Chapter VI; and footnotes 4 and 12 of Chapter VII.

3. Rutherford, p. 48.

4. Without going into specifics, the basic pattern of Biblical prophecy encompasses the smiting of Israel because she did not hearken unto God, and the subsequent scattering, shepherding, restoration, and redemption of Israel to make her the leading people through which God's blessings will flow to all nations. It is of considerable interest that the destiny of Israel has also been prophesied in the shapes of the passages of the Great Pyramid, appropriately named "the Bible in Stone." This amazing monument—the largest in the world—stands on the geographical center of the land surface of the earth. It has been said that it places the Christian religion on a scientific basis because, though it had existed 2,000 years before the Christian era, its structural form indicates the precise time of Christ's birth, baptism, and crucifixion, as well as the timing of other crucial periods in the divine plan of the ages. See in this connection the erudite Adam Rutherford's *Pyramidology*, A Great Work in Five Volumes, The Institute of Pyramidology, 31 Station Road, Harpenden, Hertfordshire, Great Britain, 1957-1974.

5. Nesta H. Webster, *Secret Societies and Subversive Movements.* (9th ed.: Hawthorne, Calif.: Christian Book Club of America, 1969), pp. 3-195.

6. Ibid., p. 207.

7. Ibid., p. 231.

8. John Robison, *Proofs of a Conspiracy*, (Orig. published in 1798). "The American Classics"; Boston: Western Islands, 1967. See also Webster, pp. 233-268.

9. Ibid.

10. Bowden, Karpovich, and Usher, p. 215.

11. Webster, pp. 200 and 202.

12. Much more has been said and written on the satanic conspiracies of world conquest than has been covered by the footnotes of this book. However, since they were either not

catalogued or not on the shelves of the Library of Congress, where I worked, I could not refer to them here.

13. Bowden, Karpovich, and Usher, p. 240.

14. The alliance between international finance and communism becomes less astonishing when it is realized that Jewish influence has played a role in both spheres. I must point out, however, that Jewish financial, political, and intellectual organizations have played no more than a limited role in these spheres as well as in other plans for world domination. The evil ones who dream of conquest over all nations incarnate in every nation, people, race, land, and clime, and eventually go into the sea of forgetfulness.

15. One of the books I found most useful in my researches was drawn to my attention by a cab driver during a casual conversation.

16. Webster, p. 177.

Chapter IX

MORE ABOUT THE ANTI-CHRIST

What Followed World War I

That World War I was a turning point in the history of man has been widely recognized. In 1954, the British historian, H. R. Trevor-Roper, said: "The first (World) war . . . closed a long era of general peace and began a new age of violence in which the second (World) war is simply an episode. Since 1914 the world has a new character: a character of international anarchy." In 1964, Konrad Adenauer, chancellor of West Germany, pointed out that security and quiet have disappeared from the lives of men since 1914. A year later, in 1965, President Dwight D. Eisenhower said, "A deterioration has been going on since the First World War."[1]

Individually and collectively people everywhere want improvement, security, and peace. Why, then, have they had deterioration, turmoil, and conflict? The answers the experts give to this apparent paradox leave much to be desired. They say that man cannot have his heart's desire because of ignorance, lack of resources or resourcefulness, mistakes in judgment, accidental circumstances, and the dead hand of the past. The labels they place on these reasons change with the times. More recently, the fashion has been to speak of overpopulation (not enough resources) and the failure of institutions to change fast enough to keep pace with the rise of popular aspirations stemming from advances in technology.

If scientists understood how divine justice and balance operate, how reincarnation assures the orderly progression of life through the different races and cultures, the reasons they give for social problems would be completely different. There are two basic factors which alone account for all the fundamental disturbances in the divine order underlying life. These are the evil forces in high places and the hybrid nature of divine-animal man who knows right from wrong but does not care to follow the right course. The animal has no concept of good or bad; divine man does. The mixture of these two different natures mentioned in Chapter III has given rise to selfish cleverness, with its obvious potential for destructive action. All other reasons for human disorders are either unimportant, or they can be traced to the interplay between evil's plotting and man's succumbing. The only way out of this predicament lies in overcoming the animal in us through love and evolution. Negative forces do not have a chance where there is both righteous concern and patience.

Even those who pull the puppet strings behind the scenes would get nowhere if a righteous few—and it would not take more than a few—would take their stand with God, as Davids facing their Goliaths and say, "This much and no further." There are people in government now who have been divinely guided to the positions they hold for the express purpose of stopping the evil in their land and in the world. Today they are not listening to their inner promptings. What they may choose to do tomorrow is another matter.

If only our leaders would realize how easy it can be to oppose and overcome the negative powers they face through righteous acts of valor! However, the universities and seminaries which are supposed to show the way do not themselves know how to define, let alone cope with the evil influences in the world. As a result, the multitudes suffer. Therefore, while not holding the average man blameless for his wrong deeds, we do not condemn him or think of him as a sinner. Rather we recognize the least of them as brothers, since we are equally sons of the Father in Heaven. This we do because it is literally the Father's wish to see all His children eventually as great as He is and even greater. Which genuine father would wish otherwise?

Not yet having learned to think of themselves as invincible children of God, men were fated to suffer at the hands of luciferian forces until the good in them—like a rubber ball submerged under the water—would bounce to the surface again, to bask in the sunshine and in the life-giving forces of the Father. Thus we still believe that it is best to think of man as essentially honest; we know he can learn to live with his neighbors comfortably and decently. Given a fair chance, he can learn to govern himself equitably without big and oppressive government.

At the peace conference in Paris, however, the hidden hand was far from giving people a fair chance. I realize that the powers behind government do not particularly think of themselves as villains who like to make others suffer, but the very process of solving problems through international intrigues, economic sanctions and hidden controls involves endless suffering. Moreover, to work toward one international system of money, law, and government violates human nature and divine plan alike. Even if it succeeds for a while, it would stop the growth of the human soul and block man's endless creative possibilities. Of course, people will say that the League of Nations was not intended to be a world government. The point is, however, that the long-range intentions behind the scenes were different from what was made to appear on the surface.

In arranging a peace to follow their war, the mammon interests were determined to protect their puppet in Russia. To avoid adverse reactions, as usual, they had to extend their support through a variety of ruses. After all, Bolshevism was supposed to fight capitalism instead of depending on a faction of super capitalists for its very survival. True, some insignificant contingents of Allied troops were sent to Russia. Such moves, however, were intended to strengthen rather than to weaken the Bolsheviks by fomenting nationalistic sentiment among the Russian people. These expeditions, moreover, were followed by such surprising peace and trade proposals as to make one writer say, "The attitude of the Allied Governments toward Russia is either treason or madness."[2]

So much false information was spread about the real nature of the Bolshevik takeover that, on March 11, 1918, in a cable of greetings to the Congress of the Soviets, President Wilson said, "The whole heart of the people of the United States is with the people of Russia in the attempt to free themselves forever from autocratic government and become masters of their own life."[3]

Moreover, the plans the international mammon forces had for Germany could not have made the peace stable. They wanted to be in a position to have the militaristic German nation and her partners plunge the world into another major war when the time would be ripe again. They needed such a war not only for the huge profits it would bring them, but also as another giant step forward in their program of regimenting all the nations under one command. Consequently, they decided to subject the German economy to a number of major controls. President Wilson and the other idealists who opposed such harsh measures and who favored a moderate and magnanimous peace were definitely outmaneuvered by the international mammon forces.

These forces had seen to it that their interests would be represented on every major delegation at the peace conference.[4] Thus having the power, they made their wishes prevail. As the outstanding authorities on the economic history of the period pointed out, "the economic activities of the Germans, the Austrians, the Hungarians, and the Bulgarians were subjected almost completely to the will of the victors: and under the guise of reparations, obligations were exacted which in reality were indemnities."[5] We saw in an earlier chapter how international bankers "sat in heaven, under a rain of fees and commissions" received in financing these so-called reparation payments.

Such unconscionable arrangements sooner or later were bound to cause adverse reactions, although people at the time did not know what had caused the consequences they had to suffer. More than thirty years later it came out with the publication of Hans Luther's memoirs that the German government, unwilling to pay its reparation obligations, in the early 1930's, wanted to see economic conditions deteriorate. It did not want to see them improved.[6] Hans Luther at the time was president of the *Reichsbank*. The famous economic historian, Alexander Gerschenkron, has started to expose some of the real motives behind the deliberate policy of creating economic hardships. Earlier, along with most of his colleagues, he had thought the monetary contraction of the German central bank to be a mistake or an over-reaction to the German peoples' neurotic fears of inflation.[7]

Perhaps one day other memoirs will be published to convince some other scholars that the truth is not what it seems about the sequence of events from the German deflation through the Hitler era to World War II. Recently an American historian changed his mind drastically about the war even without new facts uncovered from old archives.[8] Even so, no historian, regardless of how open-minded he chooses to be, can know enough of the truth to explain accurately the basic motivation behind world events in the face of well-organized attempts to distort the evidence.

It is, therefore, to divine sources from the invisible planes that I had to turn to find the missing pieces of the puzzle. In sharing this information, however, I must go back once more to 1917. As we saw earlier, the Russian Revolution was not what it appeared on the surface. This too was the product of international intrigue which involved some of the wealthiest capitalists in the world.

According to the theories of Marx and Engels, capitalism would have to go through a process of maturation before the successful appearance of socialism through a proletarian revolution. Only after such a process would the so-called inherent contradictions of capitalism make it ripe for its own downfall. To initiate a revolution in a place or at a time which did not approach this stage would be to engage in "mad adventurism." The peasant society of Russia in 1917 was very far from this stage of mature capitalism. It had neither powerful capitalists nor a large industrial working class. The urban sector constituted less than twenty percent of the population.

Moreover, the sudden seizure of the reins of government by a small group of trained revolutionists, a strategy supposedly developed by Lenin, was in fact completely opposed to his earlier thinking. In 1905, he had said, "He who wishes to proceed to socialism by any other path than political democracy must inevitably arrive at absurd and reactionary conclusions, both in the political and economic sense.⁹ Even if a strong-willed intellectual like Lenin could have changed his mind so radically on such a vital subject, the fact remains that the Russian revolution was not a genuine Marxian revolution. It was an attempt to establish the nucleus of a radical world government—a World Soviet Republic. The Soviets openly declared that they intended to use Russia as a base for worldwide propaganda, aimed at undermining religious faith and destroying all that Western civilization stood for.

Few young people today realize the extent of the social cataclysms released by the Russian Revolution. In order to radicalize a peasant society, the revolutionists cried, "Seize the land!" To this cry the Soviet Headquarters in Moscow added another, "Arm yourselves!" Issues were to be settled by nothing less than brute force. Such militancy naturally erupted in civil war.

To make matters worse, the most productive members of the formerly wealth-owning and professional classes were murdered in cold blood, incarcerated, or else they died in various epidemics or immigrated to other lands. In resisting the forced requisition of agricultural products, the peasants cut back on production drastically and slaughtered their own cattle. These acts in turn resulted in catastrophic shortages of food and large-scale famines. On the theory that it was desirable to give the workers control over their industries, manufacturing and commerce were nationalized. In less than four years, total industrial production fell to about 15 percent of what it had been before the war!

A reign of terror similar to the one instituted during the French Revolution was launched to break the people's will to resist. Fear gripped everyone. Brother betrayed brother. The Bolshevist labor laws made all "citizens" subject to compulsory labor. Coping with shortages of managers was even more difficult. In all probability the regime could not have survived without foreign help.

To save the situation that they had created, the internationalists had to provide the required assistance. Economic historians refer to this surprising cooperation between the revolutionary Soviet government and foreign capitalists as "the new economic policy." Under this novel program, foreign capital and experts were sent to Russia, excessive bureaucratic centralization was reversed, nationalized industry was reorganized on a commercial basis, and capitalistic methods were introduced into Soviet finance. This went so far as to allow the Central State Bank to issue bills backed by gold or foreign bonds.[10] As a result of these measures, for awhile, many economic gains were made.

Even so, all these policies were reversed when Stalin won his struggle for power with Trotsky after Lenin died in 1924. Stalin knew of Trotsky's ties to international finance. Believing that his knowledge of these illicit connections made his opponent vulnerable, he thought he could defeat his rival and make a clean break from foreign control at one and the same time. Consequently Stalin exaggerated his doctrinal differences with Trotsky. He stressed the building of socialism in one country, namely Russia, at the expense of the old Bolshevik emphasis on promoting so-called proletarian revolutions everywhere in the world. His ruse succeeded. With his parochial line, he gained the support of the more nationalistic party regulars and won his fight.

At this turn of events, the hidden forces started to worry that their puppet in Russia might turn into a Frankenstein monster. Consequently they decided to revive Germany's military power as soon as this could be arranged. The Nazis could be expected not only to remilitarize the nation, but also unwittingly to help the Zionists, backed by international mammon, to establish the State of Israel near the fabulous oil and mineral resources of the Dead Sea region. The anti-Semitic policies Hitler would adopt were to harden the hearts of the Jews and practically force many of the reluctant ones to immigrate. In the meantime, the Zionists would have their golden opportunity to whip up sympathy and financial support for the Jewish homeland idea. The risks involved in this plan were enormous. But it was not the first time that ambitious men would think that a good end justifies a few questionable means. We are told, however, that even the powers behind the scenes did not anticipate the monstrous extremes to which the Nazi party would go in carrying out their anti-Semitic program.

However, we still believe that at least a remnant of the House of Israel, including Judah, were destined to walk again in the former Holy Land. This had to happen. Students of Bible prophecy know that outcome to have been divinely ordained. Moreover, after centuries of persecution, it was a matter of practical necessity that the Jewish people should have a land of their own. It is a sad commentary that they should come into their ancient lands through intrigue and bloodshed. Yet, it cannot be denied that similar plots and injuries were directed against Judah in times past. In the overall picture, where divine justice must prevail, acts of infamy which occur were allowed to hurt only those who have lessons to learn or debts to pay for wrongs done in earlier lives. Can you conceive this to be true? It is the beginning of the new wisdom.

We touched on the illicit cooperation across the Atlantic Ocean to get Hitler's war machine rolling again, in a previous chapter. So few people have bothered to find out how Nazi Germany obtained the economic resources she needed for war. Carroll Quigley says that, "when Germany began the war in September, 1939, less than a third of its oil, rubber, and iron ore were of domestic origin; it had only two months' supply of gasoline at the peace-time rate of consumption and about three months' supply of aviation fuel."[11]

How could a nation in such a position fight a major war? Where would Hitler have been without the aid of hidden international cartels, which were not so difficult to spot, if only the Allied governments would care to look? The truth of the matter is that they did not dare to look.

Early in 1940, when some British members of parliament were pressing the government to bomb German munition stores in the Black Forest, the air minister asked angrily, "Are you aware it is private property? Why, you will be asking me to bomb Essen next!" The Krupp interests had their munitions factories located in Essen.[12]

To supplement their program of rearming Germany, the mammon interests controlling the international cartels also invented the policy of appeasement. This policy was bitterly criticized; it was called a serious blunder, unrealistic, and shortsighted. In fact, it was none of these. It was nothing short of diabolic. The theory behind it was that if Hitler were permitted to take enough territories, eventually he would turn on the Russians. If Russia were attacked, Stalin would have to cooperate with the Allies, making it possible once again to establish a basis for the world government the insiders had dreamed of for years. These plans were worked out so cleverly that even Neville Chamberlain, the prime minister of Great Britain, who was to implement the policy of appeasement, did not suspect that he was carrying out the war plans of the international mammon group.

It is, of course, not pleasant to write about the Anti-Christ. Nevertheless, there is no denying that the influence of dark forces has been very much in evidence in our times. The Second World War did not have to happen, but it did. The United States government did not have to drop atomic bombs on the Japanese people, but two such bombs were dropped. The United Nations organization did not have to become a giant international bureaucracy, where the "virtuous and the criminal sit side by side,"[13] but that is exactly what happened. The cold war and a series of hot wars did not have to break out, but they broke out all the same despite the United Nations. American financiers did not have to promote a strong European union which would take the mantle of leadership away from the United States, but they did, on the pretext that it would be a bulwark against the communist bloc with which they also started doing business. The freest nations in the world did not have to be maneuvered into more and more tightly regulated systems, but they were, gradually, through a series of artificial crises. Atheistic and materialistic philosophies did not have to spread, undermining faith in all spiritual values, but did they not do so at an alarming rate?

The Hidden Anti-Christ

If a hidden group of master manipulators set on destroying the individualistic order—to replace it with one they can control—did not in fact exist, future historians would find it necessary to invent one. Most modern intellectuals are unfortunately too biased to think objectively about what has been happening. Consider the world wars, the international anarchy, the social revolutions and moral deterioration, the rise of one totalitarian state after another, and the gradual erosion of freedom even in the nation with the most glorious traditions of political and economic liberty. Does it seem to you that these are natural or normal developments? Considering how fast the educational levels of the people are rising, social conditions should be getting progressively better instead of worse.

As we saw earlier, there are those who blame these abnormal developments on the new technologies which have shrunk the world, on overpopulation, nationalism, class struggle, ignorance, and the refusal to change with the times. In a world in which each nation respected the independence and rights of every other nation, the shrinking of distance would not have created perpetual conflict and turmoil. Far from giving cause for deterioration and conflict, the control the new sciences and technologies give man over his environment makes it possible to feed and clothe billions more. Thus the Malthusian theories of population, with their emphasis on wars, famines, and other catastrophes to check the excessive growth of population, should have by now become obsolete. Furthermore, if strict justice had been maintained in economic relationships, the reason for destructive class struggles and much of the destitution in the world would have been eliminated long ago.

The heart of man, though tainted with animalism, is still basically pure, and it does respond to kindness. Man has proved himself capable of wonderful works of art, marvelous inventions, amazing sacrifices, and great generosity. After the wars that the Americans were drawn into, did they not even feed their former enemies? Similar acts of kindness are not unknown in Western history.

As the world-famous sociologist, Sorokin, has pointed out, "The longest existing organizations have been those animated by spiritual and altruistic forces for realization of the supreme values of God, Truth, Goodness, and Beauty. Such are the great ethico-religious organizations (which) have already lived one, two, or three millenia."[14] Does not this support our thesis about man's innate goodness?

Moreover, regardless of what social scientists say, we cannot forget the divine supervision of world affairs. I do not have to convince the religious that the God revealed in the Bible is a potent God, very much involved in history. At His command is the inexhaustible power that spins the universe. Nothing that affects human destiny is unknown to Him. If, as some say, the great social catastrophes in the world are accidental—related to impersonal developments in demography and technology—why does not a compassionate God, involved in history, prevent these accidents from happening?

From a spiritual point of view, is it not more logical to say that it is not impersonal accidents, innocent mistakes, or unfortunate coincidences, but the machinations of evil forces which make people suffer? All higher religions recognize that there is a mysterious and devious power bent on deception and mischief. This power working through people who open themselves to evil temptations attacks nations no less than individuals. Therefore, if we find entire societies confused and despairing, it is time to ask which satanic personalities, groups, or movements have made this so and why.

About thirty years ago, an erudite and upright economist, Friedrich Hayek, wrote *The Road to Serfdom*. In this book he argued that the much-prized liberties in the West were threatened by the very social trends which the more high-minded people in Western societies were helping to promote. He asked, therefore, "Is there a greater tragedy imaginable than that, in our endeavor consciously to shape our future in accordance with high ideals, we should in fact unwittingly produce the very opposite of what we have been striving for?"[15]

His basic thesis is that it was not the congenital wickedness of the Germans but the acceptance of socialist doctrines and policies which had paved the way for Nazi totalitarianism in Germany. Moreover, he felt that the same basic causes would also create the same detestable effects in England and the United States, despite the fact that policies which are essentially socialistic were often favored by the most highly admired people of good will.

Hayek was right in believing that the socialist and communist policies set the patterns for the Nazis and Fascists to follow. The latter did not have much to invent when it came to collectivist social policy and the means needed to make it work—i.e., despotic rule and thought control.

He was also right in pointing out that prominent socialistic writers in England were paving the way in their own country for catastrophic outcomes similar to those seen in Germany and Italy. Talented intellectuals can do this, because they can change the premises on which public opinion is formed. As Hayek noted, the socialists set out to alter English society by cleverly changing the meaning of such words as "freedom" and "morality" into their exact opposites. Another approach they used was to introduce subtle distortions in historical facts and interpretations. For example, before World War II, English writers treated Bismarck, the social interventionist, sympathetically, whereas Gladstone, who stood for economic liberty, was presented in such a way that his name was rarely "mentioned by the younger generation without a sneer."[16]

131

Hayek also mentioned with alarm how the ideas which destroyed Western civilization in Germany began to appear repeatedly in English political literature. Among these were: "the increasing veneration for the state," "the enthusiasm for 'organization' of everything" (under the new name of planning), and "the inability to leave anything to the simple power of organic growth."[17]

This distinguished scholar also noted the increasing convergence in the views of the Right and Left, and their common opposition to traditional British policies of economic liberty. He was particularly disturbed by the intellectual mood created which made progressives willing to break all cultural ties with the past and stake everything on the success of radical experiments.

Two or three decades after Hayek's book came out, these conditions were more or less duplicated in America. At first, the general public did not suspect that, behind the scenes, history was being made to repeat itself. Now, the number of those who know is increasing.

There are more than a few reasons why it is wrong to consider socialism as *the* cause for the decline of freedom in the West. First, the socialistic visions which have mesmerized millions did not originate with the socialists; they can be traced to the clever deceptions promulgated by Weishaupt's Bavarian Illuminati.

We know that it was one of Weishaupt's ruses to conduct his order's program of world revolution "under other names and other occupations." Most varieties of utopian socialism, scientific socialism (or communism), and Fabian socialism have been little more than some of the other names under which his program has been conducted.

It is by no means a coincidence, therefore, that, although the nature of the social problems and grievances of the peoples in different countries at different times have varied greatly, the basic remedies proposed by most socialistic thinkers have more or less remained the same. Moreover, these have coincided with the aims of the Illuminati. These aims are: (a) replace all established governments with a universal state, (b) abolish all religion, (c) eliminate private property, (d) destroy the spirit of nationalism or patriotism, and (e) undermine the family through loose morals and the education of children by the state.

In addition, we cannot help being impressed by the contradictions in the writings and lives of socialist leaders, or in the way socialist movements have evolved. These contradictions are resolved only when socialism is seen for what it has really been—a front for the evil spirit of conquest. For example, it was pointed out that:

> even in the section of his book dealing with the origins of Industrial Capitalism, where Marx refers to the great financiers, the stockjobbing and speculation in shares, and what he describes as 'the modern sovereignty of finance' he never once indicates the Jews as the leading financiers, or the Rothschilds as the supercapitalists of the world. As well one might sit down to recount the history of wireless telegraphy without any reference to Signor Marconi! Only by recognizing that Marx was not sincere in his denunciations of the Capitalistic system, and that he had other ends in view.[18]

Nor was the erudite German historian, Oswald Spengler, overly exaggerating when he wrote in his *Decline of the West* that:

> There is no proletarian, not even a Communist, movement, that has not operated in the interests of money, in the direction indicated by money, and for the time being permitted by money—and that without the idealists among its leaders having the slightest suspicion of the fact.[19]

In England, it was asked fifty years ago where the money came from which enabled so many socialists to "dine and sup, feast and amuse themselves with as few scruples of conscience as any unregenerate Tories."[20] In the United States, we may ask the same question today about radicals in lieu of socialists.

Large-scale wars and the militarization of society which they bring about are among the most powerful forces which have led to the regimentation of the social order of the West. Who can reasonably claim that it is socialism which has been responsible for the fantastically destructive and meaningless wars which have invariably centralized power?

If there was not a powerful conspiracy to back the work of the socialists, how on earth could their efforts have been crowned with so much success? The equality which socialists advocate is the most unattainable of all dreams. Before the revolution to force equality on Russia, one socialistic experiment after another directed toward equality had ended up in complete failure.

Among these one may cite Robert Owen's "New Harmony Community of Equality," started in America 1825, and similar communistic settlements started by the disciples of Owen. The domestic association of workers—phalansteries—initiated by Charles Fourier in 1832, where complete equality was to reign, also ended in dismal failure. The experiment in Guild Socialism launched by the Saint-Simonien Buchez met the same fate. He had all workmen in his Atelier (workshop) pool their tools and their money and share their profits equally after reinvesting a sixth.

State intervention in everyday life has not appealed either to workers or peasants in whose name socialistic revolutions have been organized. If this were not so, what need would there have been to promote socialism from the top, using as agents intellectuals and students who have been out of touch with the realities of everyday life? As mentioned earlier, promoting socialism has been made a profitable venture for many intellectuals by capitalists who are supposed to be natural opponents of share-the-wealth proposals. Could these proposals have been sincere? Whatever the motives of socialist intellectuals, the fact remains that the system they glorify has sooner or later crushed the individual wherever it was tried.[21]

True, during the course of the Industrial Revolution in

England, the United States, and elsewhere, workers were at times mistreated and exploited mercilessly by their employers. There is also no denying that any power which challenges the status quo certainly has some appeal to those who have suffered under a system which has injured them. Nevertheless, during the course of revolutions started to upset established orders, the monstrosities committed have exceeded by far any mistreatment of labor or of ethnic or racial minorities.

Nor is the worst thing about the socialistic orders established through bloody revolutions the millions who die in the process. After the reigns of violence and terror come the totalitarian governments which falsify information, distort the thoughts of men, poison the minds of children, and attempt to crush everyone opposed to their will. According to Karl Marx, after the downfall of the capitalist system and the crushing of capitalist ideology, the state, as the political weapon of the proletariat during its dictatorship, would gradually wither away. That is, in time it would cease to be repressive. Nothing like this has happened, nor will it ever happen in any communist country.

In the long run, these regimes make no one happy, not even the rulers. History has shown how these rulers turn on each other. By far most of the communist leaders in Russia were shot by their own comrades or were sent to rot in jails. The record has not been much better in Eastern Europe or China. In view of these experiences, how can any communist ruler feel secure in his position?

There are many who make light of these facts. Nor will they admit that the communists who finally find themselves in the saddle establish a ruling class whose privileges, villas, and servants surpass those of the most wealthy in other lands. In the meantime, a clique of these most wealthy in other lands helps them to consolidate their repressive rule with publicity, credits, and transfers of the most advanced technology. In their own countries, the power of the super-rich keeps increasing instead of decreasing despite decades of socialistic legislation and policies aimed at redistributing incomes and social benefits.

If you reflect on any one or two of these conditions, let alone all of them taken together, would you not begin to suspect that perhaps there is something missing in the arguments of those who will not look behind the scenes? If a powerful hidden force were not blocking the formation of honest opinion in our communications systems and in our educational or religious institutions, why would people be left in the dark about the absurdity of these apparent contradictions?

If we are to find the most important reasons for the decline of freedom in the world, we must look for them in the plans and machinations of the international mammon forces. As I have shown in this book, they are the ones who have supported the totalitarian systems of both the Left and Right, although those who will deny it are legion.

These mammon souls are a group of their own. We are not reluctant to mention that some of them are known as Jews; there are others, however, who are nominally Christian. Regardless of their ethnic or religious background, they are all in reality atheists who would banish from the face of the earth the very concept of a God of righteousness. They care for neither Jew nor Gentile, neither white nor black, neither poor nor rich, neither Left nor Right. Their plan is to rule the world by controlling what finances they can gather surreptitiously, by overtaxing and otherwise exploiting the peoples of the world. Access to the fabulous wealth of the Dead Sea region also plays a big role in their thoughts. The riches there are not confined to oil. There are also immensely valuable chemicals and jewels in that area. This is not known to the public, but it is known to the insiders, at least to some extent. Therefore, they estimate the wealth ensconced in this domain not in the billions, but in the trillions of dollars. That is why they feel that the faction which gains complete control over this area may end up having the riches to dominate the world.

This prize has been a big factor behind the unusually intense passions which have been artificially aroused, at first by the Vatican, and more recently by the Soviets, to block or to gain control over this area. The satanic forces will use any means, any nation, any faith, any ideology to gain their ends. We predict that the most ferocious battles of the Armageddon will be fought over the spoils in this area.

I would not have known these things had they not been suggested to me through ESP. Such knowledge was certainly not taught at Harvard University, where I received my Ph.D. When I studied the ESP revelations on this subject, however, I found them to be quite consistent both with long-standing prophecies and with all the facts I could find on these problems from reliable sources. I had much to relearn, which I did. Now I know what President Franklin D. Roosevelt meant when he said that in politics nothing happens by accident. If it happens, somebody must have planned it that way.

I know that there are those who feel that the planners of the current turmoil are the communists, or the Zionists, or the Rockefellers and their ilk, or the Bilderbergers, or the Council on Foreign Relations, or a combination of these forces. I know also that there are many who are innocent in the camps of every group thought to be the enemy. Nor do I ignore the fact that behind every negative force here on earth there are also negative forces on the etheric planes. As the apostle Paul wrote, "We are not contending against flesh and blood, but against the principalities, against the powers, against the world rulers of this present darkness, against the spiritual hosts of wickedness in the heavenly places." (Ephesians 6:12).

This does not mean, however, that we can shift the blame for the injuries people cause here on earth to devils on the etheric planes. Such dark souls can make no inroads whatever unless men weaken and open the doors for their influence to come in. If this were not so, you could hold no man responsible for his wrong deeds.

We also should make it clear that since the French Revolution, not all concentrations of wealth have come under the power of evil. Much good has come from the proper use of great fortunes. At the same time, the fact remains that most of the wrong in the world has been promoted primarily through the power of money. The evil forces have known that through the control of money comes the control of jobs, of financial rewards, and of channels of publicity. Through the latter, they have brought forth various forms of thought control. With such power over the minds of men, is it any wonder that they have been able to manipulate people and governments leaning both to the Right and Left alike?

There are those who say, "Tell us their identity, so we too may know the Anti-Christ." With the Teacher of teachers, we say, "By their fruits ye shall know them." The evil ones do not yet want to be known. Nor do we make them known at this time. They call themselves the Nameless 300; we call the name of the righteous legion! What need do overwhelming majorities have to know the identity of a tiny group who are too fearful to come out into the open? The Christ knows who they are and their every move. Is this not good enough? Instead of seeking concealed knowledge, the righteous would be far better off acting on the information they already have to pluck out the ugly fruits of evil from their land through legal and proper means.

We look for the manly men and noble women who know that the earth is our Prince's, and who would therefore sweep it as a household. Please know that the fruits of evil are the work of deliberate doers of iniquity, planted in every walk of life by forces bent on world conquest. We stress again, however, that millions who do their bidding are basically innocent. They have been duped by the clever arguments of the devil's disciples. That is why those who attempt to strike the evil ones in their treacheries should make sure that the innocent keep their distance.

Know, however, that there has been an overall infiltration which we label the "Seven Satanic Takeovers." These now influence all important developments in government, money, races, schools, health, churches, and communications. Others may call them by different names, if they wish, and find no association between the negative trends they face in these seven

138

fields. We submit, however, that the needless and meaningless wars, the dishonesty in government, the proposals for unilateral disarmament, the rampant crime in the streets, the inflation of the major currencies of the world, the dethroning of the dollar, the distortion of racial issues, the disorders in the schools and universities, the widespread use of drugs, the disdain for natural avenues to health, the God-is-dead type of theologies, the increasing hedonism, subversion and defeatism in the land cannot all be, and are not in fact coincidental. They are all aimed at lowering resistance to one-world government—the dream of the mammon forces who pull the puppet strings behind the scenes.

The Handwriting on the Wall

In a recent *Wall Street Journal* editorial it was asked, "What mysterious affliction has seized the minds of so many of our best people, leaving them unable to understand the simple answers, unable to recognize their own traditional values, unable to distinguish between dreams and reality?"[22]

It did not occur to the editors to think that in order for the one-worlders to succeed, it is essential for the best people in the United States to be seized by a crippling affliction. As we have pointed out in this volume, economics and politics cannot be separated from cultural and ethical ideas. The evil forces have known this better than our well-meaning editors and professors. That is why they have found it necessary to enlist the help of Karl Marx and Sigmund Freud to implement the plans of Adam Weishaupt. It is this brilliant luciferian trinity who have done more than any other to bring the world to its present state.

What is to explain the dilemmas of modern man in terms of impersonal economic and social conditions, if not another application of Marx's economic interpretation of history? Marx denied that man has free will to choose between good and evil, and to shape his destiny accordingly. He attributed both the form and content of the forces which shape the lives of men to accidental developments in the mode of production.

139

In the West, from the time of Saint Augustine to that of Georg Hegel, it was believed that world history was determined by divine orders manifesting themselves in human events. The rationalist Hegel had transformed the Kingdom of God into the Kingdom of Reason. Nevertheless, his thoughts parallel many ideas expressed in this volume. For example, he emphasized that we live in a world of opposites and that progress comes from opposition. Moreover, he held correctly that it is thought which creates things, rather than material things which create thought.

Marx, on the other hand, while accepting Hegel's philosophy in many respects, twisted it on this and other critical points to come to his materialistic and revolutionary conclusions. Today such twisted Marxian ideas have become so much a part of modern thought that they are fast displacing all philosophies of history based on divine plan and purpose.

Sigmund Freud's analysis of man's nature depicted his animal reactions, not the reactions of the eternal spark at the core of his being. He was correct in pointing to the importance of subconscious influence in man's mind. Even so, from Freud to fraud, it was but one short step. His emphasis on sexual frustrations and subscious conflicts as causes of mental illness did not result in many cures. However, it did undermine responsible moral conduct. Moreover, Freud's discovery that unconscious conflicts were often induced in early childhood made the life of the individual appear both defenseless and meaningless.

As a social philosopher, Freud thought that the irrational forces in society were much stronger than the forces of reason. He concluded, therefore, that most men are hopelessly corrupted by the societies into which they are born. The way out, he felt, was immense programs of psychological reeducation of parents and teachers. He obviously had no faith in the power of God or the experience of life itself as the best corrective influences which may be counted on to resolve the problems of struggling humanity.

To quote one of his disciples, "Freud believed that life was a roundabout way to death."[23] We may wonder, therefore, how far he would have gotten if his works were not promoted by the evil forces for reasons we have already discussed in this volume.

Given the entrenched power of those promoting the concepts of Weishaupt, Marx, and Freud, is it any wonder that we should have so many strange afflictions gripping some of our finest people? There are those who feel that now that the hostilities have come to an end in Southeast Asia, there will be a reversal in these negative trends. However, even if the social forces move to a natural equilibrium, the powers behind the scenes will not let things settle down.

The drugs and permissiveness they sponsored have already unleashed the worst crime epidemic in decades. Moreover, they have set into motion even greater forces to help them move quickly toward their objective of one-world government. Control of strategic parts of the economic system, of legislatures, newspapers, radio and television through mammon had not always moved them fast enough. Too many men in public life were receiving sparks of light from the Holy One, and therefore would not do their bidding.

Consequently they decided to use, first in the United States, then throughout the world, the black man! By placing blacks in positions of power which would have been beyond credibility twenty years ago, they are planning to create such disturbed conditions everywhere that it will become a matter of necessity to have stern control measures on all aspects of social life. An early fruit of this plan is a statement by James Forman, leader of the "Black Manifesto" movement, who wrote, "We are dedicated to building a socialist society inside the United States, where the total means of production and distribution are in the hands of the State—led by black people."[24]

Needless to say, most black people would have nothing to do with such wild plans. The fact remains, however, that the seeds of world disorder and revolution have been sown, and violent radicalism is spreading, with or without the financial support and blessing of the World Council of Churches. We see other

141

fruits of evil. Already scandalous behavior in high places, induced by the evil forces to shock the public, has been surfacing in waves reminiscent of events preceding the French Revolution and other major upheavals since then.

Mene, mene, tekel, upharsin. With the prophet Daniel again we read these words, "You have been weighed in the balance (by God) and found wanting."

There are so few truly great men left on the world scene holding high positions. Our leaders perform the letter of the law, not knowing the spirit; and the letter of the law goes amiss. How foolish they are when they rely on those who control the finances of the world rather than on the Giver of all good and perfect things!

As of old, our society needs once more to be warned: Worship ye not mammon! For what good is it when man conquers all the earth, yet loses his very soul? Even shekels in the millions cannot keep man off his crutches. When God's will is done, there shall be no need for crutches.

Do people really feel that they can keep their freedom or property if they do not change their attitude toward mammon? They must place what is right ahead of what is good for their pocketbooks to have the moral force to stop their political leaders from taking them into a tyrannical one-world government. Is it not obvious that they will not have much, if any, control over such a monolith once the masks are dropped and those in control start to consolidate their power? Even communist states today watch their steps because they have to consider public opinion in the rest of the world. What can possibly limit the power of a totalitarian state encompassing the whole world? Will they never see that events are gradually, and sometimes not so gradually, moving us into just such a super state?

Over the past ten years, the money and capital markets of the major industrial nations have been increasingly international- ized. The principal financial centers of the world are now interlocked in a way which could not have been foreseen either

142

by economists or statesmen as late as a generation ago. A principal link in the current international network is the Eurocurrency markets. These have mushroomed from very modest beginnings in 1960 to a huge proliferation, encompassing deposits amounting to over $70 billion in 1971. About $55 billion of these deposits represent dollar claims on international banks in Europe. This rapid expansion of Eurodollar and Eurobond markets has made it possible to borrow and lend dollar funds in either European or American markets, depending on relative yields, costs, and risks.

Because this widening of choices has provided financial advantages to a number of governments and companies, the majority has been led to believe that the Eurocurrency markets represent salutary additions to the facilities of the international financial system. Nevertheless, these developments have also created potential dangers of enormous proportions.

In the first place, since they are unregulated and unsupervised by any government authority, very little is known about the soundness of the financial practices in these markets. Secondly, by increasing the mobility of capital, these international transactions have made the financial systems of the major industrial countries much more susceptible to sudden large-scale flows of funds and destabilizing speculation. Finally, the pyramiding of interconnected deposits among international banks (and their branches) has magnified the danger of completely chaotic chain reactions or domino effects.

When a single large borrower or lender is suddenly made to face financial disaster, huge amounts of capital would start moving frantically from one country to another, seeking safer havens in other banks. When billions of dollars change hands within a few hours, it will not be clear which country's central bank should or would step in to stabilize the situation. At present, none of these banks have a definite responsibility to cope with such an emergency.

A severe crisis in these markets would, therefore, create overnight a thundering threat of worldwide depression. Stock markets would tumble around the world, causing a catastrophic collapse in confidence. Such an emergency would give the mammon forces an excellent opportunity to impose tight financial controls on all the major industrial countries. No one would quite know what happened or why as another giant step is taken toward one-world government. In the future, the forces of mammon would not even have to precipitate a depression to accomplish their objectives as they had to in 1929-32. The threat of depression would suffice.

In the fall of 1971, a proposal was made to have an American company build, as prime contractor, a complex of truck factories in the U.S.S.R. with a huge annual capacity of 150,000 trucks. When this deal was publicized, some disturbing memories were revived about the sale of U.S. scrap iron for steel to Japan only a few months before Pearl Harbor. At the time, as the well-known military analyst, General Ira C. Eaker, pointed out, there can be no doubt that trucks are strategic equipment. He wrote further that both Russia and China "have cheap, controlled labor. All they need are modern plants and expertise." Believing that the communists will probably not be able to pay back the long-term loans they will need to pay for the American equipment they want, he correctly concluded that "increased trade with the Reds looks like a dangerous one-way street."[25]

Since then, however, trade and investments involving the communist tyrannies have increased dramatically. In the meantime, many of the giant American business enterprises are increasingly becoming world corporations. Already some of these multinational corporations have sales which exceed by far the national budgets of a number of fairly large countries. Recently, a Belgian industrialist predicted that the impact of the multinationals on the world economy would grow even more. He said that in world history, "they are milestones which may well become more important than hundreds of names and dates mentioned in history textbooks."[26]

What or who will stop this greater and greater centralization of economic power? Effective control in the ownership of

American business is also shifting to financial institutions which have investments around the globe. Government curbs on the lending of such institutions abroad have "paradoxically" strengthened them instead of limiting their overseas operations by boosting the position of their branches abroad.

On another front, the mammon forces are busy building a one-world of finance with their Special Drawing Rights (SDR's), known also as paper gold, issued by international authority. As this world currency replaces the American dollar in financial circles abroad, the United States economy will be subjected to more and more financial discipline by international authorities. Once the "necessity" for international controls is accepted in principle, the practical circumstances that call for their application will soon be engineered.

Knowing the aims of those behind the scenes, we can also anticipate explosions in *all* the seven fields taken over by Satan's disciples. Racial riots could get worse and worse, eventually necessitating martial law. The recently enacted revenue sharing law may be made to backfire. Corruption will be found in the expenditure of federal funds by state and local governments. Federal officials will then say in effect, "Listen, we cannot have such malfeasance. We believe in state and local autonomy, and in government which is close to the people, as much as anyone else. However, we must put an end to these scandals, and to do this, we have to have tighter controls." In most instances, they will mean what they say, not knowing that all along revenue sharing was meant to lead to tighter controls over state and local policy. Only a few will have realized that this entire scheme was promoted by the mammon forces who saw in it an opportunity to control state and local governments in the same way that they control the government in Washington.

People will, of course, not like the greater and greater regimentation of their lives. Americans are born to be free. They will not suffer controls gladly. They will be worried about the future and will start losing faith in their government. Nevertheless, they will stop and think along these lines: "We

145

depend on Uncle Sam for our prosperity, for our jobs, for our contracts, for our grants, for our welfare, for our social security, for our schools and health, etc. Can we afford to fight City Hall? Besides, how much good can we hope to accomplish, anyway? Perhaps we are just going through a temporary phase. We must not make hasty decisions which we may later regret." Even so, opposition to those in power will start growing.

In the meantime, the "lights" in the "brainwashing" department of the Establishment will be working overtime to convince the American public that, because of the overpopulation, pollution, or the new technologies, their only salvation lies in giving their national government more and more powers. They will say, in effect, "Welfare must be a federal responsibility in order to equalize payments. We need more federal money to stop the deterioration of our schools and our cities. The state and local police departments are not doing a good enough job in curbing criminals. We have to have a national police force to help them. We have had enough killing of innocents. We must register and confiscate all guns to put an end to this senseless violence. The federal government must clean up our environment, solve the energy crisis, assist our minorities at home and the less-developed countries abroad."

There will be no end to their arguments aimed consciously or unwittingly at laying the foundations for a more or less disguised dictatorship. And this dictatorship during an international emergency could hand over the sovereignty of the American people to a one-world government that has been in the planning stage for years.

The trump card of the mammon forces has always been wars and rumors of wars. These will not stop until the end of this age of mammon rule. Remember, the philosophy of the evil ones is any means to an end. In line with this philosophy, they have been encouraging the Soviet Union to arm to the teeth while inducing the United States foolishly to disarm and hence leave her cities defenseless. Thus they hope to frighten the American people who may soon be subjected to nuclear blackmail by their Soviet enemies.

In the meantime there will be moves to rearm Europe, especially if she is united under German leadership. Under such leadership, the new super power may be led to clash with the Russian Bear over the breadbaskets of Eastern Europe. As mentioned earlier, however, the key to the plans of the mammon forces is in the Middle East. In due time, therefore, the super dictator of Europe, threatened by cutoffs of vital oil supplies from the Middle East, will be made to march to Israel for battle on the hills of Megiddo. This, as of the moment, is how we see World War III starting.

When the shooting starts, from the East we see marching Red China—the only major power which is not yet controlled by international mammon. The Dragon will come, hoping for the final kill when the European and Russian dictators come close to destroying each others' power.

Let us hope and pray that the United States will not be overly involved in the blood baths of a World War III. Unless current trends are reversed, however, this nation could easily capitulate temporarily to the dictates of a one-world government. To consolidate its power, such a government will in due time bring foreign troops to discipline the American public, as U.S. troops are used for similar purposes in the rest of the world.

Do you think such things cannot happen? Would you believe those who would reassure you that we are on the threshold of a generation of peace? Let us look at the record.

At Yalta, Joseph Stalin had informed Winston Churchill that his collectivization program had cost the U.S.S.R. more lives than the Second World War (estimated at 20 million persons). If we add to this the lives lost during the Civil War which followed the Russian Revolution, during the deportation and purges, and in the concentration camps, we arrive at a staggering figure. The total cost in lives of forcing communism on Russia has been estimated at more than 45 million persons.[27] This is more than six times the number of Jewish people killed by Hitler and his gang.

Nor does this represent a passing phase. As an outstanding authority on communism pointed out,

> The history of the modern Communist movement is a chronicle of treachery and deceit. The pages of that history abound with examples of individual and mass terrorism, broken treaties, infiltration and subversion of non-Communist governments and organizations, full-scale and guerilla warfare, sabotage, genocide, repression of minorities, purges, assassinations, slave-labor camps, suppression of religion, the abrogation of individual liberty, and nuclear blackmail.[28]

Is it in cooperation with such forces that the U.S. Government hopes to achieve peace in the world?

There are people who think that, even if there is a conspiracy, the culprits are not madmen or idiots. "True, there are dangers in the current trends," they say, "but the people in charge of world affairs will not let things get out of hand."

Let them think and believe as they wish. We still predict that the day will come when the evil ones in control behind the scenes will lose their grip. Faction will rise against faction to battle among themselves. As they defy God's moral laws more and more flagrantly, they will lose their wits! God shall not be mocked forever! Moreover, when our planet earth is hit once more with the type of terrain catastrophes which led to the sinking of Atlantis and Lemuria, they will be left defenseless. Observe nature and see whether we have not already had some forerunners of the cataclysmic disturbances which will be released if men will not turn to their God and stop their wars.

We repeat, "*Mene, mene, tekel, upharsin.*" Does man need another prophet Daniel to interpret the meaning of this handwriting on the wall?

148

FOOTNOTES

1. "The Year 1914 A Turning Point," *Awake*, October 8, 1968, p.5.
2. Brasol, p. 242, and pp. 243-262.
3. Ibid., p. 251.
4. As one historian stated, at the peace conference, "the political leaders were assisted by groups of experts and interested persons, sometimes self-appointed. Many of these 'experts' were members or associates of the international-banking fraternity." Quigley, p. 271.
5. Bowden, Karpovich, and Usher, p. 707.
6. Alexander Gerschenkron, "History of Economic Doctrines and Economic History," *The American Economic Review*. May 1969, p. 12.
7. Ibid., p. 10.
8. Bruce M. Russett, *No Clear and Present Danger: A Skeptical View of the U.S. Entry into World War II*. "Harper Torchbooks": New York: Harper and Row, 1972, p. 20.
9. Eugene Lyons, *Workers' Paradise Lost: Fifty Years of Soviet Communism: A Balance Sheet*. "Paperback Library, Inc.": New York: Circle Publishing Co., Inc., 1967, p. 70.
10. Bowden, Karpovich, and Usher, pp. 705-706.
11. Quigley, p. 670.
12. Ibid., p. 667.
13. The quote is from former U.N. Ambassador Henry Cabot Lodge, who once argued against admitting Red China to the United Nations because this organization "is not a place where the virtuous and the criminal sit side by side." Griffin, p. 223.
14. Sorokin and Lunden, p. 187.
15. Friedrich A. Hayek, *The Road to Serfdom*. Chicago: University of Chicago Press, 1944, p. 5.

16. Ibid., p. 183.

17. Ibid., p. 182.

18. Nesta H. Webster, *World Revolution, the Plot against Civilization*. p. 95.

19. Allen, p. 59.

20. Webster, *Secret Societies and Subversive Movements*, p. 332.

21. A recent book, *The New Totalitarians*, about Sweden, where socialism was introduced peaceably, shows how most of the symptoms of totalitarianism are now clearly visible even there. Alexander Campbell, "If This Is the Brave New World, We're in Trouble," review of Roland Huntford's *The New Totalitarians*, in the *Sunday Star*, (Washington, D.C.), (February 27, 1972) Sec. 6, p. 6.

22. Editorial, "A Mysterious Affliction," *Wall Street Journal* (New York), (December 27, 1971) p. 6.

23. Calvin S. Hall, *A Primer on Freudian Psychology*. "A Mentor Book," New York: The World Publishing Co., 1954, p. 58.

24. Clarence W. Hall, "Must Our Churches Finance Revolution?" *The Reader's Digest*, (October 1971), pp. 95-100.

25. Ira C. Eaker, "Evaluating Trade with Russia," *Detroit News*, p. 7B, (December 6, 1971).

26. Charles A. Fuller, Jr., "Role of Multinationals Seen Gaining Further," *Journal of Commerce*, (New York), (April 28, 1972), p. 9.

27. Lyons, pp. 354-64.

28. J. Edgar Hoover, *J. Edgar Hoover on Communism*. New York: Paperback Library, January 1970, pp. 100-101.

Chapter X

THE HEART TO REPLACE THE DOLLAR SIGN

The Necessity for Divine Intervention

The previous chapter seemed to end on an ominous note. We hasten, therefore, to balance the picture. True, the people have allowed themselves to be duped, but they have not meant to harm their neighbors. Consequently there will be divine intervention to help them when they earnestly seek such help. Do you not believe me? Then perhaps you will believe the Christ, who has said to those who recognize His words today:

The times for action are coming upon you; there is sound of revelry, there are voices of perjury, there are oaths that are false, there is the lore of the wicked to beguile you. . . .

There is a time for all things, as I have uttered unto you. There is a time for winning, there is a time for counselling, there is a time for auguring, there is a time for ministering, there is a time for simplicity of heart, and there is a time for righteous purpose righteously executed, that human ingenuity maketh a better report unto the Father of that which is priceless in eternity's balances. I say there is a time for feasting and a time for fasting. All things have their places in Time. But this also do I tell you: There is a time for watching, there is a time for sowing whilst ye watch. And there is a time for praying whilst ye watch and whilst ye sow that the Father may manifest through you His everlasting and righteous purposes. . . .

I tell you it profiteth you to say, standing boldly, it is a time for the Greater Accounting with our souls. . . .

I have come unto the world when the world received me not . . . Now do I come again, verily to speak as one who hath now his recognition, to address those ears that wait a speech of beauty . . . Oft hath it happened that man hath judged wrongly the time of my coming; oft hath man erred in making a meeting with revealings of vast prophecy. And is that of consequence? Is it not meet that man should so err, that coming unto true cognizance, he should defeat his former disappointments, saying, All is of past error and now correctness cometh?

Wait for its occurrence, but be diligent in waiting.[1]

Is it unrealistic to suggest that only the reappearance of Christ as men knew Him can redeem the deteriorating world situation? Let us see what we can learn from history. For this purpose, who would be a better source than Arnold Toynbee? His scholarly work on all known civilizations—past and present—has been widely recognized. Here is what he concluded about all those acclaimed as saviors of disintegrating societies:

When we set out on this quest we found ourselves moving in the midst of a mighty host, but, as we have pressed forward, the marchers, company by company, have fallen out of the race. The first to fail were the swordsmen, th next the archaist and futurists, the next the philosophe⸱ , until only gods were left in the running. At the final ordeal of death, few, even of these would-be saviour gods, h; ve dared to put their title to the test by plunging into the icy river. And now, as we stand and gaze with our eyes fixed upon the farther shore, a single figure rises from the flood and straightway fills the whole horizon. There is *the* Saviour (italics mine): 'and the pleasure of the Lord shall prosper in his hand. . . . '[2]

152

Toynbee thus confirmed the uniqueness of Jesus Christ not on religious grounds, but on the basis of historical fact. Is there any question that He cannot return? He will have to return to shock the nations back to their senses. I need not say how He will come. A great American prophet has done this already.[3]

There are those who read the signs of the times in their Bibles and declare His coming. Others know through other ways and means, through divine prophecies and revelations given at different times around the world I say that the necessity for this event is self-evident. Look and see what is happening in the world today. Look at America, the nation millions had called the hope of the world. What kind of hope does she offer for the future?

Expedient conduct in public life is now called "rising above principle." Criticism is reserved for those who are fighting deception. They are the ones who are called extremists, bigots, or hatemongers. Judges allow dangerous criminals to go free on legal technicalities. The hand of the law is raised against those who want their children to go to school in the safety of their own neighborhoods.

The reckless and cunning rise to power. The dedicated, the men of real ability, receive no publicity. Sedition, anarchy, perversion, and pornography spread. There is no room in the inn for the message of the righteous. Anthems are sung to brotherhood, security, and justice, while the public is offered divisiveness, dependence, and weakness. Who has the cure for these mysterious afflictions?

Affluent, respectable men drop out of society, doing things that would have been unthinkable a decade ago, saying they reject their worlds of impersonal decisions, make-believe bureaucracies, and meaningless work. They go to live in communes, perhaps to grow strawberries. Some roam in distant lands or take to the seas. Is this all they offer in return for their priceless heritage? Is this how they cherish the nation that has made them strong, given them abundance and boundless opportunity?

We honor and support the churches for having kept the love of

153

God and Christ alive. But, in all truth, what kind of leadership are they providing now? They will not listen to new teachings or revelations from the One they call their Lord. Instead they listen to and believe the disciples of Weishaupt, Marx, and Freud, the greatest luciferian trinity that ever lived. Far from converting the world to a spiritual way of life, they are being converted to the luciferian philosophy of seeking order and happiness through physical and political avenues only.

Is it a coincidence that the positions of the Christian churches and the communist parties in the United States and in Europe are almost identical on most social issues? Even Billy Graham admitted that "There is no doubt that secularism, materialism, and even Marxism not only have invaded the Church, but deeply penetrated it."[4] In the Soviet Union, the situation is still more anomalous. According to Solzhenitsyn, Nobel prize winner in literature, "A church dictatorially directed by atheists is a spectacle that has not been seen for 2,000 years."[5]

There are, of course, quite a few churchmen who continue to remain loyal to their calling. These brave souls provide a much-needed opposition to the majority of church leaders who no longer seem to understand what loyalty to the Christ means. They want to compromise with communist rulers who are avowed enemies of all religions. These rulers are still imprisoning, torturing, and starving hundreds of thousands of Christians for no other reason than their belief in God.[6]

In the course of all their moralizing, how often do clergymen refer once to the frauds and intrigues of those in high places which have kept half the world in war and the other half in poverty? How many criticize the atrocious decisions of liberal courts to which can be traced most of the increase in crime in our land? Instead they find it safer to pick on the average American for sins of omission or commission which are more imaginary than real.

Trapped by their own misconceptions, the churches cannot provide the answers to the questions the more analytical members ask. Therefore, most of the intelligent and independent-minded people think, if not actually say, "I do not believe the Testaments." They do not see any evidence of the Prince of Peace bringing peace into the world in one lifetime. Can you blame them?

The pendulum swings, we are told, from right to left and back again. In like manner, social and intellectual errors, again we are told, correct themselves in due time. This would be true, provided there would be no tampering with the clock, with the normal mechanisms of adjustment. As we saw earlier, there has been more than enough tampering to swing the pendulum in one direction only—regimentation and control, with or without a velvet glove.

The nations need a leader. This leader must be divine. The ordinary man will not serve the purpose. He must come to counsel the nations. Otherwise they will not survive when the cycle turns, when the great wind comes, seas groan and fall, and when nation rises against nation, making rulers totter on their thrones!

When He comes, He will indeed speak the comforting word, Peace. But He will speak these words also, "Except ye receive My Peace, O world, ye do have a sorry nest in which to raise your fledgelings." He says those who know His voice today:

Ye have said unto me, Master, how cometh it that thou showest not thyself unto all the world, that it should believe that thou art in thy flesh and manifesting still? Thus my spirit maketh answer: And why should I do it? that the world might deride me? did I not show myself unto the world and did it not slay me? what doth it benefit the world to know that one who is divine hath rulership over it, when those who are of evil receive its fond homage? I tell you that the wicked must be struck with a dumbness, they must fall by their own plottings, the earth must receive them, then shall the world say, Behold there was no rulership in them, they swayed by a might, they drove as a wineherd and we were their swine;

Now are they fallen and we see their iniquities, now come we therefore to raise our eyes higher, to see a whiter brilliance than the lure of concupiscence. The world hath marveled that evil is in it, yet where are those who will lift their voices crying, Evil is among us, it is made for our serfdom, behold they are like ourselves who have wrought it, let us arise and cast them out for they work a foul bondage?

I tell you, beloved, unless there be those who arise and cast it out, the Prince of Glory cannot enter. What profiteth the prince to make one with his swineherds? can they ever think his thoughts? do their swine's gruntings please him? is it meet that he should divest himself of raiment and wallow nakedly in mire that his presence there should cleanse it?

The prince is the prince. He calleth to his minions saying, Prepare for me the way, that I should walk in beauty. Am I not the prince? Do I not lead my people in that I *am* that which it pleaseth most of them to *be?* I tell you, my beloved, this is not pride; it is appreciating values. . . . And am I to wage a war in my person, that I should come among you knouting you to beauty? Have it as ye will it. When ye are willing to receive the bounties from a vast beneficence, then peace shall descend upon you. . . . And yet I come soon, for the time is at hand![7]

Is it a contradiction to say that the Prince of Peace comes to shock the nations? Watch and see how prophecies uttered two, three thousand years ago will fall in place. They are being fulfilled now under our very eyes, if only we dare to look at them with an open mind.

The phenomenal rise of the British Empire and the United States of America, the return of the Jews to their ancient homeland, the machinations of the Anti-Christ bent on world rulership, what are these things if not parts of an amazing drama, foretold by the great prophets centuries ago?[8]

The time is coming when ignorance about these matters will have to be a thing of the past. The ten lost tribes, led by Ephraim and Manasseh, will no longer be blind to their identity; nor will the children of Judah persist in blinding themselves to the identity of their Messiah. Even so, the new order, the promised Millenium, cannot and will not prevail as long as perverse government symbolized by the hammer and sickle continues to rule in this world.

How this experiment in rulership will end may not yet seem evident to many in the West. Nevertheless, a Russian author started expressing his view about the approaching final crisis in the Soviet system as early as the autumn of 1966.[9]

Have no fears, the mills of the gods grind slowly, but they grind exceedingly fine. And when the hammer and sickle are finally pulled apart, the followers of this false theory will gladly use their tools to reconstruct and harvest the earth as a means of penitence and as a way to reconcile themselves with their more noble brothers. Finally, when the mammon forces lose their secret throne, and the world finds out the truth about them at last, the selfish symbol of the dollar sign will be transformed to that of the compassionate heart.

Preparations for the New Order

Neither the scientists nor statesmen in our time come close to conceiving the wonders and glories that are for men to experience and master. As we saw in Chapter III, without direct revelation, no man or woman, however perceptive, can evaluate correctly where the drama of life is leading. In fact, while one is emotionally involved in this play, I question whether or not one can so much as begin to grasp the necessity for the performance in the first place.

That is why there are so few who understand the nature of the divine program for the advancement of man. Frankly, religious dogmas, rituals, and sacred adulations play a strictly limited role in this program. The Father is far more interested in the growth of human awareness and constructive talents through persistent

157

effort than in passive worship.

Guiding man to achieve these qualities of being is a more roundabout process than is often imagined. In the modern era, science has played an important role in this process. All the same, the progress of science also is carefully guided by Spirit.

Since the Renaissance, we all know of inventions which have been so potent they have changed entirely many aspects of social life. In a divinely supervised world, is it likely that such inventions could have been accidental? Consider the invention of the printing press. Printing has enabled the thoughts in the minds of some men to reach the mind of other men as never before. It has placed whole worlds of past knowledge before any man who has acquired an elementary ability to read. It has made modern forms of self-government workable by making it possible to raise the educational level of all the people.

To have this one invention of the printing press, however, it was first necessary to develop the technologies of papermaking, inkmaking, metallurgy, block printing, printing with metal type, not to mention the technology of the screw press itself. Imagine in how many ways advances in these technologies could have failed. The process of inventing the printing press could have been blocked not only for technical reasons but also for lack of financial support. Is it too fantastic to suggest that the invisible hand guiding these vast series of astonishing developments could not have been anything less than divine?

It is evident that without an industrial revolution people could not have been freed from economic serfdom. As the Piscean (Water) Age was coming to a close, it was appropriate that the revolution in techniques of manufacture should start by harnessing steam power for purposes of production and locomotion. With the advance into the Aquarian (Air) Age, electricity was also ushered into the scene.

Here was a power, like air, which one cannot touch or see. Yet it changed the whole character, first, of engineering, and then, society itself. Together with the application of mass production and assembly line techniques, electricity gave the people endless

158

new goods and services. Moreover, it made available to everyone goods and services produced for the rich only.

Economic laws also came into play in the creation of unprecedented abundance. With larger and larger volumes of production, the cost per product declined lower and lower. And the profit potential of mass markets created by low-cost items in turn stimulated the application of scientific findings to greater and greater fields of work. Thus the material progress achieved could not have been realized without organizing ever-expanding national and international markets. Therefore, we do not minimize the contributions of innovative businessmen and industrialists, who extracted from the laws of engineering and economics countless benefits for man. Nor do we oppose bankers or financiers as such but only those who are involved in plans to rule the world.

Both practical and theoretical scientists have contributed greatly to the progress of man. They are not, however, being scientific when they refuse to study the influence souls on spirit planes exert on conditions here on earth. The time is fast approaching when the laws governing such relationships will be placed on as scientific a basis as the laws governing invisible atoms and molecules.

We predict, therefore, that the scientists will rediscover this aspect of God's creation before the theologians. In the meantime, we repeat that all the constructive progress in science and in industrial techniques has been a preparation for the millennial age to come. One way or another, a physical basis had to be built to make it possible for man to govern himself in righteousness and abundance, free from the dictates of all-powerful government.

Man has always had the power to shape his life as well as the form of his external environment. In the final analysis, the individual is the only being who can generate human energy, without which nothing can be accomplished. External authority can control the conditions which stimulate, divert, or block the flow of energy through the individual. However, it cannot control the individual directly. Free will has forever been God's order of the day. Have there not been martyrs in every age to demonstrate this principle?

In modern times, applying the advances in knowledge, man has shown what his spirit can do as never before in recorded history. He has even invented a new science—cybernetics—which is the science of self-control through feedback. Thus, by developing the proper information about his internal and external environment, man will master his life more than was ever thought possible in the past.

With the invention of modern digital computers, the limits on how much information can be processed, disseminated, and digested are also stretching beyond our fondest dreams. Therefore, it is daily becoming more feasible to design feedback systems not only for selected organizations, but also for entire national economic and political systems. Once this is achieved, it will be much simpler to have every society operate on genuine principles of self-regulation.

Already, with the use of feedback in the laboratory, science is at last venturing into fields which were previously relegated to metaphysics and mystical religion. There are now electronic instruments which register visible or audible impacts of altered states of consciousness. By using such instruments, experimental subjects are finding out that by changing their thoughts and feelings, or the way in which they focus their attention, they can change their heart rates, body temperatures, brain waves, and other processes which are normally considered unconscious bodily functions. It is said that seeing is believing. Therefore, by seeing (or hearing) how much impact one's state of mind has on one's well-being, the new electronic feedback devices are opening new avenues to better health and creativity.[10]

When scientists cease following the path of destruction, the day will come when they will be allowed to create instruments whereby they shall be able to pick up Lincoln at Gettysburg giving his address. Think about it! They shall be able to pick up Washington saying "Farewell" to his troops. Yes, they shall be able to pick up in Aramaic His voice as it expounds the original

Sermon on the Mount! Spirit, of course, can see much farther ahead than we can dream. Thus we are told that, if men handle themselves properly, they shall one day have the power to perform the same miracle as He did when He brought His good friend Lazarus back to life!

These predictions are conditional. If scientists do not watch their step, if they continue to overstep in areas which interfere with God's design, their science can and will go astray once again. Their inventions, unrestrained by spiritual values, can lead once more to as much wholesale destruction as in the days of Atlantis and Lemuria.

People grow spiritually and mentally as well as in physical stature. If we keep this in mind, Christ's oft-repeated phrase, "The Kingdom of Heaven is within you," takes on a literal significance. Absorbing the lessons experience gives him by the finite, the Christ in man goes on and on into endless manifestations which eventually transcend all finite forms. At the same time, we cannot repeat often enough that man cannot achieve such progress if he allows the soul-killing despotism of a collectivist state to hold him down.

Given a chance, in the future, not only will man's mental powers increase, but also his understanding will stretch as new information is brought to his attention. In fact, there will be such a quickening of the mass consciousness that people will have memories of their former lives open on a truly large scale.

People will remember by whole racial and political groups what patterns of civic and cultural organizations they had tried in earlier lives. They will thus know what had been the concrete results of their choices in each case. Knowledge of reincarnation will be so real and universal that every child will understand it by the time he learns his alphabet.

Once men realize, when they followed a wrong course in a previous life, what a tremendous price they had to pay for their errors or stupidities, they will think twice before making similar wrong choices all over again.

Consider what may happen when the memory veil on past lives is lifted in the next century. The voters will acquire the ability to

161

know from their own memories the past achievements or mischiefs of outstanding public personalities. This will mean that when the latter run for office, they will no longer be able to deceive the electorate, as they do now far too often. The people will look at a statesman and identify him, say, as a great parliamentary celebrity in an earlier period of British history. Similarly, they will know the greatest tyrants and scoundrels in ancient Egypt, Greece, or Rome, as the case happens to be. It is conceivable, of course, that these souls may have returned to balance their karma through constructive acts of service. Nevertheless, they will have to be watched carefully, since they will naturally bring with them the same capacity that they had earlier to go astray along the very same lines.[11]

It should be understood, of course, that these things cannot happen if the trend toward world dictatorship is not reversed. Free will being always the order of the day, this possibility cannot be ruled out. I feel confident, however, that the trend will be reversed.

I wish I could also feel that there will be an easy transition to the wonders and glories of the new age we see on the horizon. However, in all truth, I cannot say that this will be the case. We can obviously do much to mitigate the evils that are bound to come. Nevertheless, we cannot avoid paying for the errors and crimes which have already been committed. We take no pleasure in having to say it. Yet, forewarned is forearmed.

Did not Jesus Himself prophesy about the dark days ahead when He said, "For then there will be great tribulations, such as has not been from the beginning of the world until now, no, and never will be. And if those days had not been shortened, no human being would be saved; but for the sake of the elect those day will be shortened." (Matthew 24:21-22). At the same time, we should know this also, that in the days of tribulation, the ones who do the Father's work will be protected. They will have to be. Otherwise, who will be around to spread the divine light that we know will never go out?

Thus, in the bedlam of confusion that is to be, there will come clear voices speaking: "This is He who cometh to absolve you! He hath power to heal you and to instruct you. Hear Him, I say, hear Him!"

During that period, to be known as the "Time of the Great Speaking," His little band, their roots far down into the golden earth of perfect truth, will say once more, "Except you give heed unto His Words the demolishment continues."

As men finally begin to listen, the Savior will then bid His disciples to arise and lead the nations. His stalwart ones, the true and faithful, though offering little physical opposition, will nevertheless challenge the evil ones. The Spirit of God will be with them, and they will perform many miracles to prove their divine calling to the people.

As all men are sustained by the power of God, no punishment would be needed for the evil ones except the withdrawing of Spirit from their being. This will be enough to make them lose their wits. Thus left defenseless, and fighting among themselves, the 300 devil's advocates will be eliminated one by one, whether through the cataclysmic geologic changes to come, or due to more normal causes.

Once this hidden source of subversion is removed, it will then be relatively easy to rid the world of its ugliest features. From then on there will be no organized effort to block genuinely constructive solutions to world problems. The takeovers in the seven fields mentioned in Chapter IX will stop. The world will be allowed once more to continue its normal pattern of evolutionary growth through trial and error.

Opposing forces will remain, of course, but the opposition that remains will be honest. Stoic, though misguided, souls will still want to hang on to the wrong concepts of the past. To win them over, once more the art of gentle persuasion will be set in motion. This approach has always been the Christ way, and it will remain so to the end.

In such a period of transition, an atmosphere of urgency will prevail everywhere. The physical and moral cataclysms which will be unleashed if man does not change his course could disturb the social order even more. In view of such immense turmoil there should be much pressure to introduce new legislation quickly. One law after another would have to be enacted at lightning speed. Otherwise man would not survive.

To help cope with the pains and challenges associated with such immense crises, to everyone's relief, will appear the Christ Host from other planets. They will come to counsel the people and the governments of the world. These extraterrestrial helpers will bring with them, and they will proudly show, photographs and moving pictures of life on their own planets. These will be the envy of all who see them. Under some circumstances, they may even assume positions of authority, until they train others to take their place. At all times, however, their aim will be to lead and to serve, not conquer and rule.

Scientists know nothing about those predictions which are bound to change the world. In general, the views scientific writers have of things to come contain little more than projections into the future of things they have already seen. If they refuse to look at direct revelations of divine plans, what else can they do?

I do not ask this question to find fault. Nor do I question that, to a degree, science can predict the future from the past and present. After all, do we not live in a world of cause and effect? My point, however, is that their visions of the future are far from adequate.

Scientists foresee correctly such things as a world of endless new materials and products, a world of abundant energy—in atomic and other forms. They predict from established trends such inventions as (a) high-speed monorails that go right into people's homes and apartments from ultramodern shopping centers, (b) giant garbage disposal machines with vents and vacuums to draw refuse conveniently into central disposal units, (c) inexpensive home machinery to circulate air noiselessly and to take dust out of it continuously, (d) education from computer-stored knowledge fed into individual points of contact, with less need for central schools, (e) ground transportation via underground air tubes and hook-on conveyor systems for private vehicles, (f) air travel by rocket propulsion and by magnet-controlled, flying-saucer-type vehicles, (g) instantaneous communication by sight, sound, or written message with anyone anywhere, (h) entertainment centers in homes and offices to bring the best in the performing arts to the people.

Yes, they can predict such technological developments that will undoubtedly contribute to the emergence of a new human type. They cannot, however, predict the fundamental transformations in social and personal values which will have even greater impacts on the lives of people in the future. Let us turn our attention, therefore, to some of these values without which there cannot be much improvement in the human condition in any part of the world.

This Pearl, Service

We know that the Christ had taught that he who would be greatest among men should be their servant. For a thousand years, it was repeated to Western man that only as he serves is he entitled to honor, greatness, and the wages of respect. The time is fast approaching when Western man will finally realize that only he who serves his brother best, seeking his brother's welfare before his own, should be allowed to rule.

For thousands of years, men have looked upon service as a form of servility, rendered by those lower in status to those higher in the social scale. A king considered himself a potentate because he was able to command, to control the lives of his subjects, his faithful servants. As a result, the one who was served grew arrogant and lazy. Moreover, he had the audacity to imagine himself to be of better clay!

At the same time, those who were forced to serve resented the fact that they had to do it under pressure. They hated themselves for their acts of subserviance. They could not help losing self-respect for having to cater to those above them. They knew, deep in their subconscious minds, that they were free spirits on a par with all other spirits in the eyes of the Father. Thus were social classes ill-formed, with the common interest centered mainly in the common predicament of having to endure the slings and arrows of outrageous fortune.

Social forces to break these chains were released by the mighty waves of change associated with the Renaissance and the Reformation. In the Middle Ages, social and intellectual life was as ossified as if the civilization of Ancient Greece had never existed. The Reformation asserted man's right to think for himself and to follow his own religious convictions. But it restricted severely political and economic freedoms, as well as the means to enjoy life, with all its excitement and beauty.

As we saw in Chapter IV, during the Mercantilist period which followed the Renaissance and Reformation, both the medieval nobility and the hierarchy of the Church lost much of their power over the people. However the new master which took their place—namely, the State—was not any easier on the individual, particularly if he happened to be among the lower orders. In every large state except England, the supremacy of the state over the individual was not allowed to be questioned. Nor did the religious and moral leaders understand the teachings of their Lord. He was the foremost individualist of all times, as is evidenced by His declaration that the very hairs of each man's head are numbered.

We saw in previous chapters how the chosen tribes of Ephraim and Manasseh (England and the United States) were destined to change the old ways and to give the world a new chance to enjoy the blessings of liberty and individual fulfillment. Nor did I hide from my readers the satanic plans and takeovers to lead the world in an opposite direction.

One cannot avoid the consequences of one's wrong decisions. Yet, I still declare that the era to follow the tribulations is one of joy! The evolving human spirit is to know a new birth of freedom. The growth of the soul is no longer to be hampered by that which is sordid and selfish. Today egoism is woven into the very warp and woof of the economic systems of the world. Therefore, hundreds of millions go to bed hungry at night while others are worried about being overweight. In the future, when selfishness is no longer glorified, there will not be less but more wealth and prosperity. Men will become more caring. Therefore, there will be no more hunger, as something better replaces the socialistic and semi-socialistic economies which have mushroomed in both East and West. These collectivist regimes are now taken for granted while lip service is paid to the merits and glories of individualistic orders of days past.

Collectivist systems would have much less appeal if people understood the true meaning of service. Men now think of service in terms of doing work for another on a quid pro quo basis. This, however, is not true service unless it is motivated by a desire to do for another something that he cannot do for himself.

There is little merit in simply doing things for another person. Frequently it merely prevents the person for whom the work is being done from doing it himself, and thus robs him of his chance for self-improvement. Let me refer my readers once more to Chapter IV. We saw there how an overly easy life led to the decadence of the citizens of Ancient Greece. From the creative heights they had achieved, too much leisure made them sink into a life of frivolity. This is by no means the only illustration one can cite to show the costs of laziness.

True service is demanding as well as rewarding. Granted that it is more rare than is often imagined. The average person is too smart to believe those who say that they are in business to serve. And the slogan, "Our most important product is progress," can only fool the simple-minded. Nevertheless, genuine service will be the hallmark of the future, as men are made to see that they can under no circumstances beat the moral law of karma.

Eventually, there will be no need to give an accounting for one's decisions and actions to an employer. The accounting one gives will be to one's self. You have heard it said that, "One man's meat is another man's poison." The individual will therefore be allowed to follow his own schedule, not that of his neighbor. But he will be taught ever to make his path one of upward climb. If he does not, the only person he would be cheating would be himself. He would know that it is to his eternal advantage to refine his thinking and feeling through selfless acts of service.

When work is performed for another who cannot do it for himself, the party who serves gains in self-esteem. He feels that, voluntarily, he is creating for another a wider and fuller life experience, an opportunity which he has not had before.

The self-esteem of the one served is also raised. He too can honestly feel that the act was not done out of necessity or out of a profit motive. Therefore, he concludes that it must have been done because he was considered worthy to receive its benefit. Thus, as the poet Lowell expressed it, "As one lamp lights another, nor grows less, nobleness enkindleth nobleness."

Nor should we think of nobility as an estate reserved for the few. There are no high nor low in the sight of the Father. He created all men of one flesh and substance. He gave them all the same gift—the gift of life. All other gifts had to be earned, although it does not seem so to those who refuse to understand the principle of repeat existence.

We therefore cannot afford to ignore karmic values, or effects which have their causes in previous lives, in the momentary estates of individuals, groups, nations, and races. Ours is a world of evolutionary progress, a world of different ages and understandings. In divine plans one estate is arranged to evolve naturally from another. Impatience, intolerance, the use of harmful means to attain good ends upset the inherent order of life. Harmful pressures—economic or political—strikes, disorders, or revolutions are of the devil. Look at God's nature—at a gentle flower or a sturdy tree—and see how much revolution you can find in their cycles of life and growth. They all follow rhythmic patterns of orderly evolution.

We do what we can without hurting our neighbors to alleviate ills, to bring in social rights or civil rights. However, if we think in terms of one life only, we miss the whole point about corrective balance, divine justice, and the sublime order underlying life.

168

We remain in bondage, chained needlessly to satanic concepts which stifle our thinking.

It is the Father's will that man evolve through self effort. One does not become a colonel by wearing a colonel's uniform. One must earn the right to command. We should be careful not to be unjust esoterically because we want justice socially and economically.

Wanting to legislate equality or to give free money to people regardless of merit is satanic in origin and essence. The fact that equality is made to appear desirable makes it even more dangerous. To hold the more advanced back in order to let the less advanced catch up is to sin in the eyes of Holy Spirit. Can you not see the deviltry involved in deceiving people with attractive ideas? The drive for equality was conceived as a political move engineered for selfish ends no matter how different it has been made to appear in order to attract the support of the righteous.

Social equality is consistent neither with equity nor liberty. It is one of the many false promises the evil forces use to regiment and control the world. Equality cannot be attained without the whip and the sword! As Alexander Hamilton said, "Inequality will exist as long as liberty exists. It unavoidably results from that liberty itself."

Receiving free money from Big Brother leads to such dependence, it might take literally decades, not years, to break the habit. This is not to advocate indifference to the needs of others. I cannot repeat often enough that the best way to refine one's feelings is through selfless acts of service. No man gives for his brother's benefit without his gift coming back to him magnified; no man takes from his brother unjustly without having to pay back to the last penny, plus interest. Please know that these are immutable divine laws. They are not said to impress the gullible.

All debts, all accounts are not settled in the course of one life. If rewards and punishments were immediate, men would be tempted to be good merely for the sake of the rewards or to avoid punishment. With this attitude, they could not develop sufficient strength of character to change the self-seeking animalistic emotions of their subconscious minds. As psychologists know, these emotions cannot be changed by sheer will power or by moralistic sermonizing. They can and do change by constructive affirmations and by living a good life, as we know from our own experience.

Moreover, let us not forget that expansion of awareness through experience is the original and primary lesson human beings came to learn from earth life. Could anything stretch one's awareness more than the necessity to make choices under conditions of uncertainty with respect to rewards and penalties?

In Chapter III, I pointed out why in the beginning the Absolute, or Holy Spirit, reduced certain parts of Itself to expressions of form. Thus could Holy Spirit's potential be explored, and in no other way. Had Holy Spirit not used this method, there would have been no standards by which to judge the growth and development of Spirit. Only through the contrasts generated, and the inevitable differentials in attainment, can the God particles (human beings) provide each other and the Father (the Creative Force in Holy Spirit) the standards with which to measure the progress of the God-process.

Now, the strange thing about this process of expansion is the following: Whereas man is given divine services to perform to help him move out of himself, to expand and reach for his godhood, in performing these services, he always tends to think of them in terms of his own narrow gain, his own status, and his own short-sighted self-improvement.

This attitude continually frustrates the attainment of divine intent. Men are meant to awaken to such a sense of wholeness that each person perceives not oneself only, but one's complete relationships to all other factors and components of life. In fact a person who has had no relationships with others—and all the joys and dilemmas they create—could not possibly have a sense of reality. Thus the All makes the one possible, as the one adds to the All.

When Jesus said, "I and my Father are One," He was expressing a form of this universal truth. The Son could not have existed without the Father—or Greater Love Force—any more than the Father could have expressed Himself on earth to show the way of perfection without the Son's presence in the world.

Loving or serving one's neighbor, therefore, is not merely a nice gesture in altruism. It is maintaining a certain karmic balance, first in one's being, and then throughout the universe. It is holding the debts and claims the different particles of Spirit have incurred to each other in equilibrium. It is giving in order to balance the receiving so that all can share the benefits which flow from conditions which everyone has helped to create and maintain.

One cannot deny the basic reality of interpersonal claims and obligations. In fact, society may be viewed as nothing other than a system of more or less permanent claims and obligations which do not always correspond to economic or legal imperatives. Some of them involve one other person, others a group, and still others a whole nation or the whole world. Each of them exerts a pressure on our wills. We can evade our obligations, but we cannot evade the attraction we feel toward them. We are drawn back to them, like a pendulum which has swung away from the center. Similarly, if our claims are not satisfied, we feel that a certain order of things has been upset. We feel cheated; we crave for restitution. There are many who literally make themselves sick thinking about the things they feel they should have been receiving from others.

In going through life, there are those who say, "How I live my life is my own business. I owe no one an explanation. I found myself in this world against my will. Therefore, I recognize no obligation to anyone beyond what I owe them legally or what I can turn to my advantage. What is my own I shall keep.

171

Moreover, I shall make people pay me what they owe me to the last penny. If I do not look out for Number 1, I am not persuaded that anyone else will."

By practicing this philosophy consistently, sooner or later some people are bound to get rich. So far, so good. Now, however, let us see what else will take place. The persons who have taken this path have been measuring their progress in terms of the piles of goods they accumulate. In place of the give-and-take of human relationships, they have been getting their gauges of self-improvement from the prices of their stocks and bonds, their houses, lands, clothes, bank deposits, in short, from things which are lifeless, and which therefore cannot react.

Their wealth has acted as a form of protection against the vicissitudes of life, that is true. However, what kind of protection has it offered them? Has it not driven them inward instead of outward? It has probably made them feel that they have no need for any god outside of them to protect them or to improve them. Their wealth has made it unnecessary for them to seek help from anyone except those whose services their money can buy. In other words, they have been induced to narrow down their experiences to a point which has led them to the habit of denying an entire universe that was intended for their good from beginning to end!

With this attitude, human beings cannot advance; they can only retreat. The load of karmic debts which their selfishness has inevitably placed on their shoulders would not lighten. They would feel an emotional weight pressing down and down and down. Whether or not they are aware of what is causing them distress would not really make much difference. The result would be the same—further and further retreat into darkness.

On the other hand, consider the person who says, "All that I can possibly share with others I shall be glad to do so. I want them to enjoy what I have as much as I do. Who can blame me for what I feel? And if anyone does, I shall consider it a privilege to suffer for my convictions."

Now let us see what will happen to this person. From the position he has chosen for himself, he will learn the potentialities in other human beings far better than his selfish neighbors. Others will be drawn to him and interact with him. Thus he will enhance his individuality into larger and finer concepts, because his external comparisons will be more varied. Moreover, he will learn the delightful reactions and the unexpected changes in character of people who are exposed to genuine altruism.

If this philosophy were applied consistently, in due time the standards of conduct which govern everyone will alter for the better. Those who start this trend would benefit from this change no less than others. Why is it impossible to explain these principles to ordinary people and then apply them not only to the social life, but also to the government and the economic systems of the future?[12]

FOOTNOTES

1. *The Golden Scripts*, pp. 765-69.
2. Arnold J. Toynbee, *A Study of History*. Abridgement of Vol. I-VI by D.C. Somervell. New York and London: Oxford University Press, 1947, p. 547.
3. For a summary account of his prophecies about the Reappearance of the Christ, see Lewis, pp. 272-303.
4. David Noebel, "WCC's 'Prophetic Role' a Facade," *Christian Crusade Weekly*, Vol. 12, No. 31, (June 11, 1972) p. 1.
5. Ibid., p. 6.
6. See the appendix to Richard Wurmbrand, *Tortured for Christ*. "A Diane Books paperback," California: Diane Books, 1969.
7. *The Golden Scripts*, pp. 538-40.
8. For an interesting reference to the latter days rule of the Anti-Christ, called also the beast in Scriptures, see Chapter 13 of the Revelation to John in the Bible.
9. Andrei Amalrik, *Will the Soviet Union Survive until 1984*. "Perennial Library," New York and Evanston: Harper and Row, 1970, p. 3.
10. Allan Smart, "Conscious Control of Physical and Mental States," *Menninger Perspective*, the Menninger Foundation, (April-May, 1970). See also: Alyce M. Green, Elmer E. Green, and E. Dale Walters, "Psychophysiological Training for Creativity," unpublished paper presented at the 1971 meeting of the American Psychological Association, Washington, D.C.
11. The basic ideas expressed in the last four paragraphs come from Discourse 88 recorded by William D. Pelley called, "What the Phenomenon of Americanism Means on the Cosmic Blueprint," *Soulcraft Scripts*, Vol. 7.

12. I am indebted to Pelley for many of the ideas on service expressed in this section. The discourses he recorded which were of particular benefit were "Service: The Mystery of Returning Value for Value from the Cosmic Angle," (Discourse 111). *Soulcraft Scripts*, Vol. 9 and "Interdependence: How Holy Spirit Seeks to Coordinate Its Parts, Thus Making for Universal Organization," Discourse 70 in *Soulcraft Scripts*, Vol. 6.

Chapter XI

PRINCIPLES OF THE PROMISED MILLENIUM

New Wine in New Bottles

Genuine service along the lines discussed in the previous chapter would be a boon to individuals in any society. However, neither a socialistic nor a capitalistic system would encourage its members to experiment with such high concepts of work and life. Thinking of these things, we begin to understand why the old orders must pass away to make room for the new.

One of the most curious notions the human mind has generated up to the present is the belief that, in order to prove one's eminence, one must act as though one is leading the lives of many men at the same time. One must have a house that can accommodate a legion, and yet dwell in it alone. One must own properties that would command the necessities and amenities for a thousand, instead of one household. By accumulating enough for a thousand, a person is led to think that perhaps he can raise his life in importance to a level equivalent to that of a thousand others.

In the past, this mentality has influenced people to want to own more and more slaves. At present it tends to stimulate desire for more and more other possessions of equivalent value as symbols of prestige.

To a reflective mind, this mentality appears quite childish. No matter how many suits of clothes a man has, he still can wear only one suit at a time. Nor can a person eat more than one meal at a time. The enjoyment of things does not depend on their quantity. It depends on the quality of one's attitude toward things.

In the future, men will not be considered great for the size of their possessions. Nor will they be considered great for the frequency of their acts of "charity" in doling from their surplus things their neighbors may beg for. They will be considered great for the character of what they do for the social or moral advancement of others.

It is only just that social rewards be made proportional to the contribution a person makes to improve the social body of which he is a part. Should not this have been the proper way of rewarding people for their efforts all along? Proper compensation is necessary to reinforce proper motivation. Compensation, however, need not be confined to money. If it is, all a man may end up having is money. The children of such people usually turn their backs on the ways of their fathers. Thus do karmic laws operate to restore a balance upset by overly stressing one aspect of life at the expense of others.

The takeovers we mentioned in previous chapters could not have been engineered if the people involved had not been overly impressed with financial success devoid of compassion. However, even without such monopolistic distortions of power, there would still have been quite a few evils associated with any system which is guided primarily by monetary incentives. Among these we may cite the proneness of such a system to periodic fluctuations in business activity. This has led some people to call competitive enterprise the system of "boom and bust."

Granted that some of the biggest busts—such as the Great Depression—cannot properly be attributed to the way competitive systems operate. As we saw earlier, the severest depressions and international conflicts were not caused by competitive forces vying with each other for a greater share of the income of some people. They were caused by international machinations aiming at greater control over the peoples of all the nations. Economists who will not recognize such skullduggery behind the scenes have yet to find plausible reasons to explain how presumably intelligent people could have acted in such inept ways and still managed to have kept their reputations. I doubt whether they ever will. A very prominent economist once told me that no one had caused the Great Depression; rather, it hit the world like the bubonic plague, out of nowhere. What reasoning! Even bubonic plague epidemics have had their discernible causes.

My purpose here is not to put my colleagues on the spot. It is to point out that even if a fundamental reform of the monetary system makes it no longer possible to manipulate money and credit to cause severe deflations or inflations, a competitive economy dominated by money values would still have a tendency to be unstable for other reasons.

Any economic system that coordinates the decisions of millions of individuals must of necessity be a delicate instrument. Unless it is watched carefully, it can be easily deranged. The disturbances may come either from external shocks or from internal distortions in the performance of its institutions and markets.

By external shocks, I do not have in mind merely wars or political upheavals. Innovations in methods of production, the introduction of new types of products, changes in taste or even in weather conditions can disturb the circular flow of economic activity. Moreover, once a disturbance occurs in one sector, it tends to spill over into others. If an economic upset is large enough, the waves and ripple effects it creates affect profits, incomes, and employment levels throughout the system.

Distortions in the internal relationships of a competitive economy can cause as much trouble as outside shocks. Overdevelopment of producers' goods industries relative to consumers' goods industries, savings which cannot find profitable outlets in investments, overconstruction of housing units, insufficient expenditures on consumer goods out of earned income are a few examples of deformities which may imbalance an economy. Once any of these start affecting profits and then employment levels, waves of pessimism or optimism are also generated which rock the boat even more.

As economists know, when the economic boat rocks far enough, one group after another lose their balance, fall into a sea of trouble and start to sink—unless a helping hand is extended in rescue. So long as it is primarily profits which animate economic activity, it is inevitable that we shall have such ups and downs in economic life. In a competitive economy a firm must make a profit or go under. Businesses must watch their prospects for profit or jeopardize their own existence. Therefore they will cut back production or expand it beyond sustainable limits, all depending upon what is happening to their prospects for profit. Thus do they give rise to the contradiction of unutilized or underutilized labor and capital resources on the one hand and ill-fed and ill-housed people on the other.

Much of the economic life in the modern world is not on a strictly competitive basis. A canopy of laws, regulations, traditional standards and practices protect the powerless. By the same token, excessive governmental intervention and bureaucracy in all sectors of the economy are stifling the individual in every direction. The average American does not always admit that he is losing his freedom. In his heart, however, he knows that neither his life nor his property belongs to him any more. An undeclared war, if not a criminal in the street, can wipe out his life as easily as higher taxation or a runway inflation can wipe off his property.

Intelligent people in business, government, or elsewhere know that the realities they see are not what they are said to be. Yet they have neither the insight nor the zeal to correct that which is wrong. They see that those above them follow a course of expedient unconcern, and they follow suit. Can you condemn them? Would you condone them?

People say that government intervention is needed to clean up the environment, rebuild the cities, protect the minorities, upgrade education, or otherwise improve the quality of life. So far, however, although we have seen much evidence of government waste, we have seen no evidence that government can change the human condition into a utopia. Does it add to the quality of life to rob Peter through taxation to pay Paul? Is the quality of life improved by forcing people to behave even if government had sense enough to know what it means to behave? Governments should be strong enough to restrain evildoers. They should never be strong enough to restrain the average person from doing what he thinks is right. It was well said that a government powerful enough to give people everything they want is also powerful enough to take away everything the people have.

The individualism we prescribe for the future, therefore, is one which is held together by the spirit of cooperation. It is not one torn apart by commercial rivalries. We believe that even bureaucracies can operate on a cooperative basis. We do not rule out competition. We say, "Let men compete to excel in performance or service, but never to the point where they begin to hurt one another."

If business had been conducted with less greed and more cooperation in the past, would we today have a polluted environment? Would we have had business monopolies, labor monopolies, government monopolies, and pressure groups in every field? In the long run, nobody benefits from these restrictive arrangements, not even the monopolists.[1]

Consider now what more and more governmental intervention has been allowed to do in these United States. While retaining an impressive authority on paper, Congress has been willing to allow the executive branch and the courts to assume immense powers over the lives and fortunes of the people. Such power has been misused not only to involve the nation in painful international conflicts, but also to promote disruptive policies on the domestic scene. Over the past decade or two, some of the most important social decisions, such as school integration and busing, permissive treatment of criminals and subversives and voter reapportionment, which changed the political balance of the nation, were made by the Supreme Court after a bare minimum of public discussion.

Americans have looked to their presidents for leadership. Have they had the leadership they had hoped for? Starting with President Woodrow Wilson, one could make an interesting comparison of campaign promises of U.S. presidents with their performance after election. In recent years, the establishment of a second state department in the White House, and now the Watergate scandal, should speak volumes. . . .

There are too many forces which prevent elected officials from representing their constituents beyond what serves their own selfish interests. The betrayal of the trust placed in them is often very subtle. A senator or congressman knows that if he sides with the political leadership, he can make more demands on them later when he wants something done. Given this opportunistic mentality, all the mammon interests have to do to get what they want is to flatter, buy, seduce, threaten, or otherwise exert pressure on the political leadership. Most of the other politicians fall in line sooner or later. The mavericks have their day in court, of course, but they are not allowed to get too far.

The blame for centralization of power is often placed on advances in technology. However, even the establishment's eminent worldly philosopher, Peter Drucker, was unimpressed with this argument, when he wrote, "It was naive of the 19th Century optimist to expect paradise from technology—and it is equally naive of the 20th Century pessimist to make technology the scapegoat for such shortcomings as man's blindness, cruelty, immaturity, greed and sinful pride."[2]

Drucker does not realize that, once the truly evil forces are finally eliminated, man will no longer seem to be nearly as blind and cruel as he now appears. We must keep our accounts straight on this matter, so we can distinguish between cause and effect and between symptoms and the related malady. All the same, his point is well taken, for science and technology do not by themselves either cause or solve social problems. It is the people who use these forces who do so.

We need not belabor the point that cooperation is better than regimentation. We propose to show that it is also far better than selfish competition. In a world of work in which people regard each other as rivals, would not any change which threatens to lower the status of some in relation to others create anxiety, if not misery? The competitive mentality allows no one to feel relaxed or secure in his economic position or social attainments. A change in a contract or a fashion, a new industry or technology, or perhaps simply a new boss, is enough to shatter the world one has built over many years.

I realize that what we have now is not, and in fact it has never been, a strictly competitive system. Nor should we equate free enterprise with an unbridled free-for-all. Rather, free enterprise refers to a system which gives everyone equal freedom and opportunity to start an enterprise and make it succeed. In such a system one can conduct one's business in a very altruistic way and still be immensely successful, as people like Milton Hershey, Henry B. Endicott, and George F. Johnson have proved in their times. These gentlemen did the right thing voluntarily and they were loved by the people who knew them for doing so. On the other hand, John D. Rockefeller Sr. was so hated in the oil fields of Pennsylvania for his selfish policies that he was hanged in effigy.

There have been businessmen who were ridiculed or pitied for their philistine attitudes and narrow interests; while others were greatly respected or honored for their enlightened and farsighted leadership. Thus free enterprise systems allow the very best as well as the worst in man to manifest. Often under divine guidance, Western businessmen and industrialists achieved fantastic marvels by making good use of their economic liberty. Even Karl Marx had to admit that "capitalists," during the industrial revolution, "accomplished wonders far surpassing Egyptian pyramids, Roman aqueducts and Gothic cathedrals."

Therefore, we do not question the tremendous benefits which can be achieved through free enterprise systems. Rather, we address ourselves now to those who make a religion out of economic competition. Is it not true that an overly competitive system tends to make people want to discard anyone who is not, or who is no longer productive? The lack of meaning in life that many retired people feel betrays a longstanding lack of purpose which comes to the fore when the busy mask is removed.

Furthermore, the educational system of a nation that glorifies competition would continue to emphasize preparing individuals for the needs of industry. In the future, the emphasis should be on reshaping industry to serve the needs of individuals. We must watch the character of our economic systems carefully if we are to avoid distortions in ethical values. There have been those who have shown their moral blindness by attempting to measure human progress in terms of economic values, instead of measuring economic progress in terms of human values.

Profit-based systems can aggravate, as often as they ameliorate, problems of poverty in the midst of plenty. Poverty need not necessarily be a demeaning experience. All the same, it will injure a soul if it makes him feel worthless. The injury will be greater if despair and self-pity are added to the indignities the poor have to bear as failures in the competitive race.

The desire to get ahead is certainly legitimate and worthy. For some people, it provides the only incentive to get things accomplished. However, if it hardens the heart, we know what a legacy of bitter feelings it can leave behind. Let others say what they wish. We say that good feelings are more important than big profits. Eventually they lead to much bigger profits and far greater prosperity.

Civilized life requires that men act thoughtfully and wisely, taking into account the effects of their acts on each other. The freedom which a responsible individualistic order promises is not a license to hurt one's neighbor. It is said that justice is blind. I want to know why justice must be blind. In the past, the blind justice of impersonal forces has caused too much injury. In the cooperative system of the future the blindfolds on justice will be removed to make it more sensitive to individual differences.

We look forward to an age when the lion shall lie down with the lamb, when swords shall be beaten into plowshares and spears into pruning hooks. Men will then come together to meet their obligations to each other, not to see what they can get from each other. When fear and insecurity are replaced with courage and real trust in the guidance of the Father, there will be no end

183

to the miracles which will redeem man's economics and politics no less than his individual failings.

We saw in the previous chapter how all constructive advances in science have been a prelude and a preparation for this righteous, cooperative age predicted by the ancient prophets. Even the preparation for this period had been foretold by Daniel, who prophesied that at "the time of the end ... knowledge shall increase." (Daniel 12:4).

I know that it is not easy for a person who has gone through an educational system dominated by skeptics to look forward to such an age. Bear with me, however, and decide for yourself whether we can have it.

As it was said of old, men do not "put new wines into old bottles; else the bottles break, and the wine runneth out, and the bottles perish; but they put new wine in new bottles and both are preserved." (Matthew 9:17).

The Father of whom I speak is the Father of all nations and of all tongues, races and climes. However, if the world is to be saved from the clutches of those who would rule it for their own profit, it will have to be saved first on these shores by the upright and optimistic people of these United States. The social and economic principles I am about to describe are therefore offered first and foremost to the American people.

Favoritism or bias has had nothing to do with this choice. How could it have? God is no respecter of persons. The plain truth is that in the eyes of the Almighty, the American people have earned the right to provide political leadership to the rest of the world. This right has been earned by the way they have conducted themselves relative to other nations, not in any other way.

Once these principles are applied in the States, however, their benefit will be as an open book available to anyone who cares to learn and to profit. The gates will be opened to people from other lands so they can come and examine for themselves how the new system operates. They will be encouraged to learn how to adapt it to their own nations in ways appropriate to their own peoples and climes. Nevertheless, in the Father's plan, the new principles are to come forth from the New Jerusalem, which we declare to be Washington, D.C.

Here, then, are the basic principles to govern the new order:

1. In the new dispensation, every human being, as a son of God, is automatically to become a citizen of the nation of which he is a part. Being a member in good standing of God's world, the United States will offer every citizen living within her borders the inalienable right to exist in safety and dignity. Thus will a standard be established for the proper treatment of all citizens of all nations under God.

2. Although universal love of all mankind is the ultimate goal, it cannot be accomplished by sacrificing the lesser goals of loyalty to family, community, and nation. Therefore, it will be the first goal of the American educational system to instill in every person an abiding love for one's family, community, and nation.

3. In order to survive and prosper, the state will become the paramount interest in the people's minds. Each citizen will be given a rightful voice to express himself not only through the privilege of voting, but also through the processes of originating legislation, registering one's protest against unwise laws, regulations and policies, and if necessary, recalling self-seeking or incompetent officials.

4. Social and economic institutions are not to be ends in themselves, but instruments calling men to a higher way of life. A balanced system of rights and obligations will replace the controls of the dictator or bureaucrat on the one hand and the dollars-and-cents calculations of the capitalist on the other. The citizen will feel free to choose to stay at the bottom or reach the heights. When God's economy is placed in the hands of good men, there will be so much abundance, no one will be allowed to suffer severe economic hardships at any time.

5. Wages and prices shall be flexible, and responsive to the changing tastes and technologies of an expanding economy. However, they shall be guided by standards of equity to be formulated with the help of well-qualified experts. In deciding

185

what to produce or what not to produce, it will be understood that the voice of God is the voice of the people, who are given the education and the means to make their wishes known.

6. An overall planning system will supplement the supply-and-demand forces operating in free markets. The planning, however, will be educative and cooperative, instead of being authoritarian and coercive. It will be done the better to harmonize the interests and performances of all participants in the economic process.

7. Every able-bodied person will be assured gainful employment commensurate with one's talents, while every retired person will have a pension, well invested and insured by either private or government organizations.

8. The sick, disabled, and the severely handicapped will be cared for. At no time, however, will anyone be made to feel that he is getting a handout from Big Brother. No one will be denied any reasonable opportunity to have a good life and to improve one's self through proper education, housing, health, and other personal or social services.

9. Property will remain private as far ahead as we can see. It will be distributed according to individual talent for acquiring and managing it. Anyone who would question this will have a difficult time explaining how the collective ownership of property can be prevented from deteriorating into witless tyranny over the people. All the same, the educational system will teach that property should be regarded as a thing to be held in trust to help others, and not as an avenue to financial aggrandizement.

10. Leaders in government, education, and industry will be trained to feel and act more like sages and philosophers, and not like shrewd, opportunistic politicians. They will be promoted into their positions of leadership after years of successful service in fields for which they have been thoroughly prepared. Appointments to discharge personal or political obligations will be considered a disgrace. Salesmanship will be replaced by servicemanship in both the economy and government of the nation.

11. The basic character of all economic and governmental

organizations will be cooperative, instead of competitive or hierarchical. At the same time, the individual will replace the organization at the center of the stage. It will no longer be, "Am I my brother's keeper?" It will be, "I must be my brother's helper, so we may together climb the stairs to greatness to our eternal profit."

12. Usury and unjust enrichment in all its forms will be eliminated by transforming the values people cherish as well as the legal systems which support economic injustice. Once unproductive extortion by virtue of economic power—which is the very essence of usury—is no longer allowed, there will be no more reason to complain about the unequal distribution of income.

13. Science will be keyed to government and government to the benefit of the people. Pure science no less than its applications to physical and social problems will be encouraged in peacetime with as much vigor as the manipulated governments of less enlightened ages have encouraged it in wartime. Those who work in the fine arts and humanities will be recognized and rewarded, each according to one's talent and contribution to the well-being of men.

14. Money will be an economic convenience, not an instrument of power. Therefore the control of the monetary system will be taken away from central bankers and placed in the hands of its proper owners—the American people. As Abraham Lincoln once said, "The privilege of creating and issuing money is not only the supreme prerogative of government, but it is the government's greatest creative opportunity."

15. A National Monetary Center will replace the double-faced Federal Reserve System, which has been instrumental in creating too many crises in money markets at home and abroad. The National Monetary Center will not attempt to be the world's central bank, nor will one be needed. Domestic monetary and fiscal policy alike will aim at facilitating steady, spontaneous growth, instead of constant intervention in the economic process.

16. Basic natural resources, such as oil, natural gas, coal, mineral deposits, or large tracts of land, will be owned by the

government. No one can claim to have produced these assets. In the past, they have been acquired all too often through force or fraud. In the future, they will be used honestly for the public's benefit, making it possible to reduce excessive burdens of taxation in all its forms.

17. Taxes at all levels shall be lowered stage by stage, as more and more functions are transferred from public to private hands. There will come a time when welfare as a governmental function will be unheard of, as will huge public debts that are rolled over from generation to generation, without any prospect for repayment.

18. It will be realized that the United States shares an interest in the expansion of international trade on equitable terms. It will also be realized that the United States should help to create a smoothly functioning international financial system. However, it will not be necessary to sacrifice important domestic policy objectives to help achieve international equilibrium. Adjustments in foreign transactions will come about through flexible exchange rates, as equitable codes of commercial and banking practices are made to work to everyone's advantage.

19. Americans will have opportunities and incentives to serve abroad, to help the less developed countries advance, and to start commercial and industrial enterprises on foreign soil. For their efforts, they will be entitled to receive good wages and profits as well as other rewards and compensations. However, they will not be entitled to receive government guarantees or military intervention to protect their financial interests. Moreover, they will not be allowed to take capital out of the country on a permanent basis, or to own the oil, the mines, the forests, or other basic resources of foreign countries. Nor will they be allowed to become dominant factors in the politics of weaker nations, claiming privileges which the nationals of host countries are not themselves permitted to enjoy.

20. The national security arrangements of the United States will not be tied to a global system, which in the nature of things would have to have a monopoly of all the weapons in the world.

The United States is destined to provide leadership to one of three regional power blocs which are to evolve naturally along cultural, ethnic, and economic interest lines. Uncle Sam is not meant to be a policeman to the whole world. Besides, such a three-way split of political power would provide a safer and more effective system of checks and balances to help prevent the abuse of military power in any part of the world.

Every one of these twenty principles has been divinely inspired to help solve the problems of the future. Those who attempt to apply them will have guidance beyond their fondest dreams. Blessed are those who will understand the benefits of these principles and glorify the Father by putting them into practice.

A True People's Government

The Father has never attempted to institute His plan for righteous government directly. Instead He has allowed men to evolve the requisite forms through trial and error. At all times, however, high masters on the Spirit side have watched carefully the denouement of world events to guide them into channels that would enrich the evolving consciousness of man.

At present, there is more of a hands-off attitude than ever, so evil can have its self-willed and self-destructive sway. Nevertheless, events are watched carefully so they will not go more astray than necessary to bring man back to the true path.

A little reflection will make it clear that a genuine peace, a saner culture, a more truly progressive society cannot prevail unless we have first better government. Moreover, to have better government, we must have standards with which to judge what is good or bad in the art and science of politics.

In the beginning, governments were instituted among men to derive their just powers from the consent of the governed. This is not always understood, partly because the politics of the most ancient civilizations were far from democratic in form. As we saw in Chapter IV, the earliest governments were typically dynastic kingships and hereditary priesthoods.

Obviously this was rule by the few. It was not, however, always harsh and exploitive rule, as the socialists would have us think. There were, it is true, definite lines drawn between the ruling classes and the subject populations. Nevertheless, it is also true that the rulers knew much more and had much greater talent than the people over whom they reigned.

It has always been recognized that some are born to lead and others to follow. All that justice requires is that the leaders qualify for their special privileges of leadership. How? By being equipped with such talents and mentorship that *they are able to inspire the governed to project through them their own unvoiced longings.*

Leaders so equipped were sent by God to rule, which they did. At times, however, corrupted by power, they ruled more harshly and selfishly than they had intended before coming to earth life. Nevertheless, the plan of the Divine Host who sent them had been all along to institute such forms of rulership as would not only have the consent of the governed, but also lead the people to rule themselves insofar as they were able.

In the early stages of society, statecraft could not have been based on the direct consent of the governed. Giving an impulsive and ignorant people the right to vote would almost certainly have prostituted government by free vote into a license to operate against the public interest. As we saw earlier, after thousands of years of civilizing life experiences, there is still much more of this type of prostitution than most professors of government will admit.

A genuine system of self-government is one where each citizen has a rightful and effective voice at all times and on every occasion. The fact that a man has the right to vote for a representative, a senator, or a president does not mean that he will automatically have a significant impact on his government. People can have their rights usurped by their representatives no less than by their institutions.

The most basic question in distinguishing divine from satanic government is the following: "Do the people own their government, or is it their government which owns them?" There are

190

principles at stake here of which scientists have no knowledge. There are great works which manifest through human lives that the eyes of men do not always see. Men have missions unto themselves to cultivate their senses and intellects, through trial and error. They have obligations to each other incurred in previous lives that they must meet or suffer. From the depths of their hearts (i.e., subconscious minds) men feel these things.

People have His will in their hearts. What need have they of a Big Brother to tell them what to do? Can you conceive that the day will come when men would have little or practically no government? All they will need and want will be traffic cops to make sure their lives do not bump into those of their neighbors.

The younger a child, the more he needs his parents to direct his life, to help him survive, and to grow. As he advances in years, parental control diminishes stage by stage. Should not the same rule apply for the guidance of human societies through the agencies of government? Eventually government will only be a means of keeping the wheels of progress well oiled and operative in a framework of law and order.

For the state to recede as man advances, we must know ourselves and we must know our God. As long as man does not believe in a God who provides all things rightly deserved, he will want to deify the state as his provider of last resort. In the seventeenth century, the pioneers of the great scientific movement, unlike their successors, did believe in a sovereign God from whom they derived their meaning and their truth.

The French philosopher, Rene Descartes, pointed out that if he did not think that his mind was created by a perfect God he could not trust the utterances of his reason.[3]

Another seventeenth century genius, Blaise Pascal, had a vision one night in which he was shown that the true God was the God of Abraham and Jacob and not an abstraction created by philosophers and mathematicians. He said this made him cry tears of joy.[4]

We saw in Chapter V the religious concepts of Washington, to whom it was given to father his nation because of his great love for his people. Washington had said that "reason and experience both forbid us to expect that national morality can prevail in exclusion of religious principle." In a similar vein, two hundred years ago the British philosopher Edmund Burke declared that liberty can exist only with order and virtue, and cannot exist at all without them.

Starting with the French Revolution, however, the new morality of nature and reason started to replace reverence for God and individual responsibility for one's moral decisions. The Divine Host allowed these winds of change to prevail for awhile so that they would sweep away the obsolete class structures of feudalism, monarchy, and ecclesiastic privilege. Moreover, through the horrors of revolution, mankind was to learn a great lesson, namely that two wrongs never make a right. Nevertheless, as the old orders disappeared, the Godless morality of reason could not prevent the deterioration and confusion caused by what we have called the seven satanic takeovers.

As a result, we find presumably intelligent scientists who say, "I cannot observe a God, therefore I cannot tell you whether He exists," or "I can tell you what is but not what ought to be."

Fortunately, the intellectual and political contradictions of our times will soon bring such absurdities to an end. Let us prepare, therefore, for the 1000-year Christ reign to follow, so we can mitigate the cataclysmic transitions to the glorious new age.

When the time arrives, there will be no shortage of ideas about how to proceed. Much will be taught by the Christ and His mentors whom He will gather from this and other planets. Many ideas will also come forth from the civilization of Atlantis, which will be rediscovered about that time. We predict the discovery of a large metal tube in submerged Atlantis. This tube contains an elevator, which is well oiled and in operative condition. It will take people down to one floor after another, where they will find specimens and documents that will provide much information on the economic, social, and governmental institutions of Atlantis. A great deal will be learned from this discovery alone.

The Christ will be available and accessible for guidance

192

whenever needed. He will appear to world leaders at meetings and conferences around the globe.

We predict further that new light will be shed on the Constitution of the United States of America. Original drafts will appear. When they see these, people will marvel at how the inspiration and the word of God has remained unmovable over the years. Other interpretations will be brought up to date.

The new government to be established in the United States within the bounds of its Constitution will be an inspiration to the world. When the evil ones behind the scenes are no more, men's minds will be released from destructive thoughts. There will be nothing to stop the sovereign will of the people from being expressed in matters both great and small.

The laws on the statute books will be equitable but few. A government that is wisely and justly administered in carrying out the wishes of the people has no need for too many codes. The laws that it will have will be by consent, not coercion.

The spirit of revolt will be gone; the youth will say, "What do we have to protest now? This is our system." The schools will prepare children for mature, responsible citizenship. It will be common knowledge that man is an eternal spirit seeking divinity. At present, people do not believe that it is profitable for them to take the long view, to work patiently for the higher values. This is the fault of the educational and religious leaders of our times. It is not the fault of the average person who follows the accepted authorities of his time.

The whole world, especially the Christian world, should have by this date advanced to the type of understanding presented in this book. It is the ethical and cultural leaders of the world who have *blocked* this advance! We know whereof we speak. Slothfulness, self-centeredness, greed, blind dependence on tradition have been allowed to dominate their thoughts. We mention these things without spleen. Nor do we feel self-righteous. We do not judge or accuse. We let their works speak for themselves.

Our concern here is to point out that man *can* have better government if he changes his attitudes, eschews evil, and knows

193

that it is possible for all things to happen with the Father, provided he takes action as he sees the light. Once he cleanses his government, then and only then will he have the freedom to put his economic house in order.

The New Economics

The guiding principles of the new economics can be expressed in two words—*cooperative individualism*. A little reflection will show that genuine individualism cannot survive without a cooperative attitude which would make people want to do the right thing voluntarily. If individualism degenerates into a free-for-all, controls are bound to be imposed sooner or later.

As the economic systems of the past have prepared the way for what is to be in the future, when the new system is put into operation, it too will be a steppingstone to something better. Ultimately, when men, through righteous living, finally develop the power to create by thought, there will be very little need for any formal system of political economy. Do you find it difficult to accept this possibility? Creating by thought is what Jesus did when He multiplied the loaves and the fishes to feed the multitudes. Did He not prophesy, "Truly, truly, I say to you, he who believes in Me will also do the works that I do; and greater works than these will he do"? (John 14:12)

In the meantime, the greater production, the faster transportation, and the more instant communication in the new age will give man a feel for what it means to emulate Holy Spirit. This awareness of the marvelous things man can do with his mind will gradually stir up in him latent memories of the things he was able to do in his original spirituality. This is the way the Father would have His children reach their divine potential.

Is it becoming clearer now why we kept insisting that the study of economics should not be confined to problems of allocating scarce resources? If a man is ill paid for his work and is troubled because of it, his economic injury causes him spiritual injury as well. A troubled person does not set a good example for his family or his friends. Thus out of economic injustice flow social injuries also.

If you examine once again the principles to govern the Millennial age, you will discover that they aim either at avoiding injury to others, or at helping man to grow by helping his neighbor. Have not these aims always been at the very core of the Christ teachings? When these principles are applied, the day will come, to be labeled as the Age of Service, when our Elder Brother no longer will need to wash His fellow man's feet to show the love of the Father *equally* for all mankind.

We recognize that every society must have its method of deciding what will be produced, how it will be produced, and who should receive its products. We should also recognize that whatever the character of its institutions, no system will function well unless certain balances are maintained between production and consumption, savings and investments, revenues and expenditures, productivity and wages, and so on. Although one need not know a great deal about how these balances are achieved in practice, it is essential to grasp the importance of having a method of achieving these balances if the system is to keep its equilibrium.

In a free society, the most important parts of such mechanisms are flexible market prices. Some people think of prices simply as sums of money they have to pay to buy the commodities they want. All the same, in a broader perspective, prices are seen to serve also as traffic signs to guide the flow of production and consumption in an economy. By deciding to buy or not to buy any given commodity in the marketplace, people in effect vote for or against its continued production at its current price. If there is not enough demand to absorb the supply of a commodity at a given price, its price will tend to fall. In due time, the lower price will encourage more consumption, discourage overproduction, and thus bring its supply into equilibrium with its demand. Similarly a price which is too low will rise, encourage more production and less consumption until the shortage disappears.

In short, fluctuations in individual prices continually tend to eliminate imbalances in the economy in the form of shortages or surpluses of commodities. Here I am not speaking of inflations or deflations, which represent movements up or down in the general price level. These are economic diseases to be avoided by all means. Fluctuations in individual prices, relative to each other, are an entirely different matter. Not to allow such flexibility in prices and wages (which are the prices of various types of labor) would be to throw monkey wrenches into the balancing mechanisms of a voluntary enterprise system.

Changes in technology, incomes, and tastes affect different industries in different ways and degrees. As a result, certain costs decline more than others; while the revenues of some companies soar, others plummet. In the economy of the future, the prerogatives of management in varying their prices and wages to cope with these situations will be respected. Decisions about what prices to charge or what wages to pay, however, will not be made on strictly economic considerations. Obviously it is pointless to engage in a transaction which is not profitable to at least one of the parties involved. Profitability in some form must, therefore, continue to be the main criterion for production or trade. At the same time, profit will come to mean something more.

In the past, profits have served as incentives to rearrange market forces and reallocate resources so as to minimize costs or maximize revenues for a firm. As men realize, however, that an enterprise which creates material values at the expense of spiritual values is doomed, they will have a broader concept of profitability. They will want their production and trade to be guided by standards of performance which work to everyone's advantage, emotionally as well as financially.

This sounds a little unusual now. Keep in mind, however, that the business atmosphere will be quite different from what we see around us today. People of good will in manufacturing plants, in banks, department stores, and even in government agencies will sit around a table to discuss information gathered from market research studied, wage surveys and similar sources of information. Qualified experts will be invited as consultants to share their knowledge and experience with those in charge. Because of such discussions, the decisions will be more equitable. At the same time, the basic attitudes and life styles of everyone involved will improve as they see how much better results can be achieved when right is placed above economic might.

So many economists feel solutions which satisfy everyone do not exist because they think human nature is essentially grasping. Recently a well-known economist vividly expressed what his profession believes in a tactful way when he said that "at its best, economics seeks to harness man's very human motivations to the public interest."[5]

Once people start to understand what it means to live forever, and how they must personally suffer the consequences of their every blamable decision which harms their neighbors, is it not fair to assume that their very concepts of what constitutes profitable behavior will start to change? And when their higher insights lead to more socially responsible attitudes, would it not be equally fair to assume that their free enterprise systems will work even better than they have in the past?

In the new age, we emphasize again that the truly evil souls shall be removed from circulation. This means that the motivation and drive which results in big business, big labor, big crime, and big government will be largely gone. Nor will the genuine experts in the social sciences feel that they have to limit their investigations to problems of interest to those in power in order to get so much as a fair hearing for their views. Therefore, their methods and techniques of analysis will have more exciting and productive applications.

Free enterprise, operating in an equitable permanent framework, will still be called upon to handle most of the problems of the nation. At the same time, business enterprises will be placed on a more scientific basis. Moreover, the market system will be supplemented with a limited amount of national planning. The planning, however, will not be *for* the people but *with* the people. Here is how it would work.

At the grassroots level, the citizens, moved by the pleas of their neighbors, will become aware of social ills for which a remedy has not yet been found. They will work together to identify these ills, analyze them, and evaluate what can be done. They will not become overly emotional about what they see, however, because they will know that people are where they are because they belong there. They will also realize that as Rome was not built in a day, so the social problems of their day will not be solved in a week. Nevertheless they will want to do what they can. For aspects of the reforms which are beyond their capabilities to handle, or which require coordination, the people in local communities will organize a system of representation to get the attention of those whose consent or participation is needed.

At the county, city, or equivalent levels, the grassroots proposals will be received. Intelligent reasoning, with attention to a broader set of facts and circumstances, will provide answers that were not possible at lower levels. Broader problems that touch on regional or national interests—clean water and air provide examples—will be referred to still higher levels. From community to city, from city to state, from state to federal government, respected leaders will take the urgent pleas of the people to the proper level of decision making. Bitter conflicts of opinion will be almost inconceivable as the Spirit of God will go with them, counseling, encouraging, and blessing all sincere efforts made to improve the social conditions of the people.

In the federal city, the plans submitted for additional universities and laboratories, highways, cultural centers, monuments and parks will be coordinated. Special measures will be considered to help the people in industries which are not able to survive on their own. The most creative people in the nation will be given a chance at the top level to provide additional leadership, suggesting new initiatives, new standards of conduct in the business world, and better public policy measures to improve the structure and operation of the nation's economy.

Planning at all levels will be by the free consent of all the parties affected, not by coercion or clever salesmanship. The art of gentle persuasion will be developed along with the art of consultation with the Divine Host on important public matters through tested and certified prophets. The latter will be revered as dedicated servants of God, instead of being ignored, shunted aside or ridiculed. Much emphasis will be placed on proper education, including formal instruction in ethics. As a result, the planners as well as the people will have the background to appreciate what is valuable and worth achieving socially.

Tables, charts, projections, visual aids of all types will be used to demonstrate the concrete benefits of the proposals made. In fact, the whole social planning exercise will be one great practical experiment in adult education. The people's awareness of their neighbors' joys and sorrows will stretch and expand as never before. By appealing to the good (God) in him, rather than to his "very human motivations," man will ennoble his brother to their mutual advantage.

To do the technical work necessary for the planning process, full-time employees of the states will participate in the work of the federal government. Similarly, federal representatives in any given state will be composed only of residents of that state. They will therefore have a feel for the outlook and attitudes of the people they have been appointed to serve. This will also help to make the intergovernmental relationships personal, intimate, and warm. Township committees, members of city councils, committees of state legislatures will have full knowledge of what is going on. Thus there will not be much room for misunderstandings and friction.

Economic policies will stress preventative measures. Huge concentrations of power which can readily be abused will simply not be tolerated. What economists call perverse incentives will be eliminated from the economic structure as fast as possible. One does not have to be an eminent economist to realize that "many of our social problems arise because the current system of markets, laws, and customs provides positive incentives for individuals, business firms, and local communities to engage in what can objectively be called anti-social conduct."[6]

Above all, the new system will feature a full employment economy. There will be no if's and but's about this objective. Can you imagine for one moment that an economy built on the social precepts of the Christ would not provide a job to anyone who is willing and able to work? This, of course, does not mean that there will be a zero percent unemployment rate. A small fraction of the labor force will always be between assignments, so to speak, voluntarily looking for a change. What there will not be are cases of long-term or hardship unemployment.

Think of the benefits which can be realized when every able-bodied person is assured gainful employment commensurate with one's talents and experience! We are not speaking here of what it means to the individual to have a meaningful job. We assume everyone knows how work adds to one's dignity and provides a chance for self-expression and participation in the social order. Rather we have in mind the social benefits of full employment. If managers accept the challenge of finding appropriate jobs for workers who are out of work, they would become more respected in the community. Arrangements would be made for more varied on-the-job training, which is the best way of training most nonprofessional workers in a rapidly changing world anyway. The need for welfare, the inclination toward crime, and the deficits in public budgets would all decrease, as more people become productive citizens and taxpayers. Moreover, with greater percentages of the labor force employed, the economy would create both a greater abundance of products and services and more purchasing power with which to buy the additional commodities.

To help achieve full employment, there will be governmental funds to retool firms so they can make the transition from one pattern of production to another. Another way of handling the overflow of labor will be to have employers hold on to their surplus work force on a contingent basis during the less active periods. There will be so many ingenious *natural subsidies* to

200

assure people the jobs they want, there will be no need for too much governmental involvement in this field. Moreover, with monopolistic practices and positions of power in labor markets having been eliminated, the relentless drives for higher and higher wages will have stopped. Consequently, employers will not be discouraged from hiring all the workers they can absorb.

Furthermore, a shortened workweek will make it easier to attain the nation's full employment objective. At the same time, it would enable people to devote more time to civic affairs, ecology, and to cultural or humanitarian interests. There has been a persistent secular trend toward shortened work hours for over a hundred years. Prior to 1860, the weekly standard was over seventy hours. By 1910, the average had declined to between fifty to fifty-five hours. Since 1946, it has been forty hours. By 1990, it could well be thirty hours or less.

In the meantime, much of the work that will need to be done will be of a pushbutton variety. Furthermore, with insecurity, worry, and fear reduced, if not eliminated altogether, work will become more creative. At the same time, the basic causes of disease will gradually disappear. Is it not true that it is financial worries which give rise to most of the anxieties people have to bear?

The medicine of the future will become essentially preventive, with the emphasis on proper nutrition, right mental attitudes, emotional self-control, physical exercise and wholesome recreation. Consequently, the need will be mainly for health centers for rest and recuperation, instead of expensive specialized hospitals and clinics. The severe handicaps of psychoanalysts and psychiatrists who think in terms of one life only will be so obvious people will wonder how they could have been so blind for so long. The best physicians working in this branch of the healing professions will tend to be mediumistic, or they will work with mediums to diagnose emotional causes of illness originating in previous lives. This will speed up the therapeutic process enormously.

In short, tremendously burdensome health and welfare problems will be a thing of the past. Disease and dependency will be considered essentially preventable abnormalities. Physicians will teach people to live a sane, healthy life. They will not concentrate, as they do now, on clinical medicine.

Believe it or not, one of the most common causes of illness is the unconscious projection of people into situations which have nothing to do with their life plans. A balanced life is carrying out no more nor less than the plan or chart prepared prenatally for that individual. You may say, "The average man knows nothing about such a plan," and we agree. Our point is, however, that such a plan is nevertheless embedded in his subconscious mind, and expresses itself through his feelings.

A person may get out of balance either by leaning too far backward to avoid the uncertainties or pains of the life one has come to experience or by tipping too far forward in one's impatience to try to help in areas where one has no business interfering. As a man errs in either direction, he will feel that somehow something is quite wrong in an area of his life. Lack of balance is always loss of power. Thus the harder he works and strives in the wrong direction, the less headway he will seem to be making. Therefore, sooner or later, he will return to fulfilling his prenatal plan, to regain his balance.

To get back to the loss of balance which makes people sick, consider the way millions have been taught to look at the so-called underprivileged about them. Not understanding the universal laws at work in letting the poor suffer, they dwell constantly in their imagination on how cruel human beings are to let such things happen. It does not occur to them to think that the poor have a different conception of their situations. The following story, told by Mrs. Rose Wilder Lane, illustrates this point.

When American Red Cross workers went into the Balkans after the First World War, they found families living in a clay bank at Montenegro's largest city. They were horrified. So was I. I wrote a piece about these homeless victims of war that should have wrung dollars from the stoniest American pocketbook. Only, before I finished it, I went back with an interpreter to give some first aid to those miserable refugees. My sympathetic questions bewildered them. They were living as they always had in their ancestral homes.[7]

Here is an example of habitual poverty which persists as a form of psychosis. This state of mind, referred to by Jesus, when He said, "the poor you have with you always," keeps a man or woman in conditions of destitution year after year, and life after life. It is a disease of spirit which cannot be cured so long as a man refuses to recognize and correct the deficiencies of spirit which cause his destitution.

The first step in helping these persons is to make them realize how far behind they are falling in the human procession. The second step is to have them understand that they have no one to thank but themselves for their lack of enjoyment of life's better things. The third step is to help them overcome their limitations. Instead, what is being done now? The blame for their failures is placed on society at large, while checks are sent to social misfits out of the pockets of the socially productive who have rightfully earned the funds these checks represent.

Furthermore, this abortive gesture is regarded as charity, or as a highly commendable humanitarian act. Meantime, what of the spirit that prompts it? If the ugly truth were known, those who favor these handouts are more often than not attempting to buy immunity from their own tortured imaginings. They are not concerned with the poor, but strictly with themselves.

The givers are reading into disorganized persons' plights their own imaginings as to how they would feel if the order of society were suddenly reversed, and they, with their finer endowments and sensibilities, were cast into the roles of the poor. Not believing in a God of order and justice, the modern mind does not understand that *all persons are where they are in life because they need the specific lessons they should be learning from their predicaments.* Welfare checks may give the recipients something approximating the physical well-being the morally sensitive givers think the improvident welfare receivers should have. Can this type of giving improve the spiritual development of the poor, or the relations between givers and receivers?

True charity removes the cause of the improvidence in the individual by setting up a tutelage, either privately or publicly, so the improvident can feel the benefits of improving himself in his own experience. In the economy of the future, the perennially destitute will be surrounded with such stimuli and incentives for effort that, over a period of time, they will be in a position to overcome their deficiencies. Those who cannot make the grade will be taken care of in a personal way, along with the aged and the ill. As for the doctrine that they are being victimized by society, it will be exposed for what it has always been—an atheistic misconception or a fraud with effects worse than foul venom on the human consciousness. If this assertion flies in the face of most "expert" opinion, so be it!

Let us not ignore the fact that it is also possible to be thrown out of balance by having too many possessions. As Disraeli said, "Money is power, and rare are the heads that can withstand the possession of great power." Do not people know instinctively that things do not go well with the wealthy who refuse to give a part of their affluence to help advance spiritual causes?

If a man's efforts are rewarded with profits, he will be a better man and a more stable citizen. But balanced against material reward for well-directed effort must be the spiritual nobility expressed by service as we have defined it.

Collective ownership of property—the aim of the socialists— can never achieve the diversity and creativity of individual enterprise based on private property. As the famous nineteenth century economist, Alfred Marshall, pointed out:

Starting from the fact that the growth of the national divi- dend depends on the continued progress of invention and the accumulation of expensive appliances of production, we are bound to reflect that up to the present time nearly all the innumerable inventions that have given us our command over nature have been made by independent workers, and that the contributions from government officials all the world over have been relatively small. Further nearly all the costly appliances for production which are now in collective ownership . . . have been bought with resources borrowed mainly from the savings of business men and other private individuals.[8]

Developments in economic history during the Twentieth Century have essentially confirmed "Papa" Marshall's generalizations, despite the enormous growth in the role of government. As for the celebrated achievements of the Soviet system, even Stalin was reported to have said that the United States had helped to build approximately two-thirds of all the large industries of the Soviet Union.[9]

A people will not give its best without compensation according to ability. And ability includes know-how in managing capital. Neither can there be freedom of expression or new cultural movements challenging the status quo in a socialistic system whose capital is collectively owned. For these things to happen the mavericks must be provided first a livelihood and then channels of publicity. Do you believe for one moment that the rulers of a socialist state who control not only the jobs of the people but also the newspapers, magazines, radio and television stations of the land would finance such anti-social individuals and their activities?

It is a great fallacy to contrast human rights with property rights. It is an essential part of the human rights of individuals to earn and own property. Jesus knew that property rights, being very much a part of the sum total of human rights, should not be tampered with arbitrarily. When one of the multitude asked Him, "Teacher, bid my brother divide the inheritance with me." He said to him, "Man, who made me a judge or divider over you?" Then, turning to the people, He said, "Take heed, and beware of all covetousness; for a man's life does not consist in the abundance of his possessions." (Luke 12:13-15).

The natural tendency to order and balance in all things is a universal law. Men of great wealth who come into earth life on a financial vibration are destined to turn everything they touch into gold (the Midas touch). Otherwise they could never earn so much money in such a short time. The rich, however, throw themselves greatly out of balance if they do not use their fortunes to support those who come to earth life on spiritual missions. In the future, the wealthy will understand consciously those laws which they have always known subconsciously. They will realize that they are the ones who are expected to finance most of the schools, health centers, cultural enterprises, and other human institutions of society. That is why the man of capital of the future will be glad to cooperate with the righteous government of the people. As a result, they will be respected and glorified for their generosity. Their new attitudes will thus greatly improve the government of society. As Benjamin Disraeli wrote, " . . . that the tenure of property should be the fulfilment of duty is the essence of good government." After the evil few who have set the wrong standards of conduct are eliminated, why should not true benevolence become the general standard? Even in less enlightened ages, many among the rich and super rich have been true benefactors of mankind, building schools, churches, parks, and backing many other worthwhile causes.

Maintain an equitable balance in all economic and social relationships, and you will be amazed at the prosperity which will inevitably follow! In the past, business enterprises have cared little about the human use of human beings except where it would help them to reap more profits. When strict equity is observed in the economic world, businesses will not be run primarily in the interest of their stockholders, nor yet of their employees. They will be run first and foremost in the interests of those whom they are created to serve, i.e., their customers or clients.

If, say, 1,000 customers who patronized a business have maintained it in existence over a period of ten years, is it not fair that they should be rewarded for their patronage? We suggest that they are entitled to whatever of value is left in the business after the employees, managers, creditors, and owners are justly compensated for their talents and contributions.

There are those who argue that customers who receive goods and services at prices they are willing to pay have already been rewarded for their role in the productive process. The values changing hands in such transactions, however, are entirely different from the values involved in making it possible for a business to exist in the first place.

Granted that a business could not exist without its sponsors or employees either. Even so, while the rights of these groups are widely recognized, is it not true that the patrons of a business are often kept outside the pale? The commercial psychology in the main has been to consider customers as the prey of the owners and workers to be charged without mercy as expediency commands.

In recent years, under the rubric of "social responsibilities of business" some recognition is being given to the obligations commercial enterprises have to the various segments of the society which makes it possible for them to exist. At the same time, we should also realize that, in attempting to make them socially responsible, there are businesses which are being forced to reduce their efficiency, almost to the level of a governmental agency.

For the new age, we do not have in mind confrontation politics or socialistic legislation. We have in mind spontaneous cooperation, induced by appeals to the good in man. True, we are advocating a threefold balance among patrons, employees, and sponsors. But we are not advocating organizations where responsibility for what is decided cannot be traced to specific individuals. Fixing responsibility on the individual for his own acts is the beginning of administrative wisdom. Nor are we advocating weakness in management. We know that it is executive-minded men with the incentive, the financial backing, and the authority to act who make things happen.

Resolving the Money Question

Important as it is to maintain the right equilibrium in the

organization of production, it is doubly more important to stabilize monetary conditions. The Federal Reserve System was not only conceived in sin and misused by international mammon interests as discussed earlier, it has not even been effective in accomplishing its officially stated aims. Evaluating the overall performance of the "Fed," an outstanding authority on money, Milton Friedman, pointed out that, "... even if the war and immediate postwar years are omitted, and we consider only the peacetime years from, say, 1920 through 1939, and 1947 to date ... the stock of money, prices, and output was decidedly more unstable after the establishment of the Reserve System than before. The most dramatic period of instability in output was, of course, the period between the two wars which includes the severe contractions of 1920-21, 1929-33, and 1937-38. No other twenty-year period in American history contains as many as three such severe contractions."[10]

There is no shortage of economists who are constantly advising the Federal Reserve on how to avoid "mistakes" in monetary policy. They think they can solve with better techniques problems which are essentially political and ethical in nature. To prevent disorders and fishtail movements in money markets and in the economy, we do not recommend merely superficial improvements in techniques of monetary management. We recommend putting an end to the tinkering with the money system by nonelected monetary authorities, appointed and controlled behind the scenes by international banking interests. A man lacking proper knowledge of the intricate mechanisms of a watch should not attempt to repair it. Is there a banker or economist in the world who knows what will happen to the economy and when, as he tries to balance it, in the same way that a good repairman knows what will happen to the watch he is adjusting? Of course not. Then it is time for central bankers and their economist friends to rely less on their inevitably limited knowledge and more on the natural forces of adjustment engineered by One whose knowledge is greater than theirs.

The potential dangers of monetary manipulation are dramatized by Lenin's well-known dictum that the most effective way to destroy a society is to destroy its money. No society would have progressed beyond primitive forms if it had not achieved a stable medium of exchange, i.e., a reliable money. The world learns through trial and error, and it would be unfair to blame bankers and economists for not having in 1930 the knowledge they had in 1970. The important thing is that at least one school of economists—the monetarists—have finally hit upon an idea which would give people a stable money and at the same time control over monetary policy through their political representatives.

This idea, which is based on much conscientious, scientific research, emphasizes that historically economic instability has been due to changes in the conditions under which money has been supplied to the economy. It has not been due to undependable behavior by the producing and consuming public who use the money that is supplied.

Here we use the term "money" to mean all the currency and deposits in commercial banks held by the public (except banks). In this sense, the total amount of money available in the economy is determined by the monetary authorities and the banks, and not by the public's desire to hold more or less money balances at any given time. The public cannot change the total amount of money outstanding because no one can diminish the amount of money he holds by spending it without at the same time increasing the amount of money held by the one from whom he buys what he wants. The monetary authorities, on the other hand, can expand or contract the money supply by increasing or decreasing the bank reserves which must be held against outstanding deposits.

If the total amount of dollars, say, is kept by the monetary authorities at a constant level, the public could step up the tempo of economic activity and cause prices to rise by going on a spending spree. Similarly, by hoarding their cash and not spending enough to keep the wheels of industry turning, the public could cause economic downswings and unemployment. However, the monetarists have found that such things are not likely to happen because the behavior patterns of the public with respect to their holdings of money are fundamentally stable.[11]

This means that if the supply of money is increased steadily in line with the growth of the labor force and in productivity, there simply could not be inflations, deflations, or serious monetary instability of any kind. A question would arise, of course, as to who would decide how fast the expansion of the money supply should be. The answer given most often is that Congress has the responsibility for issuing and regulating the value of money under the U.S. Constitution.

The findings of the monetarists as well as their basic philosophy have often been challenged, particularly by Keynesian economists. Some have claimed that a simple rule established by Congress would place the monetary authorities in a straitjacket, as though the monetary authorities are not already in a bind when the lion's share of the vast quantities of the money and liquid assets of the world is controlled by a small number of multinational companies and banks who can precipitate a severe monetary crisis any time they so wish.

Other economists have claimed that adhering strictly to a legislated money supply rule would generate intolerable pressures in financial markets as business conditions fluctuate. These pressures would in turn force the central bankers to take defensive actions which would necessitate increasing or decreasing the total amount of money available in the economy. While there is merit to this argument in the context of the present economic and financial system, a steady growth in the money supply could not hurt the type of economy we have outlined for the future.

And when the value and supply of money is stabilized through this method, people will discover a new concept which seems impossible in a world of grossly distorted financial arrangements. This is the concept of an honest unit of account—a dollar in the United States—which stands for a unit of toil applied to nature to produce something wanted by man.

A change should also take place in the present system of fractional reserve banking. With the present system, private bankers can earn billions in interest on money they have never earned. Perhaps because economists are used to adapting to the ways of the world, whatever these ways turn out to be, they are not shocked by such arrangements. They explain objectively that this practice goes back to the sixteenth century goldsmith bankers who found they could lend most of the gold left with them for safekeeping without fear of objection. The owners of the gold were satisfied so long as the goldsmith establishments, by keeping enough gold in reserve, could return to the owners all the gold they wanted to take out of storage. In the nature of things, the reserves which had to be kept amounted to a small fraction of the total gold left with the goldsmiths.

Similarly, when a deposit of cash is made in a modern bank, the bank sets aside about ten to twenty cents of every dollar as reserves to meet the requirements of the law and lends out the rest through another window. This can lead and has led to the anomaly of the U.S. government paying huge sums of interest to bankers to borrow money the banking system creates for the purpose when the government could have created that money without selling government securities to the banks. We speak of the banking system as creating money because they create demand deposits which circulate as money, whether it is the government or private parties who write the checks against these deposits.

So few stop to think that it is fundamentally unfair to give away to any private group a privilege which makes ordinary people perpetual debtors to owners of government securities. Economists say, "Oh, well, we owe this money to ourselves." As for the bankers, they do not, of course, object to interest on government bonds and other debts rolling into their coffers as long as economists manage to find clever ways of convincing themselves and others that the fractional reserve system is really quite fair after all.

Here is a typical example of how the subject is treated in college textbooks:

> No banking system with fractional reserves—i.e., none which keeps less than 100 per cent of its deposits in cash—can ever turn all its deposits into cash on a moment's notice. So every fractional reserve system would be a 'fair-weather system' if government didn't stand ready to back it up. If panic ever again came, Congress, the President, the Secretary of the Treasury, and the Federal Reserve Board Chairman would all act. They'd say: 'If the panicky American people all insist on taking their money out of the banks, we'll print as much money as is needed to meet the emergency.' . . . But knowing the government is ready to act, people will never put it to the test.[12]

What we would like to know is this. If, in the final analysis, it is the government's power to print money which is guaranteeing the survival of the system, why should not the government print money *before* an emergency arises and thereby save its taxpayers billions of dollars which banks earn in interest for creating the people's money? Money is a creature of the law, a social invention, and it rightfully belongs to the people.

As early as 1929 a proposal, called 100 percent reserve banking, was made which would return to the government its prerogative of issuing money and regulating its value. Strangely enough, however, the merits of this proposal (better control of the money supply) are discussed typically without reference to the fact that, if adopted, it could save taxpayers something like a hundred billion dollars over the lifetime of one generation.[13]

With 100 percent reserve banking, the government would not have to pay interest on government securities owned by the commercial banks. Moreover, it would be the government who would be earning the interest on the debt instruments acquired in the process of creating bank deposits. In order to hold 100 percent cash against all their deposits, the commercial banks would have to exchange their interest-earning assets with non-interest-earning cash assets issued by the government. As a result, the people would benefit from the assets used to create bank deposits for the convenience of using checks.

In the new age, when the people will own their government in fact as well as in theory, commercial banks will become nothing more than financial intermediaries to put the nation's savings to work. They will not be allowed to own the nation's central bank, literally or figuratively. They will lend existing money, make prudent investments, and in general act aboveboard as they say they do, and which some of them unfortunately do not.

When a National Monetary Center is set up to replace the overbearing Federal Reserve System, money in circulation will be increased by reducing taxes or, alternatively, by paying for additional necessary government expenditures with money the Center is authorized to print in limited amounts specified by Congress. There will be no need to redeem the dollar either with gold, silver, wheat, tin, or any other commodity. Money is redeemed every time it is accepted by the public in day-to-day transactions.

If the supply of dollars—in the form of hand-to-hand currency and of bank deposits—is made to grow in line with the growth in population and productivity, there will be demand for dollars. Dollars in huge quantities will be needed, even as they are now, to carry out transactions and to hold as valuable investments. In fact, they will serve these functions better in the future, because their value will not change from year to year.

As for the management of the National Monetary Center, it will be placed in the hands of elected officials, who will be competent, fair, and executive-minded. With the admirable salaries that they and their technical staff will receive, there will be no reason why they should not serve their nation well.

After the monetary situation is stabilized, it will be much

213

easier to pursue successfully a full-employment policy. Moreover, the psychological atmosphere will have changed to make cooperation the rule, rather than the exception. Therefore, prices and taxes will be gradually lowered as costs decline with improved productivity, and as people learn to do for others what they now expect the government to do for them. Moreover when the nation's basic land and mineral resources are publicly owned, the rents to be collected on these assets will greatly reduce the need for high rates of taxation.

The prosperity of a nation depends essentially on the inspiration, energy, confidence, and skill with which people use their labor, capital, and credit to build a better tomorrow. Switzerland is often cited as a nation which has greatly prospered even though it is not particularly well endowed with natural resources, mineral deposits, or a good soil. More recently, Japan, Germany, Taiwan, or Mexico—all countries where Mother Nature has not been too generous with her gifts—have also experienced remarkable rates of growth.

To achieve better economic performance, it is more important to reduce governmental obstacles to growth than to institute new government programs to stimulate expansion. Among these obstacles we may cite high taxes, pernicious laws encouraging oversized debt burdens, and restrictive practices in business and industry, governmental roadblocks to efficiency (of which the American farm program is a good example) and, of course, enormous outlays on armament. It stands to reason that governmental intervention and bureaucratic controls tend to be all the more distorting and dangerous when several nations are involved.

George Washington's "great rule of conduct" was to expand commercial activities to foreign nations with "as little political connection as possible." Following his rule would not have hurt either the United States or other countries. As the famous Gottfried Haberler pointed out, " . . . the possession of colonies was not a decisive or even very important factor in the development of the colonial powers. If it had been, it would be difficult to explain why colonial powers have done quite well after having lost their colonies (e.g., the Netherlands) and why Germany, Sweden, Switzerland . . . developed just as well, or better than others that had colonies."[14]

Particularly the evil, exploitative aspects of imperialism have benefited mainly the mammon forces behind the throne, not the economies or the peoples of the metropolitan countries. Even the famous Hannah Arendt, who does not ordinarily think in terms of the Hidden Hand exposed in this volume, recognized "the intimate traditional connection between imperialist politics and rule by 'invisible government' and secret agents."[15]

By referring to the more sordid aspects of international politics, we do not mean to imply that international trade has not made a tremendous contribution to economic development in the past. Nor do we imply that it does not have further significant contributions to make in the future. According to the celestial point of view, however, every nation will be better off if it works out its economic destiny without overly depending on any other nation for its survival. Furthermore, it is not necessary to lower world living standards to the least common denominator to make up for real or imaginary misdeeds of the past. The correct approach is for the more advanced nations to help the less advanced to achieve a higher living standard.

Every hair of a poor Indian, Chinese, or Congolese worker is numbered as carefully as the hairs of the most prosperous American or Western European businessman. The entire "world is the Lord's and the fullness thereof," as the Psalmist sang. Nevertheless, the United States (once it is over its diabolic ills) will probably once more demonstrate the highest standard of living, even as other nations progress, because its people have experienced the highest evolvement *soulwise*. Those who are ready for the higher existence to be available here, be they Englishmen, Jews, Germans, or Armenians, will reincarnate in the United States, or migrate here with Spirit help. Whether people realize it or not, this is also exactly what has happened in times past.

We must emphasize in this connection that in order to minimize international frictions, all nations must respect the

215

natural distances between them. Not that we preach provincialism or excessive zeal and concern for the culture of one's own country alone. We know that this attitude can lead to the most falsetto jingoism or predatory pride in the armed forces of one's nation. Provincialism differs from genuine patriotism which unifies men's desires and hopes to live together peaceably and constructively. We recognize also that the more men truly progress up into higher octaves of cultural growth, the more inclined they become to look abroad and take note of the commendable traits of attainments of other people. By advocating nationalism, we wish to curb the temptation to meddle in or dominate the affairs of other nations, which are equally holy and inviolate in the eyes of the Father.

We look forward to quite a different world than the one we have now. Communism, we predict, will collapse during the cataclysmic transition to the new age. So will the one-world movement. Thus with conspiracy and the relentless drive for power gone, politically, it will be feasible to have a safe and sensible decentralized system composed of nation-states. To maintain a stable equilibrium, these states can be aligned in three regional blocks with centers in the Western Hemisphere, Europe, and Asia.

Economically, the international system will give all nations virtually complete autonomy to pursue their own domestic policies. The current fancy talk about the necessity to coordinate economic policy-making among the major trading countries because of the growing interdependence of the world economy is more than a misconception. It is a ruse to lay one more foundation to build what the international mammon forces have wanted all along—one-world government.

Even now, if a system of flexible exchange rates in foreign currency markets were adopted, equilibrium in external payments and receipts would be established through more or less automatic adjustments in the value of the dollar, the pound, the mark, the franc, the yen, etc. Spontaneous adjustments in foreign exchange rates—which are nothing more than prices of foreign currencies—serve a balancing function similar to the one domestic prices serve in a free economy. That is to say, they eliminate deficits or surpluses in a nation's balance of payments the same way that fluctuations in prices of individual commodities eliminate shortages or surpluses of such commodities in domestic markets.

Central bankers have given every conceivable reason in objecting to flexible exchange rates to achieve balance in international payments except the most important one. Since genuine exchange rate flexibility would make the adjustments between currency values more or less automatic, it would loosen the grip the money barons have on the economic systems of the West. The higher financial powers (who now operate mainly from New York) share some, but not much, of their power with central bankers to make them feel important. Thus do they lure them to do their bidding, often without even appearing to do so. In the final analysis, therefore, it is not the people's interest but mammon's interests which are served by monetary authorities who on the surface appear to be perfectly honest and legitimate. There are those who know these things, but think it is the only way a government can be made to operate.

Nevertheless, we say that there is a better way. With the twenty principles of government and economics presented in this chapter, we have outlined this better way. We do not care what people do with these principles or when they put them into operation. We do our part and leave the rest in the hands of the Father.

FOOTNOTES

1. During a recent interview, the well-known Professor Milton Friedman explained why one must "separate the correct statement that business controls government from the false statement that business profits from that control." He granted that, "in most cases, during the earlier period of government intervention, the then existing concerns probably do benefit. But after the government control has gone on for a while, no one benefits at all." To illustrate his points, he cited the effects of the regulatory activities of the Civil Aeronautics Board and the Interstate Commerce Commission. Friedman claimed that since the CAB took over control of the trunk airlines in the 1930's, not a single new airline has been allowed to be established. Given this monopolistic restraint, evidence was cited to show why "there is no doubt that today's fares would be about half of what they actually are if there were no CAB regulation of fares." Yet the airlines are now making perhaps half a cent more profit on a dollar of sales than they would have, had they allowed more competition in this field. The remaining portion of the higher fares goes into wasteful practices. This libertarian economist pointed out also that, as a result of ICC regulations, the railroads, perhaps, did make higher profits for the first 10 or 15 years. He concluded, however, that, "in recent years, it is quite clear, the ICC has been a hindrance to the railroads' making a profit." See: Milton Friedman, "A Libertarian Speaks," *Trial, the National Legal Newsmagazine,* (January/February) 1972, p. 23.

2. C. Lee Walton, Jr., "A Balanced View by a Realist," a book review of *Technology, Management and Society* by Peter F. Drucker, in *Business Week,* (April 25, 1970) p. 10.

3. Tomlin, p. 144.

4. Ibid., p. 145.

5. Charles L. Schultze, "Is Economics Obsolete? No, Underemployed," Reprint 223, Washington D.C.: The Brookings Institution, (January 22, 1972) p. 52.

6. Ibid.

7. Rose Wilder Lane, *The Discovery of Freedom*, Man's Struggle Against Authority, New York: Arno Press & The New York Times, 1972, pp. 20-21.

8. Marshall, p. 712.

9. Allen, p. 101.

10. Milton Friedman, *Capitalism and Freedom*. The University of Chicago Press, 1962, p. 44.

11. See, for example, Milton Friedman, *Dollars and Deficits: Inflation, Monetary Policy and Balance of Payments*, Englewood Cliffs, N.J.: Prentice-Hall, 1968, pp. 126-52 and 195-205.

12. Paul A. Samuelson, *Economics*. New York: McGraw-Hill Book Co., 1958, pp. 297-98 and p. 309. Used with permission of McGraw-Hill Book Company, owner of copyright © 1955, 1958.

13. W. H. Steiner, Eli Shapiro, and Ezra Solomon, *Money and Banking*. New York: Henry Holt and Co., 1958, pp. 269-75.

14. G. Haberler, *International Trade and Economics Development*, National Bank of Egypt, Fiftieth Anniversary Commemoration Lectures, Cairo, 1959, pp. 4-5.

15. Hannah Arendt, *Imperialism, The Origins of Totalitarianism, Part Two*. "A Harvest Book," New York: Harcourt, Brace and World, Inc., 1968, p. viii.

Chapter XII

SUMMING UP

What Lies Ahead

This volume was not written as an academic exercise. It was written to explain why the world is in such turmoil, why there are even greater storms to come, and what is the way out of the crises of our age.

Through this work we meant to speak to every responsible person—from the highest to the lowest. We meant to speak as much to the President of the United States as we did to the secretary pounding her typewriter in the smallest office.

In previous chapters we revealed much about the machinations of evil forces behind the scenes. Now we shall tell you a little more. Using the concept of Atlantic union, the one-world designers, on the pretense of achieving peace, are planning a global system of controls. They want a strong world court, a universal church, a one-world monetary system, and a unified order of worldwide government.

The people of the United States in particular should be on guard against these trends. We call this nation to vigilance especially because it is still the most powerful in the world, as it was meant to be when the Father's promises were made to Ephraim and Manasseh. Moreover, we want this nation strong because we know where the world would be—the older nations as well as the newer nations—if the United States were to go down. When some of our intellectual friends begin to understand what a power vacuum a weak United States could leave in the world, we know they would play a different tune.

We realize, of course, that the Americans in the conspiracy do not want communism, at least not the Russian brand. Nor do they wish the Chinese hordes to take over. But this does not stop them from using communism and its methods to advance their overall program.

In their hearts, what these conspirators feel is this: "Let's face it, man is not capable of governing himself. It takes brains to run a government. We are the only ones who have brains. What do the people know about how governments really operate?"

We admit that, given their premises, what the plotters feel makes sense. However, their premises are widely off the mark. When man, working with God's laws, learns to create by thought, he will no longer be bound by the limitations which circumscribe his life. Thus the conspirators cannot understand how great even their own potential really is.

Moreover, they do not know how to cope with rival factions in their group. It is normal for men of good will to cooperate with each other to achieve a common end. The evil ones have a demonic urge to flight among themselves. So it is that they eat each other's dinners, drink each other's wines, smoke each other's cigars, and still think, "We wonder how we can get this other bunch out of our hair."

In the final stages of their takeover program, when the conspirators appear to stand together more than ever as a group, they will, in reality, be more divided than they are now. The international mammon forces think they have much control over the Russian Bear. The Russian rulers, however, think they can in due time shake loose from all foreign influence. Regardless of what favors are given to them out of the pocketbooks of a bemused American public, they plan one day to strike to win when they are good and ready.

As we mentioned earlier, the conspirators do not yet control the Chinese Dragon. On the recent "peace" mission of the American President, at least a third of the United States would have been offered to China, if China would sign over controls to international mammon. China still wills her own way. The Chinese rulers may be barbaric, but they are not stupid. They have their own plans to rule the world. Nor can Japan be trusted to follow international mammon's lead. If war broke out tomorrow, Japan would join the Red Chinese as the oriental enemies of the occidental world.

There are those who would build world peace through law. What can such law accomplish when the Russian Bear begins to throw a scare into the council of nations? It is not international obligations, but the Chinese Dragon, which stalls the Bear from making overly hasty moves. However, when the nations of the Common Market rearm, the Bear, in alarm, will prepare for an onslaught. And as the threat of atomic warfare stalls the overall conflagration, the one-worlders hope to speed up their action of spreading fears, lies, and despair, in order to effect their insidious takeover.

World peace through law means nothing without government to enforce such law. Nor is global government possible without a global system of money and of economic policy. Steps in this direction have already been taken with diabolic cleverness. As a recent issue of Chase Manhattan's bi-monthly economic review pointed out, "A world central bank is evolving. Indeed, in some respects, it is already here. This is the conclusion drawn by former Federal Reserve Chairman William McChesney Martin, Jr."[1]

The International Bank for Reconstruction and Development (the World Bank) and allied international institutions have been busy at work since World War II building the infrastructure for worldwide direct investments by multinational corporations. More recently ecological issues have been raised to unify the world economically as a major step toward unifying the world politically.[2]

On another front, the evil forces have been pressing for United Nations treaties and conventions which would make a nation's treatment of its own people no longer its exclusive concern. Among these the worst one so far is the Genocide Convention passed by the U.N. General Assembly in 1948, but not yet ratified by the U.S. Senate.

To illustrate how much this convention can be abused to restrict national sovereignty, it may be sufficient to point out no more than one example. Shortly after the U.N. passed this convention, the Civil Rights Congress accused the United States before the United Nations of Negro genocide. They charged the United States with the "willful creation of conditions making for premature death, poverty, and disease among Negroes—because some Negroes live in slums!"[3]

It is undoubtedly possible to use such legal ruses to build a world government. Moreover, if, in the meantime, people are demoralized by artificially created scandals such as Watergate and are offered unlimited opportunities for drugs, pornography, and other ways to stimulate the lusts of the flesh, popular resistance to political takeovers would be thereby greatly diminished.

Let us see, therefore, what we may expect when some form of political integration of the world is finally engineered, through these and other devious ways. This may be particularly interesting because those who favor global union are often regarded as idealists. Creating such illusions is not a new phenomenon by any means. Since the French Revolution, the Illuminist plans for a new world order have been made as appealing to men of learning as the fruit of the tree of life was made appealing to Eve in the mythical Garden of Eden.

The great philosopher, Immanuel Kant, for example, had hailed the French Revolution with such enthusiasm that he had exclaimed, "I can now say like Simeon, 'Lord, let thy servant depart in peace, for mine eyes have seen thy salvation.'" We note further that when Kant wrote his essay on *Perpetual Peace*, to him the chances for universal peace seemed better than ever. History has shown how wrong he was.[4]

Even the erudite Hayek, quoted in Chapter IX, had thought that "in Germany it was largely people of *good will* (italics mine), men who were admired and held up as models in the democratic countries, who prepared the way for, if they did not actually create, the forces which now stand for everything they detest."[5]

For more ancient references to appealing but false teachings, we may turn to our Bibles, where it is written that, in the days of the end, "false prophets will arise and show great signs and wonders, so as to lead astray, if possible, even the elect," (Matthew, 24:24).

Knowing these things, what can we realistically expect to be the fruits of peace through world law or government the idealists advocate? First we can expect economic conditions to deteriorate and eventually to stagnate. This would be a natural consequence of regimenting and taxing individual effort more and more to bring conditions everywhere to equal an acceptable world standard.

Centralized controls—be they national or international—do not generate economic progress. They contribute to economic retrogression. Does not the experience of Great Britain illustrate this point? Selling their birthright for a mess of porridge will leave the people with an empty bowl. This is not a piece of poetic fiction. It is a spiritual law.

Secondly, in a world held together by force of government, people would become more and more dehumanized. Dostoyevsky had prophesied what would happen when the socialist dream would come true, saying, "Men would suddenly realize that they have no life any more, no freedom of spirit, no freedom of will or personality, that somebody has stolen all that from them. People will become depressed and bored."

In the workrooms of Mother Nature, every individual evolves differently from every other individual. Can you find two fingerprints out of three billion which are exactly alike? One cannot deny the uniqueness of the individual without paying a tremendous price.

The march toward socialistic equality has already taken its toll. As the philosopher-psychiatrist, Dr. Erich Fromm, observed, "Our contemporary Western society, in spite of its material, intellectual and political progress, is increasingly less conducive to mental health, and tends to undermine the inner security, happiness, reason and the capacity for love in the individual."[6]

Expanding on this, the author of *Brave New World Revisited*,

Aldous Huxley, pointed out that "the really hopeless victims of mental illness are to be found among those who appear to be most normal . . . living without fuss in a society to which if they were fully human beings, they ought not to be adjusted."[7]

Thirdly, in a one-world political order, thought control would be practiced with greater thoroughness and on a wider scale than ever before. There is already more manipulation of the popular mind than most people realize.

Consider what has happened to freedom of the press. There was a time when every major Western city had a large number of competing local daily newspapers. Their editors somehow found it possible to express a great variety of independent opinions on every conceivable subject. Now, even in the largest metropolitan centers, there are only a few daily papers which look more and more alike.

This trend toward a distressing sameness in the field of mass communications is in sharp contrast to the greater and greater product differentiation in virtually every other industry. There are those who claim that the disappearance of divergent points of view from the market place of ideas is purely an economic phenomenon, related to the rising costs of publication. The unpleasant truth is that most of the channels of mass communication are now effectively controlled to block resistance to the takeover programs of international mammon.

Conducting a large "smearbund" operation through clever editors, columnists, critics and book reviewers, radio and TV commentators, entertainers, motion picture producers, and TV program directors, the mammon interests make all their serious opponents look ridiculous, stupid, or malicious. In academic circles, they use highly sophisticated pressure tactics to silence all those who speak of a conspiracy. One favorite trick is to call such brave individualists paranoids.

The mass media—who rely on advertisements for survival—are of course subject to greater economic censorship than the universities and other opinion leaders elsewhere. But ways and means have been devised to have almost everyone whose opinion

225

counts support the current trends or at least remain in a harmless neutral position.

As the eminent historian Harry Elmer Barnes observed, "In Communist Russia and Nazi Germany, as well as Fascist Italy and China, the tyrannical rulers found it necessary to suppress all opposition thought . . . in the United States, with almost complete freedom of the press, speech and information down to the end of 1941, great numbers of Americans followed the official propaganda line with no compulsion whatever."[8] Things have not been any better since then.

Thought control in the United States has indeed been a remarkable operation. The public at large neither knows, nor seems to care, whether there are powers behind the scenes who want them to think along certain directions and not in others.[9] Oswald Spengler had written: "Formerly a man did not dare to think freely. Now he dares, but cannot; his will to think is only a willingness to think to order . . . a higher will puts together the picture of their world for them."

Thus, as the aims and plans of the one-world designers keep changing, the public thinks the *same* communist system is a terrible menace to be fought at one time and a force with which to cooperate at another. The taboo concepts of yesterday—such as one-world money, a universal church, government by executive orders—become the key concepts of today with so few wondering what on earth made these changes come about anyway. Events to make the new trends appear necessary are arranged behind the scenes so carefully that even we who know how these things operate are tempted to think that what is happening was a natural outcome of world events.

The millions who blindly do the bidding of the hidden forces do not really want to know about the plots they may unwittingly be involved in. Some say, therefore, that they are not completely innocent, or very bright, for that matter.

As far as we are concerned, we do not condemn or condone. We merely observe how the desire for quick rewards or undeserved power and glory makes people susceptible to the evil influence of Satan's cohorts. When the truth finally surfaces one day, oh, how many red faces there will be!

In an afterword to *1984*, Erich Fromm, who finds Orwell's "doublethink" prevalent in the West also, points out that "in a successful manipulation of the mind, the person is no longer saying the opposite of what he thinks, but he thinks the opposite of what is true."[10]

Consider the notion that one can eliminate wars by eliminating nation-states or nationalist feelings. Is this not as absurd as believing that one can eliminate poverty by printing more money? The existence of nations like the United States, France, India, or China is no more a cause of tension in the world as a shortage of money is a cause of poverty in this as in any other nation. Yet through the sheer power of repetition in the mass communications media, this idea has already gained acceptance.

Psychological research has demonstrated that, under normal circumstances, one gets better results by positive reinforcement of desirable behavior than by threats of punishing undesirable behavior. In view of this, the forms of thought control in the future will probably take increasingly pleasant forms, which of course would not make them less evil. Nor will thought control be confined to repeating the "big lie" or confusing the public with "doublethink" in the mass media.

In his fascinating book, *Brave New World Revisited*, Aldous Huxley has shown what a variety of forms political and commercial propaganda can take. Anyone interested in finding out what a despotic government could do with the truth should read about the amazing new techniques of chemical persuasion (through drugs which increase suggestibility and lower psychological resistance), subconscious persuasion (through subliminal projection, hypnopaedia (suggestion during the light sleep stage), and brainwashing (indoctrination during appropriate stages of nervous exhaustion).[11]

Fourthly, when power is centralized in a world body, as international mammon moves to converge with the Reds on the pretext of achieving peace, we foresee the rulers becoming more and more mentally deranged. Too much power has done this before to overly ambitious men. In fact, on the basis of their extensive researches, the famous Pitirim Sorokin and Walter Lunden have concluded that "the moral behavior of ruling groups tends to be more criminal and sub-moral than that of the ruled strata of the same society." Moreover, Sorokin and Lunden found the ruling groups to "contain a larger proportion of the extreme mental types of the gifted and the mentally sick than the rank and file of the ruled populations."[12]

As power is abused, we may also expect a drying up of the stream of inventions without which there could have been no material progress in the first place. As these creative sparks go out, the stagnation of the world economy we had warned about earlier would become more and more hopeless. Constructive inventions are never accidental. They are the product of divine inspiration received through the sixth sense of inventors. Such inspiration will not be given to be used by those who would rule the world for Satan and his cohorts.

If a "citizen" could not stand the stagnation, exploitation, or tyranny of a world state, what could he possibly do? Where could he go? How much power would he have to change that which would be degrading to his very soul?

Sooner or later, all the weapons in the world would end up in the hands of the government; none would be allowed to remain in the hands of the people. Under such circumstances, who indeed would guard the guardians of the people?

The peace the idealists would establish through such a universal state would soon become a universal war in disguise of the state against the people. What is the purpose of war if not to impose on the vanquished the stronger will of the conqueror? Would not a world government have every means to impose its overmastering will on all the people at all times?

Think about these things as never before. True, free will is forever the order of the day. Yet it is also true that time is running out. There will be such stupendous changes in the conditions of earth life that the evolutionary process as we have known it to date will be abruptly interrupted. Thus in a thousand years, we are told, there will be such vast cataclysmic events as to make stars literally perish and reassemble in the presence of the Father. In comparison with these events, the momentous geologic changes which we had said will accompany the transition to the Millenial age will seem like minor upsets. At that portentious time, out of the mouth of the Father will come a new creation. Those who have graduated from their earthly labors will be taken to this more nearly perfect planet, so they may learn higher lessons without being addicted to the pleasure-pain experience. Woe unto those who will not by that time have advanced sufficiently to adjust to the rarefied atmosphere of the new location! They will have to return to a completely devastated earth or a planet like the earth for thousands of more cycles of rebirth up the ladder of Jacob's vision.

The Father cannot or will not destroy Himself. Nor will He destory His children, who are literally parts of Him. Therefore the whole painful process of evolution will go on and on wherever life can find a habitat till the Father's will is done.

We repeat, everyone is free to grow at their own pace. Still we point out that human beings do not have forever to make the grade on this plane. If they allow their growth to be stunted by despotic rule, they cannot and will not be ready to graduate when their school of pleasure-pain experience disintegrates.

Are these events too far in the future for us to think about now? Then let us focus on the immediate future, when we must face the consequences of the wrongdoings of our not-too-distant past.

In our recent wars, we fought atheistic aggression on the one hand, and on the other, we allowed blatant infiltration of dedicated enemies into our government, into our churches, into our schools, and into our overall culture. The blinding desire for easy profits and the callousness of conducting business as usual in times of national peril has *overshadowed* the good we have done. And so the evil rooster has come home to roost. *Thus we stand today in the shadow of world dictatorship!*

Nor is this the only danger we have to face. As the evil forces turn the world upside down, they will leave behind them a growing trail of havoc and destruction. We would not dwell on these so that they may not dominate our thoughts. We would rather brush them aside and abide in Him until the Father's Will is done. Yet burying our heads in the sand like ostriches would not mitigate the disorders that are sure to come, or shorten the days of calamity. Forewarned is forearmed. That is why we feel it is our duty to sound the needed warnings in the face of all opposing forces and pray that the people may wake up.

What Can the People Do?

When their father Israel died, the brothers of Joseph were afraid that Joseph would hate them for having sold him into Egypt. But it is written that Joseph said to them, "You meant evil against me, but God meant it for good, to bring it about that many people should be kept alive, as they are today," (Genesis 60:20). In this text we can see described the law of transmutation which can turn the evil intentions of man to the fulfillment of His divine word. The same law may be put to work again to turn the evil plots of mammon into the wholesome plans of God.

How can this be done? It can be done by placing Him before us in all we do, and by giving His word power through belief, faith, and proper action where indicated.

As we said in Chapter I, God does not punish; He educates. In order to have mankind advance to greater heights of accomplishment, the small, parochial people had to be somehow jolted out of their shells. They had to stretch their awareness far enough to be concerned with the welfare of their brothers, even though they live thousands of miles away. The turmoil in the world since World War I certainly helped to jolt literally millions out of their shells. They no longer ask for whom the bell tolls. They know it tolls for them.

The much greater upsets which are to come will educate many million more to understand as never before the meaning of the brotherhood of man under the Fatherhood of God. Through this harsh, but effective, way the human family is being conditioned to desire relief from the mounting tensions. In no other way can they reach for the heights of the promised Millenial age.

Man does not understand how great his potential is. Nor does he realize how much the Heavenly Host rely on him to accomplish His work on earth. Even the *timing* of the reappearance of the Christ *depends* upon the attitudes of men. Can you conceive this to be true? Yes, this event depends on how fervently men desire it, and how willing they would be to work with Him when He comes. This new teaching, which was implicit in what was said before, is now made explicit, so that no one will miss the point.

Is it not almost self-evident that man cannot have his Millenium unless the negative forces in control are eliminated first? Therefore man's mind and man's will must be bent to that effort—and the sooner, we say, the better. It is true that success lies in the hands of the Host. But the deserving and earning of this success lies in man's attitudes, man's will, man's courage, and man's actions. We must do our work first so those on the celestial planes can consummate theirs. We provide them a spiritual ladder, so to speak, without which they *cannot* climb down to and up from our plane of thought.

The first thing then that people can do to shorten the dark days is to work on their attitudes. And what are the essentials of a righteous attitude? We name the following: (a) To resolve never, never, never to accept, at least in one's heart, the evil influence, (b) to view the negative forces with a passive (harmless as a dove) militancy, knowing that their days are numbered, (c) to believe the promises of the Father, (d) to stand firm in the right, willing to take action when and where called upon, provided the action is legally and ethically proper. As world conditions continue to deteriorate, the time will come when many will find such an attitude to be the only means with which to keep their mental balance.

In this one short volume, we have offered much new knowledge, beyond what is considered the norm. After one learns to view the world through this new understanding, it becomes preposterous to want to continue business as usual.

In the eyes of the Almighty, particularly in international relations, the distinction between the sheep and the goats has by no means been erased. It is moral blindness for the sheep to say we must normalize relations with the goats and trade with them or work with them for mutual benefit. The goats do not believe in live and let live. They look for ways to victimize the sheep. The goats are known by their works. They cannot hide their nature. The sheep who see them and who see their works are frightened. Thus they cannot relax in their company. How then can there be peace with the goats and the sheep mixed in one fold?

The sheep can never gain by placating the goats, who have shown their true colors, hoping thereby to achieve a greater good later on. This has been the error of Franklin D. Roosevelt; it has been the error of every president since FDR. What exactly have the American people gained by their international involvements with elements whose shameful records are public knowledge?

We are not opposed to genuine international cooperation on every front. We say, let nations meet in brotherhood and understanding. Let them share and share alike, if they so wish, the fruits of their thinking and of their labors. Let them go back to their native lands better for having had such communion. But let them leave each others' lands holy and inviolate to their own, united only in Spirit, not in government.

We advocate strong military defenses for the United States and other nations threatened by external enemies who respect nothing other than force. We quote the living Christ when we say, "Be ye not fooled by hypocrisy. When a strong man, *armed*, keepeth his palace, his goods are at peace."[13]

Similarly, we recommend government firm enough to drive crime off the streets. When evildoers are chastised on every turn, they will not dare to disturb the peace. What better way can there be of loving a criminal than to save him from his own folly?

Above all, people should be warned not to be captured by the one-world sentiment. From here on everything which leads in

232

that direction will be made to seem either compelling or enticing. As an antidote, therefore, we would advise bold and resolute stands against further concentrations of power, economic, religious, or political. Moreover, we would advise imaginative attempts to expose and curb the seven satanic takeovers. These things can be done. Some patriots have already done so in various subtle and not-so-subtle ways. Miracles are possible when issues are raised against great odds. They are not possible when there is not even a struggle to defend one's birthright from those who would trample on it whenever it suits their convenience.

Another desirable avenue would be to elect righteous men to public office, especially at the State and local level, where they can do more to influence policy. A parallel approach would be to back leaders in every field who are willing to take ethical stands and battle evil with proper means.

Still another way is to speak or write the words of correction whenever there is an attempt to distort the truth. Also in order is fervent prayer and eternal vigilance . . . the price of liberty. All these methods involve certain difficulties and obstacles. Those who dare to take right actions for selfless reasons find out, however, that the divine help they receive exceeds their fondest dreams.

We are approaching an era of brilliance, when the world shall shine with the Father's glory. It would be well, therefore, for people to accustom their eyes to the light. In Chapter XI, we described what the order of the future would be after the light of Christ begins to reign. Why not start *now* doing on a small scale what it will be possible to do later on a large scale.

More than a hundred years ago, a brilliant French economist, Mr. Frédéric Bastiat, pointed out that, in the economic sphere, an act, an institution, or a policy produces not one but a series of effects. He wrote:

Of these effects the first only is immediate; it appears simultaneously with its cause, *it is seen*. The others are only developed successively, *they are not seen;* it is well if they are *foreseen.* Between a bad and good economist all the difference is this: one considers only the effect *seen;* the other considers both the effect which is seen, and effects which ought to be *foreseen.*

But this difference is enormous, for it happens almost always that, when the immediate consequence is favorable the ulterior consequences are pernicious and *vice versa.* Hence it follows that the bad economist seeks a small present good, which will be succeeded by a great future evil—while the true economist seeks a great future good, at the risk of a small present evil.

Thus it is not only in economics, but in hygiene and in morals. It happens often that the sweeter are the first fruits of a habit, the more bitter are those which follow. For example, debauchery, idleness, prodigality.

Two very different masters teach the same lesson—Experience and Foresight. Experience teaches efficiently, but very severely. . . . For this harsh teacher, I would substitute, as far as possible, one more gentle—Foresight![14]

Since the days of Franklin Delano Roosevelt's New Deal, America appears to have decided to learn from the harsher teacher, experience, avoiding the more gentle. Had foresight been his teacher, FDR would have exposed the evil forces of international mammon, as he actually came close to doing. His administration and subsequent administrations would have followed a policy of righteous national leadership, instead of getting enmeshed in sinister conspiracies to rule the world. Equal justice for all would have been achieved through honest law honestly interpreted and through responsible, individual action, not through clever political promises, countervailing power, confrontation politics, and angry movements, which sooner or later cause injury, recrimination, and chaos.

We do not deny that the use of harmful means to achieve good objectives did at times have immediate favorable effects which were clearly *seen.* We say, however, that they also had and will continue to have, extremely injurious consequences—some discussed in earlier chapters—which should also have been *foreseen*.

Ture, we said that time is running short. But we did not say, nor do we think, that it is too late to change the trend. Otherwise we would have kept our peace. Instead, we wrote this volume to correct the errors of President Franklin D. Roosevelt, to show a new and higher way for the people to follow. And now that we have written it, we are looking for the honest men and noble women who would make the necessary commitment, put forth the required effort, and with God's help, stem the satanic influence that this nation under God may start to move once more in the right direction.

What we have proposed in this volume may seem a little farfetched and perhaps what we advocate is a little harder course to follow than people appear to want at this time. But it is the only course which we think will save the day. It is the straight and narrow path the ancient biblical prophets spoke of in somewhat different words. It is the way that the good economist, Frédéric Bastiat, would recommend to receive "a great future good, at the risk of a small present evil." In short, it is the more demanding but the nobler plan of the Father which leads to the Millenium.

What of the opposite path, the more popular, easier path which is paved with good intentions? Is it not obvious where this path will lead? We say that it is headed from the welfare state to the police state and then to the slave state. Along the way, the obstacles to complete, though subtle, political tyranny will continue to be removed one by one. This could take place amazingly enough with the blessing of most major religious denominations. Can you sense how misguided and weak are the spiritual leaders who cohabit with the enemy in their minds? As the universal church, now in the planning stage, becomes more and more powerful, it would allow *no* churches to exist outside of its pale. Bibles could be confiscated and become as rare as they are in the Soviet Union today.

Is it impossible for these things to happen? How many people thought Nazism could take over Germany ten or fifteen years before Hitler was raised to power? Conditions in the West could soon become worse than they were in Germany during the 1920's. Violence could become so rampant, taxes and inflation of the currencies could assume such alarming proportions, and corruption could spread so far that people would virtually beg to be taken over by anyone who promises them a little stability and order.

No man can serve two masters. Neither can one espouse two conflicting principles of economics and government—as it is the fashion today—with one clumsy confused embrace. In the end, one or the other must give way. Nor can the choice be avoided. Those who would straddle the fence and wait to jump to the winning side will end in the celestial orders lower than those who sincerely support *either* side.

Let people attend and support their local churches by all means. They are needed there. But let them banish the thought that church membership or attendance will automatically place them on the right side of the fence. Churches are no longer elevators to divine protection, let alone to Heaven. Only the righteous deserve and will earn exemption from the sting of the troubled days that are bound to come.

The leaders of some of the larger denominations particularly should see to it that the next generation does not turn to them in resentment, accusing them of withholding knowledge they possessed, but which for reasons known only to themselves, they decided not to give out. We speak no further on this. Let each one face his own karma, according to the Father's eternal justice. This moral law of cause and effect is God's initial and immutable law, in constant operation.

We have a very deep-seated difference with our economist friends. They would take man's wants and desires for granted and go on from there to put his economic house in order. We say that if man's economic house does not change his wants, his desires and his basic attitudes, it fails to fulfill its divine purpose.

In the Father's plan, man is destined to change and to

grow—eventually, as Jesus said, to be as great as He is and even greater. In view of this, economic and social arrangements which have evolved over many, many centuries and millenia should do more than satisfy the current selfish wants of misguided men. They should provide him with stepping stones to a higher and more altruistic way of life.

Given a fair chance, men are able to transcend their animalistic limitations. They are able to rule themselves by mastering their passions, their temperaments, and their unseemly appetites. They are able to balance their lives and overcome their weaknesses. Through the Christ teachings presented here and elsewhere they can express and ennoble the wonderful God power that lies dormant at the very core of their being. By changing their thoughts, we predict men will do these things in the next thousand years. We predict further that the fantastic riches of the Dead Sea area—over which the evil forces are now fighting—will be discovered and used by the "true Israel" (the chosen people from all twelve tribes) for the benefit of all mankind. It is this combination of inner riches with outer treasures which will make it possible for man to have his Economics of the New Age.

Finally, we offer the most glorious key to genuine success which economists seldom speak of. This key, simply stated, is love. Without love there is darkness. And yet there is no darkness except as we close our eyes to the light. Love is a vibration of infinitely higher rate than any known to our present world of science. It is able to transmute and recreate all things that feel its power. There can literally be no limitation to its power.

One must equate love as righteousness in all things. One cannot bow to evil or wrongdoing in the guise of love and have love manifest. When one insists on righteousness, when one can say yea to righteousness and nay to wrongdoing with great firmness of purpose, then we can say, "Greater love hath no man!"

Patience is another manifestation of love. It has no kinship to

237

resignation. The former is positive, the latter negative. Humor is also an essential ingredient of love. It brightens up many a life. In this volume, however, we have stressed the aspect of love we call understanding. Cherish this understanding, apply it, share it, and spread it to the far corners of the earth. Be the first one to benefit from its wisdom by giving of yourself and sharing your substance to the last penny you can afford that the world may rise up and call you blessed. Amen.

FOOTNOTES

1. "Toward a World Central Bank," *Business in Brief*, No. 94 (October 1970), p. 6.

2. Wait and see how the energy crisis and food shortages will also be used to promote world government.

3. "Genocide," *The Dan Smoot Report* vol. 12:31 (August 1, 1966), p. 155.

4. Tomlin, p. 222.

5. Hayek, *The Road to Serfdom*, p. 3.

6. Huxley, p. 20.

7. Ibid., p. 21.

8. Barnes, p. 9.

9. See this connection: "The Media: A Look at Establishment Newspapers," *American Opinion* (September 1970), and "Teleslick: Television and the Mass Slicks," *American Opinion* (October 1970).

10. George Orwell, *1984,* with an Afterword by Erich Fromm "A Signet Classic," New York: New American Library, Inc., 1961, p. 265.

11. Huxley, pp. 58-95.

12. Sorokin and Lunden, p. 37.

13. Lewis, p. 285.

14. Frédéric Bastiat, *What Is Seen and What Is Not Seen: or Political Economy In One Lesson* trans. W.B. Hodgson, London: W.H. Smith and Son, and Manchester: Alexander Ireland and Co., 1859, pp. 5-6.

Chapter XIII

POINT, COUNTERPOINT

When people I know found out what I had been writing about, they started asking me questions or expressing their opinions on my project. In the course of these conversations, it occurred to me that if these thoughts had crossed their minds, they may also cross the minds of my readers. Therefore I decided to include some of them with appropriate answers in the last chapter of my book. If my readers have further questions of their own which they would have me answer, they may write to me at:

910 Crescent Drive
Alexandria, Virginia 22302
United States of America

I hope to be able to comply with the requests made.

About the Spiritual Perspective

Q. "Your book is quite odd. An amalgamation between hard practical economic theory and a nebulous philosophy of 'divine plan' will not come off."

A. Woe be it unto those for whom it will not come off! Come, let us reason together. Is there or is there not a God who reigns over our world? If He reigns, does He not ordain? If the Father's Will were done in every area, all things would tend toward perfection. The fact that man's hard, practical economic theories are failing to solve his problems indicates that there is something "nebulous" about man's present thoughts—not about our philosophic conceptions.

Q. "Who are the divine forces you mention and what do they have to do with world events?"

A. They are souls like you and me. Let us start from one of our basic premises. People do not die; they simply pass over. They pass from one side of the veil of mortality to the other. There are many reasons for wanting to come down to earth life as there are individuals. A select few, however, come mainly to serve the human race, or a branch of the race, in some significant way. These we call the divine forces.

They do the Father's work whether in the body or out of the body. Out of the body, they inspire and guide kindred souls who have come to earth on missions similar to theirs. They may be artists, statesmen, scientists, teachers, soldiers, or businessmen. They may be Jewish, Christian, Hindu, or temporarily atheists. We know them by their fruits, not by their outward appearances. They are truly the salt of the earth. Without them, civilizations would decay and life would lose its savor.

Historians say that great leaders rise to meet the crises of their age. Such persons do not rise; they are sent. Just as a receiver is asked to run into a designated position to complete a pass that a quarterback is planning to throw, the divine forces are sent by their companions in heaven to certain places at just the right times to meet the specific challenges which are foreseen to arise.

In the same way, the satanic forces also come into flesh and go back again to do their work as they choose as directed by their cohorts on the etheric planes. Historians do not know or want to know about what takes place behind the veil of mortality. Consequently they regard the most carefully coordinated moves as accidents of history. Shakespeare, however, felt otherwise, when he wrote, "I hold the world but as the world, Gratiano,—a stage where man must play a part."

Q. "Why do you propose going back to a religious conception of life when you know that all religions have been riddled with dogmatism, superstition, and fanaticism?"

A. Our conception is not religious; it is spiritual. We advocate no dogmas, nor do we hold a brief for any particular religion. We point to spiritual laws which can be tested, as one would test a chemical reaction in a laboratory. It would be a mistake to equate our philosophy with the sophistries, conjectures, and dogmas of so-called theologians. Our philosophy is logical and individualistic; it does not lean on or depend upon external authorities, infallible or otherwise. Our leadership is by example, not by coercion, or salesmanship. Had others believed as we do, there would have been no religious dogmas, superstitions, or fanaticism at any time.

Q. "I did not understand what you were saying at first because I could not conceive that anyone with your background could take Old Testament myths and fables seriously enough to let them influence your judgment on current events."

A. Wait a minute now. Perhaps after seeing predictions made more than three thousand years ago come to pass in modern times, it should be inconceivable that intelligent people like you should continue to call them myths and fables.

We recognize, of course, that often truth in the Bible is expressed in allegorical, rather than in literal form. It is also natural for errors to have crept in through numerous translations. Moreover, what Emperor Constantine and others have done to eliminate from the Bible explicit references to reincarnation, to give to ecclesiastic authorities the keys to the Kingdom, is still another story. All the same, we revere Holy Scriptures as a source of much spiritual as well as practical knowledge.

Q. "Are you not saying that your way is the only way? Does not this type of intolerance lead to tyranny, to which you seem to be strongly opposed?"

A. The different races, nationalities, religions, social traditions and cultures provide the many ways to reach the heights. Through trial and error, over many lives, goes the evolutionary process that lifts man to more glorious states. Those who aspire to the highest, however, sooner or later must take the path of the One Who said, "I am the way, the truth, and the life; no one comes to the Father but by me." (John 14:6)

Is it intolerance which makes a graduate student want to attend higher classes than kindergarten or sixth grade? Allowing each one to take the path placed naturally in one's way does not lead to tyranny. It is treating tyrants as the moral equals of righteous men which does. Lack of belief in spiritual truth also opens the door to tyranny. If man is simply an animal whose life is shaped by an accidental environment, why bother standing on ceremony to assure each man his freedom and dignity as an individual?

Q. "Can you really be objective in your judgments when you are bound by one particular faith?"

A. We question whether one can be objective if one does not have a faith like ours. If a person believes, nay, knows that right makes might, as we do, he does not allow fears to influence or dominate his thoughts. On the other hand, a person who is afraid of the reactions others may have to his judgments loses his objectivity very fast. The process involved may not even be conscious. Nevertheless, it is very real.

Q. "Your views are not scientific."

A. Is it unscientific to speak of things the scientists do not yet know about? Nothing we have said contradicts the findings of science. On the contrary, we have quoted scientific authorities whenever appropriate to support our point of view. We are great believers in science and rationality. At the same time, we know that science and reason, when divorced from a high spiritual understanding, can go off the track and can be badly misused. Thus, instead of depreciating science, we have tried to enhance its value by showing its true peace in the greater reality of life.

Q. "Frankly I am not too anxious for the Messiah to come because I know of the terrible things it is written will happen in the 'days of the end.' If these things would happen a hundred years from now, that I would not mind too much. But personally I am not anxious for Him to come right now."

A. After the impending physical and moral cataclysms finally start to disturb your comfort perhaps you will be more anxious for Him to come.

Q. "I really do see how you can make a moral issue out of every social dilemma we face. Nobody has yet found all the answers to the problems of a complex and technological society. We have a lot more learning to do. In the meantime, are you not confusing social problems with moral problems?"

A. In 1937, when Nazi propaganda was at its height, an American philanthropist founded an Institute of Propaganda Analysis in the United States. This Institute sponsored several textbooks at the high school and university levels. When the war came, the Allied governments started engaging in psychological warfare of their own. Thus, as Aldous Huxley said, it became a bit tactless to continue such an enterprise. Even before the institute was closed in 1941, there were many objections to its activities.[1]

Some educators claimed that propaganda analysis would make adolescents unduly cynical. Military authorities feared the training of recruits might be jeopardized if they start to analyze the logic of the orders they receive. Clergymen were opposed to propaganda analysis because they thought it may undermine belief and reduce church attendance. Advertisers objected to such instruction, fearing it might undermine brand loyalty and reduce sales.

As long as people feel this way, how can there be effective education for responsible self-government? In fact, it is often taken for granted that people will stretch the truth when their personal interests are at stake. They say, "We don't blame them for saying things which make them look good. We only wish we would have an opportunity to do half as well ourselves."

Even without special instruction in analyzing propaganda, if people would stop and think, they would realize how many distortions are introduced into most pronouncements on public policy issues. These become increasingly obvious or glaring to those who know of the satanic takeovers mentioned in earlier chapters.

According to official explanations, for example, revenue sharing was designed to transfer power from the federal government to state and local governments. Thinking of it objectively will make it clear that revenue sharing will have just the opposite effect. Having to come to Washington to get their money would tend to make the states and cities more dependent on the federal government. It would not help them become independent of Washington. When federal aid was first offered to local school districts, it was also said that there would be no strings attached to such aid. Subsequent history showed how much credence can be attached to statements of this type.

Those who benefit from financial and political machinations at the expense of others do not realize that one way or another they must pay back every cent they acquire by less than rightful means. So they do or say nothing to correct the situation. They feel, "Why should we volunteer any information? It is not our fault that the world is not perfect yet. Let others watch out for their interests, as we watch out for ours." When more and more people take this attitude, who ends up being the losers? The very same people who thought they could benefit from their indifference to the problems others have.

It is now widely recognized that most of the community action programs of the U.S. government have been dismal failures. These efforts were based on the notion that federal funds could be used effectively to bring about social change despite the resistance and disapproval of local communities and local government organizations. The poor themselves were to help plan and lead local action groups. These were often to be organized against the wishes of the majority of the people who were expected to subsidize them.

The federal community action programs were based on the Mobilization for Youth effort designed to combat juvenile delinquency in New York's East Side. As Daniel P. Moynihan pointed out, the MFY was already in crisis at the time the federal programs patterned on the MFY were being launched. Why did the government go ahead with them anyway? Evidently because the public officials in charge had other motives than helping the poor.

Moreover, according to Moynihan, the social scientists who were acting as advisers would not admit the limits of their knowledge in prescribing measures to guide practical conduct.

In analyzing why the community action programs aborted, reference was also made to "the pressure to take all action on a national scale," and the "apparent necessity to overpromise and oversell an idea in order to gain political acceptance of it."[2]

Why are we mentioning these things? To show that we are not confusing moral problems with social problems. Rather we are pointing to moral failures which aggravate or prevent the solution of social problems.

Q. "How do you know that your revelations are authentic?"

A. First, because the things revealed or prophesied work out in event. Second, because they explain both the past and present with an amazing consistency, unmatched by other theories. Third, because they are in harmony with the perennial philosophy expressed in all the higher religions. Fourth, because they are edifying, consoling, and beautiful from an esthetic point of view. Fifth, because the recorder and channel who have received these ESP revelations have had no personal interest in falsifying the information given to them. On the contrary, they have done this work at considerable personal sacrifice. Let me ask you, "Do you have any reason for thinking that they are not authentic?"

We are not suggesting that people should accept what we say because of the infallibility of our heavenly sources. Let people read what we say, square it with the facts they know, test it, evaluate it, be as skeptical as they wish in the process—as we were at first. Then let them reach their own conclusions.

Q. "I do not know what you mean when you speak of righteousness in connection with economic or political issues. Why not back policies which work?"

A. "Integrity and firmness is all I can promise; these shall never forsake me although I may be deserted by all men." Do you know who said that? George Washington. Contrast this with what our public leaders say and do today, and you will know what we mean by righteousness or the lack of it in reference to politics and economics.

We live in a universe of cause and effect. "Be not deceived; God is not mocked: for whatsoever a man soweth, that shall he also reap." (Galatians 6:7) This is not an idle statement. It is an expression of a universal law. An act or a thought which is not righteous reverberates throughout the universe. In the process, it upsets many a delicate balance in human or physical relationships.

By the same token, the influence of every sincere thought, prayer, or act of a righteous man travels round and round the world, healing, harmonizing, and perfecting every disturbed relationship. With our present methods of science, cause and effect in these fields cannot yet be linked with precise mathematical accuracy. The day will come, however, when effects will be seen to flow from their causes with much greater clarity.

In the meantime, let us look at the record. Did George Washington's policies fail to work? He was not a military or political genius, or overly talented, for that matter. Yet he struggled against great odds and won. Did the policies of Abraham Lincoln, Honest Abe, who placed principle above expediency, fail to work? On the other hand, are the policies of pragmatic modern statesmen—who will rise above principle at the drop of a hat—working in our times?

Q. "If these prophecies are from God, why have not people heard about them?"

A. Many people have heard about them. Whether they have been open to them or passed the word on to others is another question. A chain is no stronger than its weakest link. Following blindly the intellectuals and the theologians of their times, many simply rejected the new doctrines which they heard. Thus they made the word of God void through their tradition.

This sad performance reminds me of Isaiah's prophecy, quoted by Jesus, when He said, "This people honors me with their lips, but their heart is far from me; in vain do they worship me, teaching as doctrines the precepts of men." (Mark 7:6-7)

Q. "What you say could convince me. However, how do you expect to convince the people in the ghettos?"

A. The people in the ghettos believe what they are told over and over again, like everyone else. When the world believes what we teach, so will the people in the so-called ghettos.

We do not see why a poor man would welcome the new doctrine of each man's divinity with less eagerness than a rich man. True, we would have each man earn his way every inch of the way. But this is what happens anyway, even though it may seem otherwise to those who are not aware of the spiritual side of life. Moreover, earning one's way is what a normal person wants to do in any case, provided one is given a fair chance. It is far more satisfying to live that way.

Q. "How will you prevail against the great forces pitted against you?"

A. How did the children of Israel prevail? How did the early Christians prevail? How did the early Moslems prevail? The majority prevails in the end. And even one with God is a majority.

Knowing what we do, is it conceivable that we should allow ourselves to be deterred by what our opponents may wish to do? Are we men? Are we Americans? Or are we cowards or creeping vermin? One cannot do the Father's work in attitudes of crouching. Suppose David had assumed such an attitude when he saw his Goliath. Suppose it were possible to intimidate the early Christians. Suppose our founding fathers had started worrying about not prevailing. Suppose Abraham Lincoln had given in to the foreign financial influences which would divide and rule his nation. Where would we be today?

This is not the age of crucifixion. It is the age of manifesting the Father's Will that the world may profit and prosper. Extreme hardships or persecution are neither required, nor are they in store for those who would usher in the Millenium. We look forward to a happier culmination of our work.

If we place a little yellow circle on a huge black canvas, do we not change the entire appearance of the picture? Which would attract our attention more—the bright little circle or the vast blackness? So we take a little thimble and fill it with a little water and pour it where there was nothing but dryness before. Others perchance see us do this, and decide to follow suit. Then some more join in, and they too fill their little thimbles and pour their few drops of water until a huge torrent is formed. And this torrent changes the entire course of human affairs. This is how we work and how we prevail until the Messiah comes.

Q. "Your concept of man as a God-in-training sounds like a piece of fascinating but totally useless abstraction. What practical application can it possibly have?"

A. Spend one hour, or perhaps one day, or, if you can, one week imagining yourself to be a god-in-training. Think like one, feel like one, act like one, and see how much power it has to change your life. Carry out this experiment with an open mind, and then decide whether this concept is useful or not.

249

When you play this role, however, be sure you do not attempt to be a god over others. This is what the Hitlers and the Stalins try to do. Be a god over yourself. Reign over your own passions and tempers. Command your own ailments, disappointments, and failings to vanish into thin air. Create by thought your own opportunities and future, and let events fall in place to prove for you the value of such constructive thoughts.

There is power within each man which may be stirred up by taking thought. Call it divine energy, if you wish. Call it hidden force and strength in each man that comes forth when called upon. Call it the god within. Call it what you will. It is there. Witness the man who swims away from the sinking ship, never before having the ability to swim. Witness the men or women who perform feats of immense strength in an emergency that would have seemed impossible at any other time.[3]

When men start to think of themselves not as economic calculating machines, but as gods-in-training, they will call upon this hidden power. And when they do, they will make greater and swifter progress than ever beore.

About the Evil Forces

Q. "I don't see any logic in your thesis about a conspiracy to rule the world. You say it started about two hundred years ago. Thus it must have been a long-range plan. Why would the people directing it start something they could never finish in their lifetimes?"

A. We offer the following explanations to resolve your quandaries:

1. They do not have to accomplish their ultimate goal during their own lifetimes. They are satisfied to see their descendants carry on.

2. Some among them in the top echelons believe in reincarnation as we do. In fact, after they pass over, they cannot wait to come back again to continue the work they had left unfinished.

3. Their conspiracy is enormously profitable, even in the short

run. Thus they enjoy going up in the esteem of the world for having been greatly successful.

4. There are some who do it out of sheer love of power. After one accumulates hundreds of millions of dollars, the extra things more money can buy do not mean very much. The desire for power has no limit.

5. Others involved in the conspiracy have a demonic urge to manipulate people and governments to precipitate disaster.

6. Still others have dreams and ideals just as we do. It so happens that they are impossible dreams and false ideals that would turn men into robots.

7. After such plans get institutionalized, they gather a force of their own. Moreover, people get hooked and think falsely that they cannot safely break away.

Q. "Are you not giving people more credit than they deserve for displaying a type of intelligence which no one really has? I have never seen anyone or any group smart enough to carry out undetected a global conspiracy. Have you?"

A. I do not doubt that you have never seen such people. How many of us have? We are speaking about the most brilliant minds that ever existed. Yet we should have enough sense to realize that it is a psychological fallacy to evaluate the potential —for good or evil—others have in reference to our own experience alone.

Q. "What do the evil forces you mention want? Do they want to preside over a prospering world order, regimented though it may be? Or would they be captains of the ship, even if they have to sink it first?"

A. They want a well-fed, well-clothed and well-behaved population, reacting as Pavlovian dogs to their commands. They would prefer to have this come about through the gentler methods of a bloodless revolution. However, if need be, they will not hesitate to force such a system upon men by leading them into chaos and despair. Thus do they plan to sit in the driver's seat. There is so little room on this driver's seat at the front. How many souls can it seat? And yet each conspirator feels that he will be amongst those in this seat. How foolish, how sad!

Q. "Is there not a real danger in speaking of a conspiracy? I do not only mean a danger to you personally. I also mean a danger that it will bring out the worst in man."

A. We have been aware of what seems to be troubling you. That is one reason we have not mentioned names, dates and places. There is always some danger in saying things which may be misunderstood, or misconstrued. There is a much larger danger in not saying things which could help to avert calamities that need not happen.

Even the highest government officials are not aware of the tragedies we see ahead—both for their nation and for them personally—unless the current trends are reversed. The average person thinks the disorders around him are temporary. He thinks they are caused by mistakes which can be avoided in the future. If he were to realize how he is being taken by plotters behind the scenes and how serious the situation is, he will not allow himself to be victimized so readily. Thus, discovery of what the problem is may constitute in this instance more than half of its solution.

The conspirators do not fear God. They do not even fear governments, which they have ways and means of controlling. Their one fear, more than any other, is the power of public opinion. Paul Revere came riding with his message to warn the people of Massachusetts. If the people he tried to reach had not responded, his efforts would have meant nothing. Thus, there must be a warning once more to the people so they may have a chance to hear it and act upon it.

We admit that the die has been cast. The disasters are fast

252

approaching. We realize that none of the negative things we have said would happen must happen. But nevertheless they are in the cards. They will not disappear by keeping silent about the conspiracy. On the contrary, they are bound to happen unless the righteous put forth the effort, based on accurate information, to stop them from happening.

If enough people stay in a positive frame of mind, the Christ Host in turn would not allow the conspiracy to hold sway. They cannot move, however, unless man's consciousness awakens and sends forth the necessary calls for help. Thus through man's prayers, constructive disciplined thoughts, and the actions of the righteous, much can be mitigated, if not stopped altogether. Always and forever, where there is life, there is hope.

You have heard that most people in their climb upward reach a stagnation point, because they lose their faith, and because they no longer remain loyal to their ideals. Thus do they go the way of all flesh, corrupted by greed and self-seeking. This often happens to countries set on an upward climb also. To prevent the decline and fall of this great nation, its people must hold the faith in God's plan and in the Elder Brother's leadership, as expounded in this book. They must be loyal to their Constitution. It is loyalty to the Constitution which gives us the confidence that we shall be free to fulfill our destiny as a nation. It is faith in the plan of God that gives us the courage and stamina to resist one-world slavery.

We are not pessimistic. We say we have a good apple. If we take the worm out of it, we can eat this apple and enjoy it. To do this, however, first we must be aware of the fact that there is a worm in the apple.

Q. "The picture you draw of satanic takeover is not consistent with my experience in government. I find the average bureaucrat to be a decent person who does his job as well as he can. There are human errors, misunderstandings, and conflicts of interest in government as well as everywhere else. But I just cannot see a conspiracy."

253

A. The conspirators apply pressure at the very top levels. At your level, you would not necessarily come in contact with any of them. They pose as public-spirited leaders, business or financial, farsighted experts and advisers. They are often greatly respected because they make things happen.

The average bureaucrat is a decent person, but he usually does what his boss tells him to do. And his boss is given the necessary instructions by his boss to implement policies formulated at the top.

You say that you cannot see a conspiracy. How often have you watched closely and objectively to see whether you might see one? Are you familiar with the arguments used by those who have studied the conspiracy we speak of for years and years? Can you knock their arguments down? Perhaps you are simply assuming that there cannot be a conspiracy because you have never heard your teachers or friends speak of it.

At a professional meeting I questioned the speaker about the possibility of a global conspiracy. He was applauded when he dismissed my question with a glib remark. Why are intelligent, rational people so anxious to deny even the possibility of a plot, without giving it a moment's thought?

Q. Do not the exposures associated with the Watergate scandal make the implementation of the plans you speak of less likely?

A. No, I am afraid not. From the Spirit planes the Watergate hearings appear as a farce. As of this writing (September 4, 1973), they have completely failed to uncover the real motives behind the seemingly senseless actions that led to the crises involving the President and his aides. In 1967, with very little publicity, a 25th amendment to the Constitution was passed. This enables the President of the United States to appoint his Vice-president, in case of a vacancy. Thus having paved the way for their takeover, the international money powers engineered the Watergate scandal, unearthed unholy incidents from the Vice-president's past, and are thus attempting to elevate Governor Nelson Rockefeller to the presidency. If and when this

254

ambitious internationalist is allowed to become first president and then dictator of the United States, the plans to unite the world politically will move that much faster.

About Government and Economics

Q. "Ideally, should we not all be living under one flag?"

A. Whose flag?

Q. "Why would a world government not be a good thing, since nations no longer serve a useful purpose?"

A. Because a world government would necessarily have to be a dictatorship. It could not be otherwise since men from different parts of the world having had widely differing experiences could not agree on common policies voluntarily. Moreover, its conspiratorial origin would bar effective checks on the evil use of power.

Also nations do serve a useful purpose. First, they provide a variety of schools for the spiritual growth for billions of individual human beings, each with a different level of awareness and understanding. Second, nations offer a legitimate way to have people accept their differences, which are very real. Third, nations make it possible to bring governments close to the people and give the people pride and joy in their distinct heritage.

Q. "Why not leave well enough alone? Despite all you claim is taking place behind the scenes, are we not making progress? Our Gross National Product is growing, our minorities are advancing, people are becoming more tolerant. Are these not signs of progress?"

A. In God's moral universe there is no such thing as leaving well enough alone. One either goes forward or backward. Look at a ball one throws into the air. When it stops going up, it starts coming down.

Most of the progress we are making now is the result of

physical and moral investments we have made in the past. Our Gross National Product is growing, of course. Its growth, however, is marred with unemployment, inflation, wars or preparations for wars, economic injustice, growing burdens of debt and taxes, international and domestic monetary crises plus a host of other tensions and headaches.

Our minorities are advancing, but so are crime, discontent, fear, distortions and divisions in our national life. Yes, people are becoming more tolerant. At the same time, they are becoming more indifferent to evil and less aware of or confident in their own heritage.

We are not prophets of doom. We are harbingers of the Millenium. We do not emphasize the negative at the expense of the positive influences in the human family. We see both the doughnut and the hole in the doughnut, if we may be allowed such a homely metaphor. Still, is it not almost self-evident that we are living on borrowed time? There is no way in the world we can sustain the forward momentum toward worthwhile achievement unless we start combating the evil forces bent on destroying us from within and without.

Q. "You criticize economists and political scientists because they see the world in a different light than you do. Is it not normal that scholars, like the rest of us, should see things from a point of view which appeals to them?"

A. I do not criticize my colleagues for the reason you mention. I say they are not sufficiently interested in the truth. Can scholars in such fields be more objective and less doctrinaire than they are today? Cervantes seemed to think so when he wrote, "Historians should be and must be exact, truthful, and altogether unimpassioned, and not diverted by interest or fear, affection or rancour, from the path of truth, whose mother is history, the rival of time, storehouse of man's deeds, witness of the past, example and lesson to the present, and warning to the future." The same standards apply to economists and political scientists as well.

Q. "You speak of reversing the current trends. Are not these trends, like it or not, irreversible?"

A. They are not indeed. It is an old ruse to make it appear to be the case. Hayek has devoted an entire chapter of his book, *The Road to Serfdom*, to showing the fallacies in the argument that it is circumstances beyond our control which are compelling us to move toward a planned society. He traces this belief to the Marxist doctrine of the "concentration of industry." Hayek calls the notion "that we are embarking on the new course not out of free will but because competition is spontaneously diminished by technological changes which we neither can reverse nor should we wish to prevent," a deliberately cultivated myth.[4]

Consider the strikingly divergent paths followed by the two postwar Germanys, the two Chinas, the two Koreas, and even the two Vietnams. These examples show how right Hayek was when he said "in social evolution nothing is inevitable but thinking makes it so."[5]

Q. "Your systems will stifle the competitive spirit which has made our country great."

A. A food industry executive, viewing the human stomach as a merchandising target, once said at a Congressional hearing, "There is extreme competition for space in the human stomach."[6] Are you sure that it is this type of competitive spirit which has made our country great?

Q. "If the haves had enough compassion for the plight of others to be willing to share their wealth with the have-nots, would the world today be in the mess it is in?"

A. What is true compassion? The haves cannot feed, clothe, and house the have-nots regardless of how much of their wealth they would be willing to share with them. There are too many have-nots in the world to make this feasible. The more affluent, however, can show their poorer neighbors how they can prosper if and when they make up their minds to do so.

When people start to think from a spiritual point of view, they will realize that those who are haves are not that way by accident. They have earned their talents, their inherited possessions or opportunities no less than what they have earned with their talents and circumstances they have prenatally arranged to have in their current lives. We are not speaking here of those who cheat and steal. The law of karma will take care of them. As for the ill-gotten fortunes of the satanic families which they have been allowed to keep for several generations, these will be wiped off during the cataclysmic events to come.

We know, of course, that it is more blessed to give than to receive. We know also that giving has no karmic value unless it is done voluntarily. To help others, it stands to reason that the giving must also be intelligent. Would it be intelligent or right for a person to deny the proper needs of his own family to help someone living 3,000 miles away? This does not mean that we advocate hardness of heart. But we do not believe that share-the-wealth schemes provide automatic answers to the economic dilemmas of our times.

Q. "Since it does not make much sense to obliterate the communist countries with nuclear bombs, which they could shower back on us, why not accept them the way they are and start to profit from mutually profitable investments and trade with them?"

A. Come now, do you really think that these are the only two choices open to us? We know that it may seem a bit cruel to be opposed to exchanges of goods and services, or modern technology and information which may raise the living standards of other nations. We realize also that the ultimate purpose of economic policy is, or should be, to help people. But can we afford to ignore the type of governments we shall be dealing with in the process? After all, the economic ties are to be worked out, not with the Russian people, but with their government.

Let me quote to you a question and answer from a recent

interview with a foremost British authority on communism, Robert Conquest:

Q. Do the Russians still think the world is going to go Communist?

A. Certainly. Their view of the world is that nonCommunist governments, and even aberrant Communist ones, are completely illegitimate. You see it in all their policy speeches, in the formal instructions to local party branches, in the theoretical pronouncements in their journals—everywhere except in one or two ambiguous pieces put out for Western dupes. They must believe what they profess to believe; otherwise they could not justify their activities—or their positions and power. They would have no moral status.[7]

Secondly, what sense does it make to spend $75-80 billion a year on defense, most of it against the communist rulers, and then to increase their military capabilities with transfers of strategic commodities, capital or technology? Do not deceive yourself that what American companies are sending to the U.S.S.R. now has no military significance. Equipment to manufacture trucks which are being sold in large quantities for the Kama River project is only one example. According to the *Journal of Commerce*, the pact signed by the General Electric Company with the Soviet Union placed "major emphasis on exchange of technology in the power generation field, including steam and gas turbine and nuclear energy technology."[8] The oil and natural gas resources which Occidental Petroleum Corporation and other companies propose to develop in Soviet Russia certainly have military value. Need we go on citing more examples?

There are those who say, "If we don't trade with the communists, other countries will." Can you imagine what type of example or leadership people who think in this fashion provide to the other nations in the free world? Others argue that greater economic ties with the communist countries constitute a practical experiment in reducing misunderstandings which contribute to international tensions.

Is it a misunderstanding that the Red rulers maintain a tight

259

dictatorship over their people? Is it a misunderstanding that they discourage political or religious dissent with incarceration in jails or mental institutions or trumped-up charges? Is it a misunderstanding that since Franklin D. Roosevelt recognized the Soviet Union in 1933, they have not once honored an important treaty commitment to the United States?

It is bad enough that Americans should want to do business with such remorseless tyrants and torturers. What is worse is that from a national point of view, it is doubtful whether any deals can be made with the Soviets on even halfway decent terms.

The capital needs to develop the liquid natural gas fields in Siberia alone are said to be in the $20 billion range. Just as the American consumer felt the pinch of huge U.S. shipments of grain to Russia in terms of higher prices for food, the world capital markets are bound to feel the pinch of huge foreign investments in the Soviet Union in terms of higher interest rates for capital.

Moreover, so-called East-West trade is being developed on credit, which may never be repaid. As a well-known proponent of and specialist in such trade, Sam Pisar, pointed out, "the anticipated U.S.-U.S.S.R. trade would be vastly different than conventional buying and selling of each other (sic) products." He indicated that, without extending most-favored-nation tariff treatment to imports from Russia and without "extreme credits" through the Export-Import Bank, "there simply wouldn't be too much trade" developed[9] The Export-Import Bank incidentally is supported by the U.S. taxpayer.

Is it really necessary to have involvements of this type with people who have never stopped scheming against our form of government? Of course not. There are many investment opportunities right here at home. Moreover there are many peoples around the world who could benefit vastly more from U.S. assistance than the people living under communist tyranny. Economic exchanges with the communist rulers are more likely to result in better tanks than in better people. Watch and see whether or not events prove us to be right.

Finally, consider the following set of contradictions. Christians call Jesus Christ Lord and yet fraternize with the most dedicated enemies of the Christ for profit. Officials swear on the Bible that they will defend the Constitution against domestic and foreign enemies and yet go halfway across the globe to encourage trade and investments which bolster the prestige, increase the power and solidify the positions of the most ardent enemies of the U.S. Constitution. A nation places "In God We Trust" on its currency and then thinks nothing of reaching one accommodation after another with the devil's worst disciples.

We were perhaps a little wordy in answering your question. We felt that we had to say these things in view of the importance of the issues you raised. When the skulduggery behind the scenes—which inspires East-West trade as well as most other absurd moves in foreign relations—stops being a compelling factor in American policy making, free trade could cease to be an issue. In the meantime, we wish people would realize just a little more what acres of diamonds the Father has placed in their own back yards.

Important as foreign trade is, particularly for the smaller nations, there are many other means also through which a country can achieve economic progress. When people learn to live righteously, they will discover so many opportunities for domestic production and trade that economic dependence on foreign supplies and markets will gradually turn into a vestige of the past. International economic relations will then become mainly a matter of sharing with other nations the unique genius and divine endowments with which the Father has blessed each and every nation.

FOOTNOTES

1. For more details on this enterprise, see Huxley, p. 106.

2. Henry W. Riecken, "Quick Thinking," a book review of Daniel P. Moynihan's *Maximum Feasible Misunderstanding: Community Action in the War on Poverty.* New York: Free Press and London: Collier-Macmillan, 1969, published in *Science* Vol. 164 (May 9, 1964) pp. 663-65.

3. For a partial, although very interesting description of this power, see Napoleon Hill, *You Can Work Your Own Miracles.* "A Fawcett Gold Medal Book," Greenwich, Conn.: Fawcett Publications, Inc., 1971.

4. Hayek, p. 43.

5. Ibid., p. 48.

6. Beatrice Trum Hunter, *Consumer Beware! Your Food and What's Been Done to It.* "Bantam Books," New York: A National General Co., 1972, p. 3.

7. "What Kremlin Wants from U.S.," a copyrighted interview in *U.S. News and World Report*, Vol. LXXII, No. 21 (May 22, 1972) p. 34.

8. "Cooperative Pact Signed by GE, USSR," *Journal of Commerce*, (January 15, 1973) p. 13.

9. "Flanigan Urges MFN Authority for Nixon," *Journal of Commerce*, (February 28, 1973) p. 1.